In memory of my father
Samuel
who excelled in calmness of mind
and kindness of heart

META

METAPHYSICS

Methods and Problems

George N. Schlesinger

BARNES & NOBLE BOOKS
TOTOWA, NEW JERSEY

© George N. Schlesinger 1983

First published in the USA 1983 by
BARNES & NOBLE BOOKS
81 ADAMS DRIVE
TOTOWA, NEW JERSEY, 07512

Library of Congress Cataloging in Publication Data
Schlesinger, George N.
  Metaphysics: issues and techniques.

  1. Metaphysics. I. Title
BD 111.S32   1983   110   82-24408
ISBN 0-389-20380-7
ISBN 0-389-20381-5 (pbk.)

Printed in Great Britain

Contents

Acknowledgements

I wish to thank the Editors of *American Philosophical Quarterly*, *Mind* and *Philosophical Quarterly*, who permitted me to experiment with some of the ideas developed in this book on the pages of their journals.

Introduction

The three topics of this book

In this book I shall try to do three different things: first, to provide a
general characterization of metaphysics, to describe some of the unique
features shared by all metaphysical assertions. In particular I shall
endeavour to state clearly what distinguishes metaphysical beliefs from
other, more mundane empirical beliefs. In the hundreds of books
devoted to the discipline in the past 20 years we find statements that
successfully describe certain features that may be characteristic of one
group of metaphysical beliefs, but not of any other. We also find
statements that describe not only metaphysical assertions but also some
hypotheses that are clearly down-to-earth scientific hypotheses. It is,
however, very hard to find a book that throws light on any one condition
that is necessary or sufficient to define a given statement as
metaphysical.

In the first chapter we shall discover that one of the central
characteristics of metaphysical statements is the unique way in which
they are related to experience. The aim of both science and metaphysics
is to account for experience, but the roots in observation and experience
of metaphysical statements are palpably more tenuous than those of
scientific statements. One of the implications of this basic difference is
that in science we can always rely on the accumulation of evidence to
adjudicate between rival hypotheses, while in metaphysics controversy
may go on for ever. A given scientific hypothesis may have looked
plausible in the context of the knowledge available a hundred years ago
but may appear absurd in the context of the greater knowledge we have
today. On the other hand, a metaphysical hypothesis that could
reasonably have been held in the light of experience a hundred years ago
would appear basically just as reasonable today in the context of a much
richer experience. The great increase in our empirical knowledge does
not have an appreciable impact on its status.

Since the accumulation of empirical data hardly affects the credibility

1

of rival hypotheses in metaphysics, we are forced to rely more heavily on what arguments can do for our case. Consequently, unique techniques, argument forms and principles of reasoning are widely employed in metaphysics. These methods may also be used in other areas of philosophy, but not in any other discipline. This fact brings us to the second purpose of the book, the description of some of the major tactics and techniques employed by metaphysicians and the investigation of their nature, scope and method of application. It is a large topic, and I do not propose to offer a comprehensive study. But because so little attention has been paid to this matter in the past, I hope that the discussion here may be regarded as a substantial beginning.

To give some hint of the complexities involved, let us consider for a moment just one of the many typical forms of argument, the infinite regress argument. Even a cursory glance reveals that though many people talk about the infinite regress argument, a number of widely different arguments go by that name. On looking more closely at these arguments we see that not one of them is deductively valid. This raises a general problem affecting many of the argument forms that are particular to philosophy: what exactly is the force behind them? Another major problem is the intrinsically ambiguous nature of the most frequently used member of the family of infinite regress arguments. In the standard case where a philosopher has generated a regress R and used it to support his claim that p is true, a different approach, and one no less plausible than the first, could show that it supports the denial of p. As we shall see, there is wide scope in choosing the correct approach to regresses of this kind. In addition, there are cases where disagreement arises as to whether any real regress occurs; some philosophers may contend that they have generated a regress which consists of an infinite number of steps, while others claim not to be able to see the need for taking even the first step.

A good illustration of the complexities involved in this particular argument form is provided by McTaggart's startling assertion that time is unreal. McTaggart's famous argument was that the most basic temporal predicates are self-contradictory, and any effort to eliminate this contradiction generates an infinite regress which ensures its failure. Several philosophers objected, claiming that in fact no regress arises at all. Others were prepared to admit that one step along this regress may indeed have to be taken, but no more. And to complicate matters even further, a fourth view held that an infinite regress *is* being generated, but is not vicious as McTaggart had claimed, that is, it does not prevent the elimination of the contradiction. Additional intricacies also need to be untangled before one may hope to grasp the nature of regress arguments. Other arguments involve difficulties of the same order. Clearly, therefore, the study of the methodology of metaphysics is a large undertaking.

The third task I attempt in this book is to discuss the nature of a number of the major metaphysical issues themselves. While I do not claim to discuss every metaphysical topic, I believe I discuss a wide variety of them, wider than is normally studied at length in books on the subject.

The metaphysical issues investigated fall into two basically different groups, each studied in a different part of the book. One group contains issues that are all controversial, one example being the problem of universals. Realists maintain – and have maintained since early antiquity – that universals exist, whereas nominalists have denied it. Ever since the beginning of this debate eminent philosophers in every generation have in more or less equal numbers taken one side or another in the controversy. Today, no less than in the time of Plato, it is not obvious which view is correct.

The second group contains issues about which everybody takes the same position, knowing it to be the right one; however, many philosophers will maintain that there is room for debating how best to justify it. Whether we succeed or fail in our efforts to provide such a justification will not determine whether we do or do not continue to hold any of the beliefs in this second group. The belief in the existence of other minds is a typical example. While different writers have attempted to defend this belief in widely diverse ways, virtually all agree that other minds exist. A genuine solipsist – someone who believes that his own mind is the only mind that really exists – is hard to find; even mere sceptics who would admit to a reasonable chance that others are mindless robots are rare.

In the first part of the book we contrast the general nature of metaphysics and science. In science, if a certain hypothesis is true and the belief in its truth is perfectly justified, it is irrational for me to want to affirm its truth so long as I happen to be ignorant of the particular justification. However, when it comes to metaphysical beliefs – at least, to those belonging to the second group – we are all rationally justified in holding them, regardless of whether we can offer a justification.

We shall find that even in societies that proclaim the complete freedom of conscience there is still pressure to hold such beliefs; or at any rate, those who act as if these beliefs are false are likely to be severely punished.

The interconnectedness of the topics

The reader is likely to agree that treating these three topics jointly has advantages; they are after all interrelated. The insights we may gain about the general features of metaphysics are bound to help us obtain a better understanding of the methodology employed by metaphysicians, as well as of some of the individual arguments advanced in support of a particular metaphysical position.

Let us look at one example which illustrates the interconnection between the various topics of this book. One well-known, ingenious attempt to justify the metaphysical belief that it is reasonable to rely on the conclusions of inductive reasoning is that of Reichenbach. His argument, which is somewhat technical, amounts to saying that he can offer no reason why the future is likely to unfold in one way rather than another, but that he can show that if any method of predicting the future is going to work then the inductive method will also work. Thus we have every reason to employ the inductive method. For surely there are two possibilities: one, that some method of prediction is effective; the other, that none is. In the first case, we can certainly use induction safely, since we have assumed that it will work; in the second case, it does not matter if we use induction – it will not work, but then nothing else will work either. In sum, we have everything to gain and nothing to lose by employing the inductive method.

Reichenbach has been attacked on a number of grounds. Several philosophers have claimed to have found a flaw in this or that part of his argument. However, no one has made the obvious objection, one that does not mean entering into any of the details of his arguments. Reichenbach does not offer any reason at all that might justify our having anything like the kind of firm confidence we do have in the conclusions of inductive reasoning. Indeed, he himself would readily agree that when I predict a particular outcome for a given experiment on the basis of induction, then, because it is merely one of infinitely many logically possible outcomes, I am entitled to be utterly sceptical about the accuracy of my prediction. But, of course, part of the ingenuity of his approach is to sidestep the question of *how likely* it is that the conclusions of inductive reasoning are true, and to show that in any case induction is necessarily the most reasonable method to employ.

The point is this: when, for example, I am in the path of a speeding car, I do not say to myself 'There is no basis for believing that I am likely to be run over if I stay where I am. The car may very well swerve to the right or left, stop, rise into the air, go underground, change to dust or evaporate. Inductive reasoning, however, suggests that if I do not at once change my position I am going to be run over. Reichenbach has convincingly shown that it is reasonable to accept the results of inductive reasoning; thus, wishing to be reasonable, I shall calmly step aside.' No; most likely I shall be frantic with fright and jump out of the car's path with every ounce of my strength. I shall behave on the assumption that in jumping quickly out of the way, I am escaping certain death. If I were offered a fortune to stay put for just two more seconds, I would resolutely turn it down. In other words, my behaviour shows that I am absolutely convinced that prediction based on induction is correct. Reichenbach's argument does nothing to support such an absolute conviction.

However, when we understand certain general features of metaphysics we are able to solve this difficulty. As I have suggested, we shall find that metaphysical beliefs fall into two basically different groups. The first group contains beliefs from which we adopt those that we can prove to be well founded. We adopt beliefs from the second group without any such preliminary; we all have a strong natural propensity to hold them. We would not relinquish them no matter what conclusions philosophers arrive at concerning their rational foundations.

The belief in the uniformity of nature, which is presupposed by our use of inductive reasoning, falls into the second group. Reichenbach's argument ought not to be taken as an attempt to justify the great confidence we all feel in the reliability of the inductive method. This confidence is not based on – and in fact is completely independent of – the availability of such a justification. Yet if there were not the slightest foundation for preferring induction to other methods, we would have difficulty understanding why philosophers tacitly endorse this common approach. Why not expose it as having no root in reality? But the answer is that it does have roots in reality. Reichenbach has shown that induction is a uniquely privileged method of forecasting the future, and, therefore, trying to shake people's confidence in it serves no good purpose.

Another example of the interconnectedness of the topics we are considering is provided by our discussion of the general nature of metaphysics. I stated that the central feature of metaphysical beliefs is that they cannot in principle be conclusively verified in the way scientific hypotheses are. But there is no reason why a belief should not be confirmable in the sense that certain observations show it to be more plausible than its rivals. A metaphysician can therefore subscribe to the confirmability principle. In the last chapter there is an illustration of how we can make effective use of this principle in attempting to establish one of the most fundamental metaphysical beliefs.

The reason for polemics

A few words can perhaps allay the uneasiness some readers may have when they see so many old positions abandoned and arguments reformulated. They may well be wondering whether it is reasonable to contend that so many new approaches need to be initiated, that such a large number of important and elementary questions have not occurred to anyone before, or that such a variety of useful and seemingly simple solutions to problems have been overlooked.

First of all, to say that a philosopher's argument is faulty does not amount to condemning it as silly; it does not even amount to claiming it to be unworthy of study. Zeno's proofs that motion is impossible, for example, were always regarded as absurd, yet for over 2000 years students of philosophy have found them interesting enough to study closely. The purpose of philosophy is not merely to discover true propositions or to acquire correct solutions to as many problems as possible. Its aim is also to inquire into the ingenious ways that are constantly being devised for handling highly abstract concepts and to gain a grip on elusive ideas inaccessible to the more direct methods of the natural sciences. The unique argument forms and techniques employed by metaphysicians may be an instructive subject for philosophical investigation in their own right, regardless of what they have helped to achieve. A building may be architecturally satisfying, and thus worth preserving, even though it is of no functional value. To some extent, philosophy is intellectual architecture, and, therefore, ingenuity of design and structural elegance of argument may engage our interest independently of the concrete conclusions they may or may not yield.

Furthermore, many arguments, though not fully adequate, are worth close attention since they may incorporate valid points and take us some way towards our goal. But even those that do not advance us towards a solution often contain valuable insights, make important distinctions, initiate fruitful ways of looking at matters and propose novel techniques that may be profitably employed elsewhere.

Finally, however, I must point out that considering unsatisfactory arguments also leads to one of the main objectives of this study: to draw attention to some of the strong forces tending to lead philosophers astray. Many authors presuppose that certain approaches will serve for any purpose, making indiscriminate use of various argument forms and techniques that ought to be employed with greater restraint. Clearly those who follow a given type of philosophical methodology are to some

extent forced to handle a particular set of issues and problems and
pursue particular lines of arguments simply because the special
characteristics of their approach tend to prevent them from dealing with
other issues and arguments. A faulty argument may be advanced
because it is the kind that flows naturally from a given approach. A
simple solution may be overlooked by a certain school of thought
because it has features that hide it from their view. From a different
perspective that solution may be better founded than any other. I shall
endeavour to expose such cases.

For example, I shall spend some time discussing the method of
counter-examples, arguably the technique most frequently employed
today. We shall see how its indiscriminate use has led to undesirable
results. For example, it has often been unthinkingly assumed that to
find the correct qualification to the statement that is refuted by the
counter-example, we need only concentrate on ensuring that the
qualification avoids the counter-example. No thought is given to the
question whether there is anything in the nature of the relevant notions
demanding the proviso that has been suggested.

A second example is provided by the widespread use of formal
methods, whose introduction into philosophy has on the whole had
beneficial effects, greatly increasing clarity and rigour. Inevitably, as we
shall see, these methods, as with all good things, can be and have been
misused.

Metaphysical issues and techniques

Let me enumerate some of the issues and techniques that will be
discussed. Among the metaphysical issues are:

1 Religious beliefs – how they may be confirmed and disconfirmed.
2 Temporal becoming and the question of the moving NOW.
3 The status of possible universes and in particular extreme realism,
according to which all universes are equally real.
4 The question why the basic laws of nature are what they are, and a
defence of the view that this is not a useless or meaningless question.
5 The ancient problem of universals and the debate between the realist
and the nominalist.
6 The question of the existence of other minds and the more particular
question as to whether, for example, others' experiences of seeing red
are the same as mine.
7 The belief in the intelligibility of nature and the belief in the
uniformity of nature.

8 The belief that material objects exist outside us and independently of our sense experiences.

The following are some of the techniques to be discussed:

1 The use of some of the scientist's practices, such as the rule that when a given event is more likely to take place according to one hypothesis than another, then that event confirms the first hypothesis rather than the second; the use of thought experiments; and the use of the principle that the hypothesis that best explains a given observation is confirmed by it.
2 The method of counter-examples.
3 The verification principle.
4 The principle of sufficient reason.
5 Occam's razor.
6 The various types of infinite regress argument.
7 The application of the methodology of mathematical logic.
8 Linguistic analysis.

To conclude, I do not propose to advance any such thing as a metaphysical system in this work. Naturally, I have no hesitation in taking an idea or argument found useful in one context and making use of it in any other context where it also proves to be useful. Consequently, the book forges many connections between its different parts. However, I have not constructed any principles (at least, not consciously) to which everything has to conform, and there is no preconceived pattern of thought into which all the ideas relating to each of the diverse topics have to be forced.

1

What is metaphysics?

The lack of a satisfactory description

Metaphysics has been studied for longer than most current disciplines. It is surprising therefore that it is so very difficult to find an adequate answer in the relevant literature to the elementary question 'What is metaphysics?' In fact, if we consult any of the vast number of treatises devoted to the subject we shall find either that no attempt at all has been made to characterize metaphysics, or that what the author has offered by way of characterization seems quite obviously wrong, and that at most it fits some metaphysical statements, but not all. It is natural to compare and contrast metaphysics and science, since both are enterprises whose aim is to understand the nature of the world around us. But while it may not be easy to give a complete characterization of science, any scientist or philosopher of science can make a considerable number of statements which will accurately describe some significant feature shared by all scientific hypotheses. The nature of metaphysics, however, seems so much more elusive; we may search the vast literature and find not a single statement that is both informative and true of all metaphysical hypotheses.

I shall consider some typical statements made by contemporary philosophers, ranging from those who regard metaphysics as the profoundest kind of inquiry to so-called anti-metaphysicians. I shall then confine myself to raising obvious objections to these statements. In most cases, when serious and competent thinkers, after considerable study of a subject, make pronouncements on it which appear untenable, it is a mistake to dismiss what they say as just so much groundless nonsense. These statements have more often than not been prompted by features of our topic which are genuine but may not have been correctly identified. In the last section I shall attempt to identify the legitimate bases of some of these seemingly misguided pronouncements.

9

Let me end this introduction with a brief statement that most philosophers will not dispute of what metaphysics is:

> Metaphysical problems are problems about how the world is that scientists do not tackle, leaving them to philosophers to investigate.

Of course, this definition gives little insight into the nature of metaphysics as it does not tell us what intrinsic features of metaphysical statements set them apart from scientific statements. The definition is useful however for classification.

Some inadequate characterizations

1 One of the opinions most often heard is that metaphysics, just like science, is concerned with the nature of reality. However, the former deals with much more general questions. For instance, K. Campbell says 'Metaphysics is concerned with the overall framework of reality'[1] and goes on 'Metaphysical inquiry is distinguished from science. . . only by attempting a more comprehensive and more systematic theory'.[2] Among the many other philosophers who have expressed similar views are B. Wilshire,[3] J. Hospers[4] and A. Quinton.[5]

It may be true that some metaphysical problems are very general, but greater generality is by no means a universal characteristic. The problem of the nature of minds, for instance, which all will agree is outside the scope of the scientist, is certainly much narrower than the physicist's problems of determining the ultimate, indivisible constituents of matter. The latter, after all, concerns the nature of all matter, while the former is related only to the properties of a tiny proportion of it, namely humans, or at most some animals too. Those who ask what precisely are mental properties seem less concerned with 'the overall framework of reality' than are the experts in quantum mechanics.

2 Another view, perhaps even more widespread, is that metaphysics is an attempt to penetrate beyond the surface of experience and discover what lies beneath. Campbell, for instance, says 'the very task metaphysics sets itself is to pierce the veil of appearance, to pass beyond how things seem, to reach to the basic, inner, and perhaps hidden part of the world'.[6] Carnap[7] and Ayer[8] also characterize metaphysics as an attempt to gain access to what transcends observation, an enterprise they find objectionable. E. Agazzi,[9] in a recent review of the opposition of logical positivists to metaphysics, regards the latter as an ill-conceived enterprise since metaphysicians are not content, as they should be, to

know only what is experienceable. Similar characterizations are found in the writings of B. Blanshard[10] and W. H. Walsh,[11] among others.

It seems that these authors were even less successful in depicting the most salient feature of metaphysics, the one that sets it apart from science. It is hard to see how a hypothesis postulating that seemingly solid, continuous and stationary bodies actually consist of tiny particles rushing about at enormous speeds can be said to pass less beyond how things seem than the metaphysicians' attribution of mind to other bodies. On the contrary, the physicists' microparticles are the kind of entities that will for ever be remote from my direct grasp, whereas minds are not so unfamiliar to me as I am intimately acquainted with at least one member of the species, my own mind.

But there are even more poignant examples. The status of temporal becoming is a typical metaphysical problem. Some metaphysicians have insisted that time flows. They have contended that a given instant of time, namely the NOW, is momentarily 'alive', is more real than other temporal points. Events that are in the distant future keep moving towards the NOW until they momentarily coincide with it and subsequently recede further and further into the past. Unquestionably, this claim does not at all represent an attempt 'to pass beyond how things seem'; on the contrary, it is very much an attempt to affirm that things are basically the way they seem to be.

Then again it seems that the realist metaphysician's claim that chairs and tables – and not merely sense impressions thereof – actually exist is less removed from immediate experience than the physicist's claim that these chairs and tables are assemblies of all sorts of imperceptible particles.

3 It is not uncommon to hear various versions of the claim that metaphysical statements are not straightforward statements about facts. Wilshire, for instance, tells us that 'metaphysics is thought about thought-about-the-world; it is talk about talk-about-the-world'.[12] Campbell expresses similar views. Walsh[13] thinks that metaphysical assertions are not strictly true or false at all. G. J. Warnock[14] also seems to think that such assertions are more correctly spoken of as illuminating or exciting rather than true or false. Strawson[15] explicitly states that metaphysics is concerned not with the nature of external facts but rather with the structure of our thoughts about these facts.

There is no need for lengthy arguments to convince the reader that on the surface it is very hard to see why, for instance, the assertion that others are not robots but possess a mind expresses a less solid fact about the nature of external reality than assigning a certain value to the mass of the electron.

4 It has also been said that all other inquiries begin where metaphysics leaves off. This means that when we investigate particular phenomena we take for granted certain presuppositions that have been established or are supposed to be established by metaphysicians. The ultimate foundation of all other intellectual enterprises is metaphysics. Thus John Kekes, in the course of his discussion of Collingwood, says:

Absolute presuppositions occur in clusters; the combination of them determines the nature, purpose, and the scope of a particular way of looking at the world. To understand a world-view is to understand the absolute presupposition that underlies it. Collingwood conceives of the task of metaphysics as the achievement of this understanding. The method of metaphysical enquiry is to render explicit the implicit presuppositions of a particular world-view. [16]

It is quite true that the metaphysical doctrines of the uniformity of nature or that every event has a cause are presupposed by the practical scientist. But what about the assertions that universals are – or are not – real or that time does – or does not – flow? These assertions are not fundamental to any theory, or world-view; they are completely irrelevant to nearly all other beliefs we may hold. In no sense of the word are these assertions 'presuppositions' of anything else.

5 Finally I should like to mention that a great deal has been said about metaphysics in a nebulous language that is quite mystifying to read, making one wonder whether it has any meaning at all. This feature of the subject must be mentioned, since it is by no means an insignificant or accidental phenomenon. Hardly any other subject has attracted this kind of pretentious, opaque writing that strikes the level-headed reader as so much empty verbiage. One of the more serious results has been to turn some of the most gifted philosophers against metaphysics altogether, which they have judged beyond the realm of the meaningful. Later I shall touch upon the views of those who seem to have overlooked the invaluable contributions of those metaphysicians who have observed the highest standards of rigour and clarity. Here I wish merely to state that throughout the book I shall confine myself to examining the arguments of this latter type of writers. However, I should like to cite an example of a passage that seems to lie just on the borderline between the two types of philosophizing. I shall return to it in the last section of this chapter to suggest that some of its puzzling features might make sense.

For a definition of what metaphysics is we could perhaps go first to history. We should then discover that the term 'metaphysics' carries with it a wide range of meanings: it is the science of the non-material, of the real-in-itself, of the unknowable, of the absolute; a systematic universal knowledge, *a priori* knowledge, and so forth.[17]

The term 'non-material' makes complete sense, of course, but it is somewhat puzzling that it should be applied to metaphysics. For example, there is a well known metaphysical view according to which material objects are bundles of properties; surely that view is as much about the material as anything can be. The second term, 'the real-in-itself', is the kind of term that has made many sceptical about the intelligibility of the discipline. The third term, 'the unknowable', is perhaps the most astonishing: why have thousands of books been written about something unknowable? Sensible people do not talk about what they do not know and even less about what is unknowable. In the last section of this chapter we shall have another look at this and other puzzling passages.

Scientific theories and evidence

Let me begin with a relatively short description of what I believe is the crucial difference between science and metaphysics, a description I shall soon elaborate on. What I suggest is this: both scientific and metaphysical hypotheses purport to account for experience, but in the case of the former the empirical situation is dynamic and gradually forces upon us the hypothesis that we eventually accept. On the other hand, while the empirical conditions relevant to a metaphysical hypothesis may not be entirely static, changes they undergo are not decisive; there is no relentless accumulation of evidence in favour of any one of rival hypotheses. The situation in the case of scientific hypotheses is dynamic in the following way. There may be as much evidence to begin with in favour of h_1 as there is for h_2. However, if in fact h_1 is nearer to the truth than h_2 then, as we gain more knowledge about nature, more and more observations are bound to come to our notice which fit smoothly only with h_1, and in order to prevent them from clashing with h_2 extra hypotheses will have to be postulated. As time goes on these extra, ad hoc hypotheses will grow indefinitely in number and make it increasingly difficult to maintain hypothesis h_2. Eventually a state will be reached where it will be much more cumbersome to maintain h_2 than h_1, so that everyone will abandon h_2 in favour of h_1.

In the case of a metaphysical problem, however, the empirical situation is more or less frozen. Consider the famous controversy between McTaggart and Russell concerning the question whether there is a moving NOW, and the many well-known arguments that have been advanced in favour of their respective positions. Each one of these arguments could have been put forward equally well in the context of scientific knowledge as it stood 50 years or even 500 years ago. The empirical features of the universe that are relevant to the hypotheses of McTaggart and Russell remain virtually the same, and it is not expected that future empirical discoveries are going to have a crucial impact on the credibility of either hypothesis.

There are indefinitely many number of examples from the history of science that illustrate the structure of scientific revolutions, in the course of which an old theory, being further from the truth, is replaced by another through the relentless process whereby the adequacy of one grows steadily relative to that of the other. As time goes on and evidence accumulates, more and more complicating hypotheses must be incorporated into the wrong theory in order to keep it afloat. Sooner or later, a stage is sure to be reached when the wrong theory is so entangled with extra hypotheses that it is absolutely clear to everyone that it does not correspond to the facts.

For an example involving nothing even remotely abstract or theoretical, let us imagine a controversy among experts of ancient Ugaritic as to what the word *dats* stands for. In the nineteenth century, one group of experts hypothesize that this unusual Ugaritic word stands for 'glad'; another that *dats* translates into 'sad'. As a matter of fact *dats* means 'glad', but in the context of mid-nineteenth century scholarship both hypotheses seem equally credible. Then more ancient Ugaritic scrolls are unearthed, and the scholars manage to decipher: 'The harvest throughout the land was exceedingly good and consequently the King was *dats*.' The first group are pleased with this discovery; it seems clear to them that what is being said is that the King naturally shared the joy of his subjects at their good fortune. The passage thus confirms their hypothesis that *dats* means 'glad'. But the second group of experts will not be forced; they do not give up their interpretation at once but invent an auxiliary hypothesis to counteract this contrary evidence. They claim perhaps that the King was in a peculiar situation, one in which a good harvest throughout the land was likely to distress him. Relying on some vague clues from other documents, they postulate that the King coveted the land of neighbouring kingdoms; a disastrous harvest would have provided sufficient incentive for his subjects to wage a war of expansion.

If no other evidence is forthcoming then the dispute may remain unresolved for ever. A single relevant passage hardly has the power to force the errant linguist to abandon his hypothesis. However, if we allow the eventual discovery of indefinitely many other passages which may provide further relevant clues, then it is to be expected that the correct interpretation of *dats* will sooner or later impose itself upon everyone. Indeed, other texts are discovered in which the King in question is strongly praised as an unusually peace-loving person. This obviously has an adverse effect on the hypothesis of the second group of experts, who as a result are forced to come up with some new explanation why a normally peace-loving King could nevertheless want to start a war on this particular occasion. But then yet other passages undermine this new explanation, presenting more difficulties which have to be explained away with some further ad hoc hypothesis. In addition, increasingly more ad hoc hypotheses are required to explain sentences like 'The King was very *dats* when his first son was born' or 'The priests were not *dats* to hear that they will not be granted the gold necessary to build a new temple' which come to light with the discovery of new texts. All these extra explanations and hypotheses make the conjecture that *dats* stands for 'sad' more and more difficult to maintain, and it is therefore universally abandoned.

This example is fictitious, but there are many real examples in science. The following example is useful and easy to follow. In antiquity it was generally considered far more reasonable to assume that the earth was flat than round; common sense and observation seemed to support this. The absurdity of the hypothesis that the earth was round seemed evident for a number of reasons; for example, if the earth were round people at the antipodes would be upside down. But then people became aware of the relevance of the fact that the lower parts of receding ships disappeared over the horizon before their upper parts. This observation did not persuade everyone to relinquish the flat-earth hypothesis, although it did make its defence considerably more difficult. Nevertheless, the flat-earthists were able to introduce all kinds of ad hoc hypotheses to protect their position. Similarly, the fact that lunar eclipses are round, together with the plausible hypothesis that they are caused by the shadow cast by the earth and the supposition that shadows have the shape of the objects throwing them, was seen by the time of Pythagoras as important evidence for the view that the earth is round. This constituted a further difficulty for the flat-earthists, but they were not yet forced to capitulate, since several ways of maintaining their theory were open to them. They could deny that lunar eclipses were caused by the shadow which the earth casts upon the moon. Such a move deprived them of a neat theory of eclipses according to which lunar eclipses must always occur in the middle of the lunar month, when the straight lines from the sun to earth and earth to moon may form an angle of 180°. The flat-earth theory became much more cumbersome with the discovery of the relevance of facts such as these.

Now, since the round-earth theory is actually true and its rival patently false, this process was bound to continue in the typical manner of cases of conflicting empirical hypotheses. That is, more and more indisputable facts came to light which fitted naturally into the round-earth theory, while the flat-earth theory could accommodate these facts only at the cost of more and more ad hoc hypotheses which made the theory increasingly hard to maintain. For example, eventually travellers who proceeded far enough along a straight line found that they had returned to their original starting-point from the opposite direction. It was natural to interpret this as an indication that the globe may be circumnavigated. The flat-earthists needed to think up some auxiliary hypothesis to explain why, despite appearances to the contrary, no circumnavigation had taken place. With each new piece of evidence that the world is round their case grows more and more complicated, until at last it becomes so entangled that its falsity is clear to everyone.

The interconnectedness of scientific hypotheses

If the reader is prepared to agree that there is indeed a basic difference between the methods of confirmation characteristic of the two disciplines, he will then want to know why. The difference just described, though it may illustrate the methodologies that scientists and philosophers have to adopt, does not expose the intrinsic distinctions between science and metaphysics that are ultimately responsible for our having to approach them so differently. Let me say something about this question.

First of all, a typical scientific hypothesis has many points of contact with reality, and hence an inadequate hypothesis is bound to clash with a large number of observations. The flat-earth hypothesis, for instance, is incompatible with the shape of lunar eclipses, with the way ships disappear over the horizon, with the circumnavigability of the earth, and so on. But even more important is the fact that in science, though not in metaphysics, hypotheses are interconnected. Suppose a scientist A claims to have determined the coefficient of viscosity of a given gas G to be V, while scientist B maintains that the value of this coefficient is V′. The difference between A and B will not be merely confined to their expectation of different results from all future measurements of the coefficient of viscosity of G, but will also be concerned with measurements of the covariation of pressure and volume, of thermal conductivity and of thermal transpiration, and with many other physical parameters. This is so because kinetic theory shows precisely how all the aforementioned macroscopic properties of a given gas are determined by the same microscopic properties of its constituent molecules.

The belief in the complete interconnectedness of all natural phenomena, or what has been called the belief in the unity of science, has been a source of inspiration to many scientists. It has been suggested that eventually we shall discover basic laws that govern sub-sub-atomic particles, from which the laws governing sub-atomic particles, and hence atoms, will be derived. These laws will then be used to discover the rules observed by molecules, living cells and so on. Because of this close, systematic interconnectedness within the set of sentences that constitutes all the laws of nature, an erroneous belief about one law will have increasing effect on the way we shall be forced to handle the growing numbers of the rest as more and more are discovered.

In contrast, metaphysical hypotheses do not form a tightly knit system. Whether I believe in the existence of universals or not does not determine the position I shall take on the question whether time flows. People who believe in the fully fledged reality of all possible worlds are not any more or less likely to affirm the freedom of the will as a result. Consequently, if I happen to hold one wrong metaphysical hypothesis, that does not necessarily force me to introduce a mass of auxiliary hypotheses to neutralize its adverse effect on all the correct hypotheses which I may also hold.

Yet we cannot ignore the fact that we often hear talk about 'metaphysical systems'. The implication would seem to be that metaphysical problems are not solved individually but, since they all relate to one other, as part of an interconnected whole.

It seems however that something else is likely to lie at the root of talk of systems. As I said earlier, the essence of the metaphysical enterprise is the devising of arguments to support another argument that has been overthrown. Because reasoning, rather than experimentation or observation, is of chief importance in metaphysics we find that metaphysical writings, as indeed do all philosophical writings, contain forms of argument that are not employed in the sciences as well as those that are. The methodology of metaphysics includes argument forms such as the transcendental argument, the infinite regress argument, the principle of insufficient reason and many others. What seems common to all these argument forms is that they do not establish their results with certainty but are to different degrees 'persuasive arguments'. In metaphysics, arguments that are not strictly valid are admissible, and so a philosopher's contribution is not restricted to the establishing of results but may include the more creative work of devising novel modes of argument that seem plausible and persuasive. Thus, while the contents of different metaphysical hypotheses may well be independent of one another, they may be jointly supported by a set of arguments advanced in a unique style that lends them unity.

It is a fact worth noting that, while different scientists may use different methods of investigation determined by their temperaments and habits of thought, their conclusions are usually formulated in the manner generally accepted by the scientific community. In contrast, there does exist such a thing as a characteristic, personal style of philosophizing. A philosopher may have a predilection for a certain type of argument which he may apply to a variety of topics, thus producing what is called a 'metaphysical system' possessing a particular intellectual flavour.

The constancy of condition of metaphysical beliefs

It is only fair to mention that not only are there philosophers holding a different view concerning science, whose development they regard as not entirely determined by objective factors, but there are also those who would challenge us from the opposite direction and claim that metaphysical beliefs also rise and fall through the relentless accumulation of hard facts which militate against beliefs that are not justified. The scope for engaging in lengthy debates with these philosophers is severely limited by the fact that they usually merely state their position without trying to justify it. Take the following, for example:

While metaphysical theories cannot be refuted, they can be undermined. They can be made to die a death by thousands of qualifications. This is the kind of demise that vitalism had, that theism and dualism are having, and that behaviorism will with any luck have.[18]

No description follows of any of the many empirical discoveries that compelled vitalists, theists and dualists to pile on to their theories all the stifling qualifications that brought or are bringing about their demise. It seems to me that vitalism was held as a scientific hypothesis much like the phlogiston or any other theory, and like them was found to have no use and was rejected. Theism, on the other hand, must be acknowledged as belonging to metaphysics. It is also true that fewer people subscribe to theism today than in the past. But surely this is due not to the discovery of new empirical evidence but to a number of other factors: the corrupt behaviour of some of the representatives of organized religion, for example, and the fact that people whose lives were solitary, unpleasant and short formerly could only wait for happiness in the hereafter but can now look upon science and technology as their saviour.

It is hard to find any event in the past 300 years that could reasonably be construed as evidence undermining theism. Admittedly some writers who claim that in view of the unprecedented atrocities that took place during World War II it is much more difficult to maintain a belief in an benevolent and omnipotent being. But this reasoning is difficult to follow. The problem of evil is undoubtedly grave, but it has a long history. A number of solutions have been proposed, of debatable adequacy, but I know of no reputable solution that satisfactorily explains the sufferings of galley slaves or victims of medieval torture chambers but is inapplicable to the atrocities of the twentieth century. The evil of the Nazis is unprecedented, but it does not undermine the credibility of theism, since the value of any plausible solution to the problem of evil is not related to the magnitude of suffering.

It might be claimed that Darwin's theory of evolution has made theism more difficult to maintain. To this the brief reply is that the theory of evolution might raise difficulties for the credibility of the Scriptures, but not for natural theology, which subscribes to no particular account of creation.

Finally, concerning dualism, it could be suggested that it is incorrect to talk about its decline when there has recently been a revival of interest in Descartes and a growing appreciation of the subtlety of his arguments. But there is no need to debate the question whether Descartes is gaining or losing ground. If he has been losing ground then surely this is because capable philosophers have devised convincing arguments against dualism, while its defenders were not resourceful enough to come up with equally good supporting arguments. It is certainly not the case that adverse empirical evidence has piled up against dualism over the last few centuries of the kind that has defeated, say, the flat-earth theory or Ptolemaic astronomy.

Science and metaphysics: some clarifications

In the last and most important section of this chapter, I shall discuss the various differences between science and metaphysics that follow from the basic distinctions that I have tried to describe. In this section, I shall make several points in order to clarify what I have said so far.

1 I did not mean to imply that no discoveries could ever affect the credibility of metaphysical hypotheses. For example, with the discovery that electrical stimulation of certain parts of the brain can induce vivid, coherent and sustained impressions of events that do not actually take place in the external world, Descartes' sceptical conjecture that all our perceptual experiences lack roots in external reality – a conjecture supported by how things seem to us in our dreams – may gain plausibility. I am merely denying that a long series of empirical discoveries will systematically and irresistibly point in a specific direction.

To give one more example, suppose it were discovered that I had a number of important physical characteristics that no other human possessed. Surely this would be relevant to the inductive argument supporting the belief in the existence of other minds – it would weaken it. If I were a solipsist I would have reason to claim that my having a mind does not provide a sound inductive ground for claiming that others have one too, since it has been established that I differ significantly from others.

Apart from the fact that such a discovery is highly unlikely, it could not provide overwhelming empirical evidence in favour of solipsism. After all, I am certainly physically different from elephants and giraffes. Yet because of important similarities in the behaviour of all animals, anti-solipsists assign to all of them (to different degrees perhaps) the capacity to experience sensations, to feel pain and pleasure, and so on.

2 Neither did I mean to imply that we never come across observations that apparently militate against the scientific hypothesis that will eventually prevail. For example, the lack of observable parallax effect among the so-called fixed stars seemed to point to the falsity of the Copernican hypothesis that the earth travelled round the sun. Supporters of that hypothesis had to explain away this finding by the then fantastic ad hoc hypothesis that the distance from our planet to those stars is so enormous that the earth's orbit is minute in relation to it. What I am talking about is the overall tendency towards an increasing need to explain away evidence hostile to the hypothesis that will finally have to be rejected.

3 According to the view I have expounded, there are overwhelming objective forces that force us to accept a given scientific hypothesis. Am I then claiming that the influential view that scientific progress cannot be accounted for in rational terms, and that there are no objective factors determining the choice of a particular theory, is groundless? Not quite. When we survey the evidence there may indeed be no rigorous

procedure for assessing the relative adequacy of competing hypotheses. Yet ultimately there can be an objectively grounded decision, since there is a clear trend over time for the wrong hypothesis to become entangled in the complexities contrived by those who have struggled to save it. But there is no precise point at which this entanglement becomes evident, which explains why not everyone abandons the hypothesis at the same moment. Eventually, however, almost everyone will.

To strengthen my point, let us look at what happens when there is agreement about which hypothesis to adopt. Any evidence that may be cited by one scientist to support his belief that the earth is round will be ratified by all the other scientists who share this conviction. The same is true for more sophisticated and complex hypotheses. Any evidence cited by a competent scientist as confirming Einstein's theory and disproving Newton's will be universally acknowledged by scientists as playing such a role. The case is entirely different with metaphysical hypotheses. Different philosophers may agree that a belief in, for example, the existence of other minds is justified, but the reason cited by one philosopher as to why this is so may carry no weight with another.

4 I mentioned earlier that the set of observations relevant to the metaphysical problem of whether there is a moving NOW has remained virtually unchanged over the last 500 years or so. It might be objected that the same seems to be true of a problem such as whether there is life on the planets of other solar systems, which nevertheless is a scientific problem.

The answer to the latter question is that it is easy to imagine plenty of relevant evidence. The reason such evidence has not been forthcoming is simply that the appropriate domain of observation has been inaccessible to us since so far we have no means of communicating with these planets. But with respect to the controversy concerning time, it seems that the relevant evidence is to be found in a readily accessible domain, that of all the everyday events which lie in the past, present and future. Despite the ease of access, no new evidence has presented itself during all this time to support either side of the dispute.

5 It is most important to note that, should the future surprise us and turn out to be different from what typical metaphysical hypotheses might lead me to predict, I shall not necessarily be proven wrong. Let us suppose that through the vast widening of our conceptual horizons the question whether time flows, for example, becomes subject, in a way we cannot conceive today, to the dynamic process that governs scientific hypotheses. In other words, we postulate that successive empirical discoveries seem to point to the correctness of, say, McTaggart's position, so that Russellians will become increasingly worn down by the

task of having to invent more and more special hypotheses to protect their position. I do not believe that this would disprove my thesis; it would show rather that what was thought to be a metaphysical problem turned out to be a scientific problem.

Science and metaphysics: some contrasts

Our recognition of fundamental distinctions between science and metaphysics should help us to understand why there are other important differences between the two disciplines.

1 Perhaps the most outstanding difference between science and metaphysics is that scientific disputes, however fierce, are bound to be resolved, while metaphysical controversies go on for ever. Indeed, it is this feature of metaphysics that has prompted the hostile view that it is a barren discipline, one in which all arguments are futile and no problem is ever solved, and that in spite of the enormous amount of mental energy invested throughout history in metaphysical endeavour no real progress has been achieved. In reply, defenders of metaphysics have claimed that it can be credited with substantial gains inasmuch as original arguments are produced from time to time; further, some old arguments have been thrown out while others have been progressively transformed and refined. However, even the staunchest supporters of metaphysics will concede that none of the major metaphysical questions yet has an answer that is agreed upon.

It is understandable why this should be so. Once the basic methodology of science is wholeheartedly accepted (which of course may be an act of metaphysical commitment in itself), scientific disputes become subject to a relentless process in the course of which the inadequacy of wrong hypotheses grows before our eyes. In the case of metaphysical questions, on the other hand, if the initial observations are such as to permit different hypotheses to be postulated, then there can be little change, for the relevant observation remains virtually fixed. The only substantial movement will be the invention of new arguments, but this of course is not a straightforward progression, since one side of a dispute is just as likely to introduce an argument as the other. Thus arguments and counter-arguments may succeed one another indefinitely, and the scientific process of accumulating evidence leading to the collapse of the wrong hypothesis does not take place.

2 It is now easy to see in what sense it may be said that metaphysics deals with more general propositions than science. We have seen that the set of observations relevant to the question whether time flows is not

going to be substantially affected by any future discoveries (unless it should turn out that this is not a genuine metaphysical question after all). In all the infinite number of logically possible worlds in which the future is different from what it will be in the real world, the arguments that seem to support the claim that time flows will therefore remain unaffected by new observations. Thus if a claim that time flows is true, it is not merely true in this particular world. The assertion expresses a general truth that is applicable to any world, however different from ours in the sense that it may have any possible future.

3 A statement whose truth is guaranteed by the laws of logic is necessarily true, and, characteristically, true in all possible worlds. Laws of nature, though they do not carry logical force, have nevertheless been thought by many to be in some sense necessary. Popper attempted to explain this by saying:

a statement may be said to be naturally or physically necessary, if, and only if, it is deducible from a statement function which is satisfied in all worlds that differ from our world, if at all, only with respect to initial conditions. [19]

It is of no concern to us that this definition has been found to conceal a circularity and thus is ultimately useless. [20] What is of interest is that the assumption on which Popper's assertion is based confirms as reasonable the view that a statement S, which does not merely happen to be true in the actual world but has to be true in an infinitely large class of other worlds (not just the class of worlds characterized as 'all the worlds in which S is true'), has a kind of necessity. Metaphysical statements may then be said to be necessary with even more reason: if true, they are true in all worlds with pasts similar to ours and with any kind of future. We have then a vindication of the view expressed by a number of philosophers (e.g. Campbell[21]) that metaphysics deals with necessary truth.

4 An individual is generally thought to have accidental and essential properties. Essential properties, according to a widely held view, are those that an individual possesses not merely in the actual world but in all the logically possible worlds in which he might exist. Metaphysical statements refer to features of our world that are present in all the worlds which so far have seemed sufficiently similar to ours for the question of their existence to have arisen, and which may have any logically possible future. Metaphysicians may therefore be said to be dealing with the essential features of the universe. This has indeed been maintained by many philosophers ranging from B. Blanshard, who regarded metaphysics as a vitally important enterprise and who said that it

'requires a focussing in the mental eye on invisible and impalpable essences',[22] to a hostile philosopher like Carnap who claimed to have eliminated the scope of metaphysics, which he characterized as the search for 'knowledge of the essence of things'.[23]

5 If metaphysics deals with 'invisible and impalpable essences' and thus requires 'focussing in the mental eye' then it deals with features that exist only in our thoughts. It is not unreasonable to claim as we saw above that 'metaphysics is thought about thought-about-the-world; it is talk about talk-about-the-world'.

Campbell's assertion, also quoted above, that metaphysics' task is to 'pierce the veil of appearance, to pass beyond how things seem, to reach to the basic, inner, and perhaps hidden part of the world' no longer strikes us as so strange. If metaphysicians are not concerned with features of the universe which merely happen to belong to it but with features that must belong to a vast set of possible universes – which of course are not here for us to examine directly – then indeed they are trying to reach something that lies hidden beyond the 'veil of appearance'.

6 We saw in the second section of this chapter how a philosopher who fully acknowledges the importance of metaphysics refers to it as 'unknowable'. This should not seem paradoxical any longer. The intention was not, of course, to imply that we do not know and cannot know the meaning of metaphysical statements, for if that were the case then indeed it would be absurd to study the subject. But what the author probably meant is that we cannot know whether a given metaphysical statement is true or not. All epistemologists agree that S does not know p unless he has sufficient evidence to establish sufficiently firmly that p is true. There are a few who have gone so far as to insist that unless S is absolutely certain that p is true he does not know that p; this leads to complete scepticism, since we cannot be absolutely certain about anything. Most philosophers have rejected this extreme view and accept the kind of confidence we feel justified in having in the conclusions that are upheld by the scientific community. As I have emphasized, even this kind of certainty is unattainable in metaphysics. It is not absurd to insist therefore that in metaphysics we never achieve the degree of certainty required for a belief to qualify as knowledge because there is no process that gradually disqualifies an erroneous hypothesis and hence a clear resolution of conflicting opinions can never occur.

7 In conclusion, a few words about those who have been antagonistic to the whole enterprise of metaphysics, and who have held – basically in agreement with Hume – that the pronouncements of metaphysicians do not 'contain any experimental reasoning concerning

matter of fact or existence' and have thus advised us to commit all their works to the flames. On reading the detailed attacks of positivists like Ayer or Carnap I am astonished to find the kind of example they have chosen in order to illustrate the vacuity of metaphysics. Speaking about 'specifically metaphysical terms', Carnap warns us in his famous article 'The Elimination of Metaphysics' that they are devoid of all meaning. Among his examples we find terms like 'the Absolute', 'the being of being', 'being-in-and-for-itself' and 'the non-Ego'. [24] Later, when he comes to metaphysical statements, he selects the following passage from the writings of Heidegger to illustrate the meaninglessness of metaphysics:

What is to be investigated is being only and – *nothing* else; being alone and further – *nothing*; solely being, and beyond being – *nothing. What about this Nothing?... Does the Nothing exist only because the Not, i.e. the Negation, exists?* Or is it the other way around? *Does Negation and the Not exist only because the Nothing exists?* . . . We assert: *The Nothing is prior to the Not and the Negation... .* Where do we seek the Nothing? How do we find the Nothing?. . . We know the Nothing. . . .*Anxiety reveals the Nothing.* . . . That for which and because of which we were anxious, was 'really' – nothing. Indeed: the Nothing itself – as such – was present. . . . *What about this Nothing? – The Nothing itself nothings.* [25]

From the numerous remarkable features of Carnap's article I should like to draw attention to (a) Carnap's failure to mention genuine metaphysical hypotheses, as opposed to absurd verbiage – hypotheses such as whether there exist dynamic temporal properties, or whether all possible worlds are as real as our own, or whether universals exist, and (b) to the fact that contrary to what he says, his examples are not suitable illustrations of how we expose pseudo-statements with the aid of the verifiability principle. A claim such as 'Last night every physical object in the universe shifted a hundred miles eastwards' might be dismissed as devoid of factual meaning through the application of the verifiability principle. We understand what is being said, and we can clearly explain what it is that cannot be done to verify the utterance. We cannot measure the distance between the position before and the position after the movement took place. But when it comes to an utterance like 'The Nothing itself Nothings', we are at a complete loss to describe what it is we cannot do that, if we could, would help us establish the truth of that utterance. In brief, this sentence is meaningless not because we are unable to perform a given verificatory operation but because it is unintelligible. Indeed, it would be difficult to see in what exactly consisted the revolutionary character of logical positivism if the rejection of the passage cited by Carnap is to be regarded as typical of its achievement.

In spite of some of its strange features, Carnap's paper does contain sound elements. Even the most intelligible and vitally important metaphysical statement may be deemed unverifiable in one sense. If verification is to be understood in the scientific sense in which experience places pressure on us to accept those hypotheses that adequately correspond to facts, then metaphysical statements are unverifiable. Metaphysical hypotheses as we have seen, are not affected by the accumulation of empirical observation, though we should not infer from this that they are deficient in factual content. However, as metaphysical hypotheses and scientific hypotheses have very different relationships to experience, they are justifiably assigned to fundamentally distinct categories.

2

Justification in metaphysics

Belief and justification

A considerable part of philosophical literature deals with the question of how to justify various commonly held metaphysical beliefs, such as the belief in the existence of an external world, the belief that the universe did not spring into being five minutes ago, the belief that others have a mind, and so on. There is, however, an important problem concerning the foundations of each one of these beliefs, a problem whose investigation requires the examination of the basic nature of metaphysics but which has received astonishingly little attention in recent years. The problem is this: why is it that the question of whether a person is rationally entitled to believe in any of these propositions is independent of whether that person is able to justify them?

It seems that nowadays the amount of treatment an issue receives from philosophers does not necessarily bear relation to its importance. For instance, in the past 15 years or so hundreds of articles have been written about exactly what is required before S is deemed to know that p in addition to being able to justify his belief that p (given that p is true). Some suggest that it is necessary that S's justification should not rely on premises that contain a sentence that (though he does not know it) is false; or that his justification needs to be defeasible, a concept that has been defined in a number of different ways by different philosophers; and so on. Later I shall look again at this relatively trivial problem, usually referred to as Gettier's problem, on which such a vast amount of ingenuity has been spent, and which ultimately boils down to the question of whether to label certain states as states of knowledge. Gettier's problem in no way affects the question what beliefs a given person is entitled to hold. Virtually nothing has been said about this much more important issue, which could affect whether a person is justified in holding some of his most fundamental and cherished beliefs.

Let us consider the belief in other minds as an example that will illustrate the prevailing attitude to all the beliefs of this kind. There are hardly any solipsists in the world. Many intelligent people who are not philosophers could not if challenged give a defence of their belief in the existence of other minds. Their typical reaction would be that they have a firm conviction that others cannot be merely robots, that they surely must have minds, but when it comes to a justification, not only are they at a loss to know how to construct one, but they will admit that some arguments designed for the purpose do not even sound intelligible to them. Even philosophers who have spent a good deal of effort in justifying such a belief do not seem to regard their justification as necessary for their belief. One may ask any philosopher who claims to have constructed a sound argument defeating solipsism what he would do if it were conclusively demonstrated to him that his argument was unsound. While philosophers may rarely admit in any particular case that their arguments are actually fallacious, they all eagerly profess to be fallible and open-minded, and agree that any of their arguments could in principle be proven wrong, in which case they would withdraw them. Thus, if we ask a philosopher what he would do if his argument in support of the existence of other minds was proved mistaken, the answer will be: he would retract it. However, he would not anticipate suspending his belief in other minds as a result. He would keep hoping that eventually he would be able to come up with an acceptable justification of his belief. In other words, the typical philosopher will admit that his belief in other minds is not predicated upon his ability to justify it.

Suppose, however, that from early childhood I have been indoctrinated with the strange belief that there are enormously intelligent extraterrestrial beings who are trying to communicate with us and who by 1985 will succeed in doing so, after which I will not need to worry about anything since they will instruct me unfailingly as to the right decision to make on any matter. This is a highly comforting belief and it may be deeply entrenched in my mind; nevertheless it seems to me that, if I am an enlightened person, once I realize I do not have any evidence to support it, and that in fact there is no way to justify it rationally, I shall abandon it. I would not be likely to fabricate an excuse for persisting in my belief by telling myself that, though there does not seem to be any evidence for the existence of these extraterrestrial beings at the moment, this does not mean that there cannot be evidence that I have yet to discover, so that I shall assume the existence of adequate evidence for my belief. I would realize, if I am reasonable, that rationality demands that one does not use the kind of argument that can always provide an excuse for believing in anything that wishful thinking may conjure up, and also that, when I do not actually have positive justification for believing that something is the case, I do not simply assume that such justification exists. Similarly, when I reach maturity and realize that it is not the possession of a sound basis for maintaining the existence of other minds that has generated in me this comforting belief, I shall abandon or at least suspend it.

It is conceivable that some might reply that I am wrong, and that in fact everyone who holds that he is not the only minded creature does so, rightly or wrongly, firmly convinced that he is capable of justifying his belief. Such a reply does not have much plausibility. It is not, after all, unheard of for a philosopher to admit 'Until x years ago I really had no idea how to justify my belief in the existence of other minds, but then it dawned on me that . . .'. Yet the same philosopher will not concede that until x years ago he was not justified in this belief.

That there is a problem here is also evident from the way we treat others. Suppose philosopher A is convinced that solipsism is untenable because of Strawson's well known criterial argument, whereas philosopher B holds the same conviction through relying on the old-fashioned analogical argument. A may well regard B as hopelessly confused, but will all the same grant that B is justified in his belief in the existence of other minds. In other words, the fact that B has no idea why he is right to believe in the existence of other minds does not prevent him, in A's eyes, from being justified in his belief.

But this is not so in general. When S believes that p, if there are excellent reasons to believe that p but S happens to be ignorant of them, then S will not be regarded as being justified in his belief. A witch doctor prescribes some bizarre treatment for a new type of disease because of a dream he has had. If it later turns out that medical scientists discover through careful experimentation that the treatment in question is effective, we shall not admit that the witch doctor was justified in believing his prescription to be useful.

The role of empirical evidence

I shall consider eight different suggestions for solving this problem without insisting that any particular solution is the correct one. In the course of the discussion it will become evident that the investigation of the problem involves probing into more vital issues than we would have initially suspected. Indeed, it is impossible to arrive at a sound solution before we have understood a number of basic features of metaphysics.

All these suggestions – except the sixth – are based on the view that the generally held presupposition (which in most cases is merely tacit) concerning the rationality of holding a number of basic metaphysical hypotheses is correct. I find it hard to believe that our prevailing attitudes are wrong; surely rationality does not require that we regard the many people who subscribe, without being able to justify their position, to such propositions as that there are other minds, or that the universe did not spring into being five minutes ago, as not entitled to their beliefs.

The suggestion I wish to consider first is that if there are empirical facts attainable through straightforward observation that are required for the justification of p, then S himself must be aware of them; but, when it comes to the arguments or logical facts that are used in arriving at p, S need not know them in order to be entitled to believe that p.

It is possible to produce some arguments to support this contention. First of all, it might be claimed that to obtain information through observation is a relatively straightforward matter and it is easy to determine whether one has done so or not; therefore we may well insist that S undertakes all such relevant observation. However, the question whether one is aware of a certain logical procedure is much more difficult to determine. It is a common phenomenon that mathematics students can prove a theorem without really understanding what they are doing. When can one really be said to understand that a certain theorem follows from another? Should a person who can make the right mathematical moves to derive a theorem without having the slightest idea how to justify any of them be regarded as capable of justifying his belief in its truth? If so, then how do we regard a person who not only does not know how to justify every step in his proof, but skips some of the intermediate steps altogether? If, on the other hand, we insist on complete understanding, then how can an average person ever be assumed to possess it? Presumably the complete understanding of a proof would involve a perfect grasp of proof theory. When philosophical arguments are concerned it is even more difficult to determine whether someone has achieved understanding or not.

Another point to consider is that if the reasoning process whereby p is established must be understood by S before he may lay claim to know that p, then, according to many philosophers it follows that, contrary to the usual view that nearly everybody knows the basic principles of logic such as the law of contradiction, in fact very few people – perhaps none – know them. The reason is that many philosophers believe that no matter how self-evident the basic tenets of logic may look, they can and should be further justified. They hold that even the argument that a proposition that looks self-evident to everyone is indeed true ultimately requires justification. However, there is no generally agreed way of doing this, and it is quite possible that none of the ways so far suggested of justifying the foundations of logic is correct. It is not, after all, unreasonable to claim that though we firmly believe that the basic rules of logic are sound, we are uncertain as to whether any of the philosophical justifications that have been offered for these rules are correct. But then, if knowledge is justified true belief, no one can know that these rules are correct.

Nor could many people be said to be justified in believing in the truth of such a simple empirical hypothesis as 'All unsupported bodies near the surface of the earth fall to the ground.' They may of course know that its basis is the fact that in the past such bodies have been observed to fall to the ground. But when it comes to the question why knowing this fact constitutes a justification for the hypothesis, most people do not know the right answer; there are scores of different and contradictory suggestions on how to justify induction. But in fact practically everybody knows that the hypothesis about unsupported bodies is true or is very probably true, which indicates that it is sufficient for people to be aware of the empirical basis for the justification of a hypothesis without their having to know the logical arguments that enter into the justification.

Our next step is to remind ourselves that all the beliefs referred to at the beginning of this chapter are typical metaphysical beliefs. The most crucially characteristic feature of a metaphysical hypothesis, as we have said, is that the facts that are relevant to its credibility remain unaffected by empirical discoveries, unlike down-to-earth empirical hypotheses, whose fortunes may change as our knowledge increases with accumulating observational data. We may look, for instance, at the various plausible arguments that have been produced in support of the hypothesis that other minds exist: we can see that none of them use facts that were not available to us 100 or even 500 years ago. Nor is it envisaged that we shall ever discover any new data that will affect that hypothesis; in fact, it seems we cannot coherently imagine any fact, no matter how strange and different from anything so far observed, that might be discovered in the future and that would affect the credibility of any metaphysical hypothesis. It is only the arguments designed to attribute more or less weight to the evidence that may undergo changes. If anyone were to object to my claim I would submit that either any counter-example he advances will be found not really to constitute a case of a dispute in metaphysics, or contrary to his belief, there has been no change in the empirical situation which the hypotheses in question were designed to explain.

Now, I admit that philosophers do sometimes make reference to recent scientific discoveries when arguing for a given metaphysical hypothesis. But it is not that such discoveries actually affect the credibility of the hypothesis, only that they may bring about a better understanding of certain arguments supporting its credibility. In other words, they may have a pedagogical use. For example, in a dispute between idealism and realism reference may be made to recent developments which make it possible, by electrical stimulation of the brain, to induce all sorts of vivid experiences in a person who has been deprived of sensory contact with the outside world. Extrapolating from this, I may conceive the possibility of there being no external reality at all, so that none of my experiences have their origin in a world that exists outside me; all of them are generated in my mind.

But of course the discovery of the possibility of electrically manipulating the central nervous system provides no evidence whatever for idealism, except that it may be used to good effect when trying to help someone to see that no amount of statements about actual experiences logically implies any statement about the existence of external objects. Descartes' original malevolent demon, who misleads me to believe that there exists an external world, was also, according to some commentators, no more than a pedagogical device, since an idealist does not really have to rely on a demon – or any external cause whatever – in order to explain how various impressions arise in our minds.

Similarly, in trying to argue for the plausibility of solipsism, a philosopher may refer to the computer – which though capable of performing complex tasks is nevertheless not thought of as having a mind – and claim that the people around us may likewise be no more than highly sophisticated, but mindless, machines. The fact that there are machines capable of simulating human behaviour to a certain extent helps us to explain the problem of other minds to the uninitiated but has no relevance to the actual credibility of solipsism.

Still, it might be argued that there is a great difference between earlier days, when sophisticated machines could be conceived only as a logical possibility, and today, when machines acting almost like humans actually exist. Their existence might be construed as evidence from which to argue that since physical systems resembling me do exist without having minds, it is likely that other people who are also physically similar to me are mindless. But we could not really argue in this way. For as soon as we reach the technological stage at which we can manufacture machines whose behaviour is sufficiently human for the solipsist's purpose, providing him with evidence for an inductive argument to support his position, we also reach the stage at which the anti-solipsist will assign a mind to these 'machines' just because they are so similar to him. Thus, the actual credibility of solipsism remains unaffected.

At this point it may be instructive to consider the way suggested by Hilary Putnam of establishing the existence of other minds. [1] It seems to raise a difficulty in the view I have expounded, for it implies that either the problem of other minds is after all not a metaphysical problem, in spite of the fact that it has been a typical philosophical problem, or that metaphysical problems are also affected by the accumulation of empirical evidence. He points out that psychologists have produced, and are constantly producing, explanations of why people are angry, suspicious, lustful and so on, and have described the circumstances in which people have these mental properties, to what degree and so on. There exists a large systematic network of explanations and descriptions of regularities which is regarded as confirmed and in which mental properties are referred to. Now if I deny that others have a mind, that they have mental properties, then 'I am giving up propositions that are implied by the explanations that I give on specific occasions of the behavior of other people. So I would have to give up all of these explanations.' [2] But then Putnam argues that when we have an explanatory system of some power we do not abandon it unless someone comes forward with an alternative system of comparable power:

It is therefore up to the objector [i.e. the solipsist] in the case of the thesis that others have mental states, to provide an alternative explanation for the behavior of other people. It is the fact that no such alternative explanation is in the field, along with the undoubted explanatory power of the accepted psychological theories, that constitutes the real inductive justification for the acceptance of the accepted system. [3]

According to this, the situation concerning the hypothesis that others have a mind is also a dynamic one, for with the accumulation of psychologists' discoveries about mental properties, the inductive evidence in favour of that hypothesis keeps increasing. It would have to be concluded that my account of the fundamental difference between metaphysics and science was wrong, or else we would have to arrive at the dubious conclusion that the problem of other minds was not really a metaphysical problem.

In fact no such undesirable consequences follow, for Putnam's argument is based on a mistake. He may be quite right that no textbooks have so far been written in a language that reflects a solipsistic position and that all the laws of psychology happen so far to have been formulated in a way that does not avoid attributing mental properties to others. But it does not follow from this that an equally satisfactory alternative theoretical system, one that does not presuppose that others have a mind, does not exist. After all, it is a trivial matter to restate any law of psychology that refers to the mental properties of others without using such references. A statement 'Under circumstances C a subject will have property M' where M is a mental term can always be translated into 'Under circumstances C a subject will exhibit behaviour which I typically exhibit when having property M.' All the textbooks on psychology can mechanically be translated into a solipsistic language. Consequently all the laws of psychology that Putnam regards as serving his purpose confirm the existence of other minds no more than they confirm solipsism.

1 Now we are in a position to see how our original problem may be solved. Suppose that a person S subscribes to a metaphysical hypothesis p when philosophers are not in agreement as to the rational foundations for the credibility of p. Conventionally it is not the case that S believes there are hitherto unknown empirical data which could be used to support the credibility of p, since S realizes that it is inherent in the nature of p that no new observation will affect its credibility. The reason why S subscribes to p even if he is not able to justify his belief is because he hopes that an adequate argument exists – one he may or may not discover – showing that in the context of the observational situation that has existed all along p may be justifiably maintained. If we believe that this is indeed so, then we shall not deny S's right to subscribe to p, even though he does not happen to be aware of the argument required for justifying a belief in p.

Suppose, however, that p stands for a down-to-earth empirical hypothesis. Then, even though S may have developed a very strong belief that p is true, he cannot be regarded as justified in holding such a belief when he is incapable of supporting it, since what he is lacking is empirical evidence – universally acknowledged to be the sole legitimate basis for this kind of hypothesis. Thus, since I am not in the possession of genuine observational data that might be construed as clues to the existence of highly intelligent extraterrestrial beings who are about to communicate with us, and since I realize that a belief in their existence is unlikely to be established by the introduction of some new type of argument that will support it in the context of existing observations, then if I am a reasonable person I will myself acknowledge that I am not entitled to hold this belief. Similarly the witch doctor who has no idea of the experiments whereby later scientists confirm the effectiveness of his prescription does not qualify as being justified in believing that his remedy will do his patients any good. The reason is, as we have already explained, that S is not justified in believing that p, even though there is empirical evidence sufficient to justify a belief in p, as long as he himself is unaware of the existence of this evidence.

I should mention that philosophers who subscribe to the causal theory of knowledge are likely to find this suggestion quite acceptable. According to the causal theory of knowing, a person never needs to justify his belief in anything. All that is demanded is that S's belief that p should be brought about by the genuine grounds for its truth. Thus some have suggested the following definition:

> Some adequate evidence e provides S with knowledge that q (or at least a justified belief that q) iff S's belief is causally based on e.

Thus a man knows that his hat is on the peg if he believes that his hat is on the peg and if it is the fact that his hat is on the peg which has caused him to believe this.

In the case of metaphysical knowledge that p, as we have already said, we are as a rule unaware of e which constitutes adequate evidence that q and therefore p is true.

Many may find the previous suggestion unacceptable. Consider a person S who knows that q and declares that because q therefore p, where p does not at all seem to be connected to q. Even if it is later shown that by some complex logical and mathematical manoeuvring p may be demonstrated to follow from q, something S admits he did not have the slightest clue of, then our intuition seems to tell us that S was not, prior to the demonstration, justified in believing that p. Of course it is common for laymen to believe in the truth of all sorts of scientific propositions established by highly technical methods that they do not even begin to understand; however, they are justified in their beliefs since they are taking the word of experts who have established the truth of these propositions. Learning that p from authoritative sources itself constitutes one of the recognized valid justifications for believing that p. However, I am referring to a case in which S arrives at the true belief that p follows from q without having heard this from anyone who knows it to be so.

2 We shall therefore consider the suggestion that S does not qualify as being justified in believing that p unless he knows the empirical basis as well as the mathematical and scientific arguments that are required for establishing that p. As to the objection that the demand that S should understand the arguments supporting p is an indeterminate demand,

the reply may be that the full possession of all the logical facts is required, but that this may be satisfied in two ways: any mathematical or scientific argument used for establishing p must be understood by S himself, or he must ensure its validity by having learned it from a reliably expert source. What S need not know, however, is any of the philosophical arguments that may be needed for establishing p.

Whether or not one is able to produce an adequate argument to defend this distinction, it is clear that by making it we are able to account for why one is justified in believing something. Suppose S believes that p follows from q. If his belief is not based on having obtained that information from a reliable source, then we shall insist that he be able to demonstrate in detail how to derive p from q. Now suppose that in his demonstration he has employed certain theorems; we shall ask whether he knows from authoritative sources that they are true. If the answer is 'No', then he has to be able to derive these theorems from others, and so on. But we are not led to a bottomless pit, since when we reach the foundations of mathematics and logic their justification is a matter of philosophy, and therefore S is entitled to believe that there is a justification even if he does not know what it is.

Again, suppose we ask whether S knows that an unsupported body will fall to the ground; the answer is 'Yes', because he is justified in believing this since he understands that it follows from 'All unsupported bodies fall to the ground', which is a true belief of his. We may continue to ask whether S knows also that all unsupported bodies fall to the ground; again the answer is 'Yes', since he knows that this follows inductively from the premiss that all hitherto observed unsupported bodies have fallen to the ground. But what if we go further, and ask also whether S is justified in believing that a conclusion which follows inductively from true premisses is to be accepted? We no longer have to require that S is capable of justifying this belief. Here the appropriate justification would clearly have to be a philosophical justification, and S is no longer obliged to provide this before he may be said to be entitled to his belief.

Similarly, S is entitled to believe in all the metaphysical propositions I mentioned at the beginning of this chapter, even though he does not know how to defend them. The reason is that what he is lacking is not some empirical information or mathematical or scientific argument, but the knowledge of the appropriate philosophical reasoning by which these beliefs are to be established, and this cannot be held against him.

But we must provide some reasonable justification for making this distinction between the various types of argument which may be required to establish the truth of p. The first suggestion we may consider is that the rules governing the arguments employed in science and mathematics are generally agreed upon, and therefore it is not unreasonable to insist that S should be able to reproduce the proper scientific arguments to establish that p. The rules of philosophical reasoning, on the other hand, are not universally agreed upon; hence it makes no sense to insist that S must employ the appropriate philosophical arguments to establish that p when the philosophical community is itself undecided as to which of the various arguments that have been advanced is acceptable. This is what accounts for the fact that practically all disagreements in science are eventually resolved since there are commonly acknowledged rules to which one may appeal in order to adjudicate such disputes. True enough, many disputes have persisted over an extended period because the amount of evidence was limited and this permitted scientists who subscribed to the wrong hypothesis to protect it by explaining away the adverse evidence by *ad hoc* hypotheses. However, with the steady increase of experimental data, the incorrect hypothesis requires more and more auxiliary hypotheses to keep it afloat, and it becomes unmistakably clear which hypothesis fits smoothly with the observed data. Thus while the hypothesis that the earth is flat, the phlogiston theory or the caloric theory of fluid was championed for an extended period in history, enough experimental evidence eventually came to light for it to become clear that by the accepted rules determining what hypothesis fits what data, these hypotheses and theories could only be maintained at the prohibitive cost of upholding an enormously inflated set of *ad hoc* hypotheses. Philosophical arguments, on the other hand, may never terminate as there are no fixed rules that the conflicting parties can appeal to.

I am aware that there are some philosophers who deny that there are any hard and fast rules for establishing scientific theories; they insist that the progress of science and the way in which old theories are abandoned and new ones adopted cannot be accounted for rationally. Yet even they will agree that substantial areas of astronomy, physics, chemistry, and so on constitute by universal agreement a body of established science. Further, there is broad agreement as to what experimental results form the empirical basis for the various scientific theories and hypotheses commonly held today, and as to the reasoning that connects evidence to theories and hypotheses. I do not believe anyone would deny that if a large number of scientists were asked to explain why Newton's theory has been replaced by Einstein's, then all would give essentially the same account. In philosophy we do not have anything even remotely resembling such a consensus. Even when it comes to a philosophical view held by nearly everyone, such as that solipsism is false, different philosophers will offer entirely different ways of justifying it. Consequently, if we were to insist that S must philosophically justify his belief that p before he will be deemed justified in believing it, then we would be setting excessively hard conditions for believing that p. As a result we would virtually never be able to tell whether S is or is not justified in believing p when p requires philosophical defence.

3 Some may not be happy with this argument. After all, if S's awareness of the way p is to be justified is a condition for S justifiably believing that p, it is just bad luck that philosophical justification is so hard to come by; but still, if S does not know how to justify p explicitly then as a matter of principle it is not correct to say that S is justified in believing that p. Hence we shall consider a different suggestion. It might be claimed that not only is there no agreement about which particular philosophical argument is the right one to establish that p, but there is no such thing as *the* correct argument. The situation may perhaps be compared to that of several novelists offering different descriptions of a certain experience. These descriptions will be judged as being insightful, memorable, eloquent, moving and so on to different degrees, but not only will the critics abstain from rendering a verdict as to which one is the correct description, they will assume that there can be no correct description. Similarly, some philosophers hold that when philosophical arguments are offered in favour of a position these arguments may differ in originality, ingenuity, insightfulness, authenticity and persuasiveness, but there is simply no such thing as *the* correct argument. If one accepts this view it seems right not to insist that S should reproduce the correct philosophical justification of p when this does not exist.

Because the standards of rigour prevailing in metaphysics are more relaxed than those we are accustomed to in science, we permit ourselves to use a large number of argument forms that are inadmissible in science. I should quickly add that this is not because of the relative unimportance of metaphysics. If we were to insist that only what is permitted in science is permitted in metaphysics, we could hardly make any progress at all. As we have seen in the first chapter, given that the empirical world does not point unequivocally to a particular metaphysical hypothesis, we are forced to compensate by relying more on arguments. But even when we employ only the inference rules of mathematical logic to establish some result in metaphysics we cannot be absolutely certain in our conclusions. We may have derived q formally from p, yet there may already be uncertainty attaching to p, which is likely to be of a fairly abstract kind, based on unproven and unspoken presuppositions; and because of the tricky nature of metaphysical thought we may not even be sure that p adequately articulates the idea we are trying to express.

4 Another suggestion might be that metaphysical beliefs may not only be held by a person who cannot justify them, they may be held even if they cannot actually be justified. The truth of a mathematical proposition is vouchsafed by its being mathematically derivable from other true propositions, and the truth of some empirical propositions is rooted in the fact that they may be derived by the use of the rules of scientific reasoning from other true empirical propositions. Anyone who believes these propositions without being able to reproduce the method of arriving at them is only guessing and does not have a justified belief. Metaphysical facts of the kind we have considered, on the contrary, are so conspicuous and inescapable that we intuit them directly without going through any process of derivation. Consequently a belief in certain true metaphysical propositions is self-certifying and a person may acquire it with complete assurance. It might be asked why, if this is so, we have such an extensive literature of arguments designed to establish metaphysical propositions. The answer would be that these are explanatory arguments intending to show *why* these propositions are true and not *that* they are true.

What is being claimed is that certain metaphysical features of the universe are completely transparent so that from infancy all of us have gained a firm confidence in their existence. For example, from the time we began to reason we all took it for granted that induction is valid and never entertained any real doubt about it. Suppose for a moment that Reichenbach's argument is valid: it is safe to use induction since if any method for predicting the future works then induction works. Then the function of this argument is to be understood not as providing the actual reason for relying on induction, but to demonstrate that there are logical considerations which make it inevitable that induction is a rational method of inquiry. Reichenbach provides an argument which we could use to arrive at the conclusion that induction is reliable were it not that we had already learned that this was so by a more direct method. The situation is comparable to what we are doing when we demonstrate that Galileo's law of free falling may be derived from Newton's more basic laws of mechanics. Galileo's law had been established long before on the basis of a large number of experiments in which it was noted how the distance fallen corresponded to the time elapsed. Our purpose in deriving it from Newton's laws is not to show that Galileo's law is true but to give a reason why it is true. We also show that were it not for the fact that we already know Galileo's law, we could have established its truth by deriving it from Newton's laws.

One can find support for this fourth solution to our problem in the writings of Wittgenstein, among others. According to Wittgenstein in his last book *On Certainty*, some metaphysical hypotheses are not based on grounds; they are not reasonable or unreasonable, they are just there.[4] They are just there, like our own very lives, without the possibility or the need for justification. Quite the opposite: he who wished to cast doubt on such beliefs would have to provide positive grounds for doing so.[5]

It should be noted that according to this view there are some metaphysical beliefs that cannot justifiably be held unless one is actually able to justify them because they are by no means transparently true. For instance, the question of how to give a correct account of temporal becoming is still widely debated; whatever the correct answer might be, it cannot be said to be immediately obvious to everyone. Also it seems that while certain metaphysical beliefs may indeed not require justification, it does not follow that the assertion that this is so itself needs no justification. If it did then it would seem one could ask: if S believes that *p* – where *p* is an allegedly manifest, directly knowable metaphysical proposition – and S is unable to reproduce the justification of the position that *p* requires no justification, is S still justified in his belief? A plausible answer to this might be that he is not, but this means merely that S is not justified in believing that he is justified in believing that *p* without being able to defend it; but he would still be justified in believing that *p*, even though he cannot defend it. The question which would then have to be asked is: do we in fact regard most people as being justified, for example, in believing that there are other minds, but not as justified in believing that they are justified in believing that there are other minds?

5 In the first chapter I discussed a radical view of the nature of metaphysics according to which our problem is easily solved. As we have seen, some positivists have claimed that since there are no agreed rules as to how to demonstrate the truth of a metaphysical hypothesis, such hypotheses are unverifiable in principle and are hence neither true nor false. Metaphysical sentences do not express cognitive propositions. If this is so, a positivist may claim that S is not entitled to believe that *p*, where *p* is a cognitive proposition, unless he is able to reproduce fully the reason why he is justified in believing that *p*. This permits subscription to metaphysical propositions without justification.

However, as I said earlier that is an extreme thesis, and it is not even certain that its originators wished to apply it to all metaphysics. A more moderate version of their view, as discussed in the first chapter, is that while metaphysical statements are of great significance they do not have the status of empirical statements because they are not imposed upon us by the inevitable accumulation of evidence. They are therefore not verifiable in the strong sense, by which they would become irresistible and thus permanently abolish all opposition in the way all scientific disputes eventually end. Because of the different status of metaphysical statements, namely that they are not empirical in the sense described, the principle that S is not justified in holding *p* unless he himself knows how to justify *p* may be said not to apply to them.

6 The following solution is based on an extreme view suggested by the writings of L. Bonjour, among others. In a fine article 'Can Empirical Knowledge Have a Foundation?'[6] Bonjour, who is a coherentist, argues against the idea that there are basic beliefs which need no justification by the agent himself. He says:

If basic beliefs are to provide a secure foundation for empirical knowledge, if inference from them is to be the sole basis for the justification of other empirical beliefs, then that feature, whatever it may be, in virtue of which a belief qualifies as basic must also constitute a good reason for thinking that the belief is true. If we let '∅' represent this feature, then for a belief B to qualify as basic in an accepable foundationist account, the premises of the following justificatory argument must themselves be at least justified:

  (i) Belief B has feature ∅.
  (ii) Beliefs having feature ∅ are highly likely to be true.
    Therefore, B is highly likely to be true.

Notice further that while either premise taken separately might turn out to be justifiable on an *a priori* basis (depending on the particular choice of ∅), it seems clear that they could not both be thus justifiable. For B is *ex hypothesi* an empirical belief, and it is hard to see how a particular empirical belief could be justified on a purely *a priori* basis. And if we now assume, reasonably enough, that for B to be justified for a particular person (at a particular time) it is necessary, not merely that a justification for B exist in the abstract, but that the person in question be in cognitive possession of that justification, we get the result that B is not basic after all since its justification depends on that of at least one other empirical belief.

This passage clearly shows that the author – who represents a view held by quite a number of anti-foundationalists nowadays – thinks that S needs to be, in all cases without exception, in 'cognitive possession' of the justification of *p* before S is in fact justified in believing that *p*. It would follow that I may not be entitled to believe that others have a mind because I believe that the inductive argument is the most correct way to justify such a belief, and it might in fact be the case that none other than the Strawsonian criterial argument is the best way to combat solipsism.

However, as I have indicated, I am reluctant to admit that I, together with the majority of the human race, may not be entitled to assign mindedness to other bodies. I would rather urge the rejection of Bonjour's view. There are, after all, other difficulties with it. Suppose S has a belief B at time t, and

B = S has intense chest pains at t.

Suppose also that S is not a professional philosopher, and is not aware of the sophisticated arguments which assign the particular feature ϕ to B, by virtue of which S is justified in holding B. According to Bonjour, S does not know that B. This in itself is somewhat strange. But now suppose S knows enough philosophy to have heard of Bonjour's principle that one needs to be in cognitive possession of one's justification in all instances of belief. Then S realizes, according to Bonjour, that he does not know that B and that he is not entitled to believe that B. Would S be morally and perhaps even legally blameworthy if he summoned the police and the ambulance service in the middle of the night to come and save him?

But there may be a simpler and stronger argument to confirm the position we have taken from the beginning of this chapter, namely that, for whatever reason, one is entitled to hold at least certain metaphysical beliefs without being able to justify them. In fact the argument that follows seems to go even further: not only is one entitled, but one may even be obliged to subscribe to certain metaphysical beliefs. Suppose the bank produces a document signed by me a month ago in which I acknowledge receipt of their loan of $10,000. Let us also suppose that I quite sincerely believe that the universe was created five minutes ago (according to Russell's well-known suggestion that this is possible; the suggestion assumes that the universe bears all the traces of an older universe). On the basis of this metaphysical conviction, I argue that a month ago neither I nor the bank existed, and that the document sprang fully fledged into being, together with the rest of the universe, five minutes ago. So I insist that there is no reason why I should have to pay the bank any money I have not borrowed from them.

Although I do not think that there is any legal precedent for this, I have little doubt that if I were to be brought before a judge he would have no compunction in forcing me to pay, even though he may never have heard of Russell's sceptical hypothesis and admits that he has not the slightest idea how to reply to it or what the rational basis is for the generally held belief that the universe has existed for much longer than five minutes. In fact he is obliged to rule thus by law. Is it plausible to suppose that one should be obliged by law, with the approval of most decent citizens, to enact beliefs one is not rationally justified in holding?

Suppose that I drop a heavy rock from the roof; it falls on a man's head, critically injuring him. Also suppose that I am genuinely sceptical of the metaphysical doctrine that nature is uniform. Consequently, I argue that when I let the rock go I was convinced that there was hardly any likelihood that it would fall downwards in an uninterrupted vertical line so as to hit this unfortunate person, who was alone in the street at the time. After all, there were indefinitely many other paths the rock could have followed, indefinitely many spots other than the head of the victim that it could have hit. Why should I even expect it to hit anything at all? It might just as well remain suspended in mid-air, turn into dust or evaporate. Of course, I shall not be exonerated. All citizens are obliged by law to act always on the presupposition that the 'laws of nature' will continue to operate in the future. Failing to do so may draw severe punishment. No philosopher is known to have objected to this aspect of the law. Thus it seems not to be irrational for the law to insist that everyone take the doctrine of the uniformity of nature as unquestionably established, even though there are not likely to be many among the legislators who know how to justify it. Whether I like it or not, I am obliged to act in accordance with it.

7 A. Plantinga, in his widely read book *God and Other Minds,*[7] discusses at considerable length the various arguments that have been produced in support of the belief in other minds, and concludes that not one of them is sound. He points out that in spite of this it is commonly agreed that a belief in the existence of other minds is rational. Therefore he claims that a belief in theism must not be condemned simply because there are no good arguments to support it. It is not irrational for the theist to adhere to his faith without any justification.

If Plantinga is right our problem seems to disappear. People are not required to be able to offer justifications for their metaphysical beliefs, because such justifications do not exist. His argument resembles argument (3) above but is much more radical. In (3) it was claimed merely that different philosophers defend metaphysical beliefs by different arguments, and it is not possible to determine which is the best argument among them. But now we are told that not only is there no such thing as *the* best argument, there is not even any good argument. Not many, however, would be willing to adopt such an extreme view. Let me try and state what is objectionable.

We are all familiar with the impatient claim that philosophy is a useless enterprise since the same old problems are being debated over and over again, with no definite result ever being conclusively established nor any real progress made. The more level-headed view however is that when a philosopher advances an argument A in support of a given position P which then is refuted by the next philosopher who advances R, the situation is not simply back where it was before A had been proposed. Progress has been made because when the third philosopher comes along he realizes that A as it stands is untenable, yet he will often make use of the valid insight which he believes underlies A, and will formulate A′, a refined version of A not vulnerable to refutation R. The debate whether P is right or wrong may never come to an end and as time goes on more and more subtle and complex arguments will have to be adduced by both sides in the debate. Thus there is much philosophical gain from the continuing debate, for both sides develop an increasingly more sophisticated understanding of the elaborate issues that may be involved in holding or rejecting P.

Now, theism, like our belief in other minds, has been argued about for a very long time. Even if it were granted that Plantinga's objections to all the arguments hitherto devised are important, it is rather hasty to conclude that nobody will ever find fault with any of them, or even that no one will find a way to reformulate some of these arguments or find an entirely new argument in such a way as to escape his objections. Plantinga himself, even if he regarded his objections as absolutely unanswerable, did not intend them to show that in principle no argument whatever could be devised to support theism or the belief in other minds, but only to demonstrate that some specific arguments are invalid. (Indeed, it is hard to imagine how anyone would go about constructing a general proof that no attempt of any kind to combat solipsism or atheism could be successful.) He thus has no basis for concluding that his arguments constitute the end of the long histories of these two metaphysical issues.

Some may, however, go further and complain that it is not even clear what Plantinga is advocating. Is he trying to convince us that in metaphysics any view is as good as any other? Does he actually want to claim that all arguments devised to defend a metaphysical view are futile, and thus recommend the abandonment of the study of metaphysics altogether? This seems highly unlikely. One might rather suggest that the two beliefs he discusses are special in that they – but not others – may be held on faith alone. In that case the essential question Plantinga neglected to answer is: what are the crucial characteristics of the belief in other minds and theism that set them apart from all other metaphysical beliefs, some of which do require elaborate justification? Of course, had he explained this he would have considerably strengthened his defence of theism, but he would not have helped us with our problem. The latter affects all metaphysical hypotheses held by non-philosophers, who are rational in holding beliefs in spite of the fact that they cannot justify them.

But perhaps a more moderate position is being advocated. It may be assumed that both theism and the belief in other minds are capable of being adequately supported by sound arguments. However, as Plantinga's elaborate discussion in his book may be taken to show, this has not been successfully accomplished in either case. Naturally philosophers will go on, and indeed should go on, in their search for unassailable arguments to support these beliefs. But surely we cannot be expected to wait and suspend judgement until someone at last comes forward with an argument no one can demolish. Plantinga's thesis may thus be taken as saying: just as nobody has waited until a compelling argument is produced affirming that others have a mind, so with all metaphysical questions everyone is entitled to subscribe to the answer he believes to be right even before that belief has been adequately defended.

It may be noted that no interpretation represents Plantinga as producing any reason whatsoever why one should affirm theism rather than deny it. His conclusion implies that it is equally rational to maintain either position. Some readers may have expected something more from a book written to defend theism. However, our last argument does give us an adequate answer to the question why one is entitled to hold metaphysical beliefs without being able to justify them.

8 Of all the suggestions considered here, the one which will probably be most approved of, and which touches upon the most central features of metaphysics, is simply that we are compelled to permit the holding of at least some metaphysical beliefs without justification. For if philosophers insisted on maintaining that there is an epistemological principle stating that no belief of any sort can justifiably be held by a person unless he knows how to justify it, then no knowledge at all is possible. For suppose I believe

S = All unsupported bodies fall to the ground.

If asked what is the basis for my belief in S, I shall of course reply that S is supported by inductive evidence. But then I may be asked to justify my belief in the validity of inductive reasoning itself. If the principle that all beliefs require justification does not extend to metaphysical beliefs, I can point out that the belief that induction is sound is a metaphysical belief and therefore I need not justify it. However, if the principle applies to all knowledge I will have to justify my belief in the reliability of inductive inference. If I cannot then I am not entitled to trust induction as a satisfactory method, and consequently neither am I justified in believing that S. Suppose I succeed in constructing a justification of induction, J. Immediately the question will be raised: can I justify J? It is clear that this process would never end; in the meantime, S remains without justification.

This last answer basically uses the argument usually employed by foundationalists – philosophers who claim that while we may justify our belief that S_1 by deriving it with the aid of some legitimate inference rule from S_2, and S_2 by inferring it from S_3, ultimately we must reach S_n which we justify no further and which requires no further justification. The important extra point that I have drawn attention to here is that all such foundational statements upon which the rest of our knowledge is based are metaphysical statements. Of course the converse is not true: all metaphysical statements are not foundational statements. However, we treat all metaphysical statements as having the same epistemological status: namely that they may be held by people who are unable to justify them.

Metaphysics and belief: a summary

In chapter 1 I referred to the remarkable fact that it is exceedingly hard to find in the entire literature on metaphysics any statement that attempts to characterize our subject, one that applies to all metaphysical beliefs. It is conceivable that someone would claim that this is not such a disastrous omission. After all, we may search through thousands of books on physics, astronomy, chemistry, or biology and not find a single sentence which makes a general statement concerning the nature of science as a whole.

This would not amount to a very adequate defence. An investigation of the general nature of science, of its aims, methods and presuppositions, belongs to a discipline different from that which discovers and describes individual results within any of these sciences. Scientists leave the former to philosophers of science. But both philosophy and metaphilosophy are part of the subject matter of philosophy, and if philosophers do not care to examine them, who will?

We are now in a position to see a much more important point. To the extent that we fail to grasp the general nature of metaphysics, we shall also fail to understand various aspects of individual metaphysical beliefs and their justification. The investigation of particular metaphysical arguments and beliefs is logically dependent on the results of our study of the general nature of metaphysics. For example, once we have learned the important point that the set of evidence relevant to a particular metaphysical statement is essentially static, we know we must be on our guard when it is suggested – as we have seen in this chapter – that the accumulating results of modern psychology may be used to establish a belief in the existence of other minds. Similarly, in the next chapter we shall find it necessary to study more closely certain arguments concerning theism in order to be able to defend the claim that theism belongs to metaphysics. For on the surface it may seem that theism lacks the feature, discussed in the first chapter, which sets metaphysics apart from science.

Finally, with regard to the use of various forms of reasoning in metaphysical statements, principles which are not deductively valid can be understood only when we realize how different are the roles of experience in the establishment of metaphysical beliefs and in the establishment of scientific hypotheses.

3

Theism and scientific method

The problem of evil

In this chapter I shall begin to deal with individual metaphysical beliefs and with particular forms of reasoning and techniques that have been employed in trying to establish them. I shall begin with a discussion of theism which, many people will be ready to admit, is the most momentous of all metaphysical doctrines. The particular technique I should like to consider is the use of scientific methodology in the confirmation of a metaphysical belief. I should emphasize that, in spite of the fact that a profound difference exists between the ways in which scientific and metaphysical beliefs are established, we should make full use of deductive and inductive logic (except, of course, on those occasions when the very metaphysical presuppositions on which these rest are the subject of inquiry). Admittedly the scope for using the methodology of the natural scientist is rather limited in metaphysics, but there is no reason why we should regard it with distrust when an opportunity to employ it does arise.

I regret that in my book *Religion and Scientific Method*[1] I failed to stress that to use the intellectual tools human beings have developed in their effort to decipher the laws of nature (which to a theist amounts to an effort to interpret the divine will embodied in these laws) in the philosophy of religion does not represent a failure to appreciate the exaltedness of the subject. Some well-intentioned critics expressed reservations and contended that, to a certain degree, I have debased my subject by applying mundane logic to it. They find it more satisfying when a writer uses a more florid and opaque style, replete with allusions and metaphors, whereby he inspires as well as mystifies the reader and does not drag the ineffable down to the level of everyday discourse.

I venture to suggest that the tendency to eschew penetrable presentation and cogent arguments is at least partially a manifestation of the spirit of despondency that afflicts many writers who defend traditional theism. This is not entirely surprising. Beginning with the scientific revolution of the seventeenth century, after which the view that physical events have natural causes strictly governed by laws took deeper and deeper root, cherished religious assumptions seem to have been demolished one by one. The relentless onslaught of the forces of scepticism has turned the gradual retreat of believers into a rout. Smarting from too many defeats, or rather from what have been construed as defeats, many theists, unaware that there is plenty of room for religious belief based upon the solid ground of reality, have been driven to such despair that they see no other path but retreat into a world of fantasy. In the course of our discussion I shall have opportunity to refer to some arguments that seem unquestionably to have been launched from despair, from a position much further back than the line of defence that adherents of religious belief had to retreat to.

The argument from evil is one of the few philosophical arguments that are fairly well known among non-philosophers. It is also unusual in that unlike most other philosophical arguments it has had widespread practical consequences: many people have abandoned their belief in an omnipotent and omnibenevolent being in view of the all too evident evil the world contains, which they regard as incompatible with the existence of such a being.

It may not be unfair to say that the argument from evil owes its great impact on the human mind to the powerful emotions pain and misery stir up in us, not to the logical force of the argument itself. There are several ways of showing that the problem of evil admits completely satisfactory solutions. I propose to illustrate this by examining a solution which has had a fairly long history. I shall not discuss more than one valid solution so as to leave enough space for clarifying the nature of the solution and for showing how any objection that is likely to be raised against it can be fully met.

The simple form of the argument from evil can be exhibited as follows. Let

H_1 = An omnipotent, omniscient and omnibenevolent being exists.

A_1 = Benevolence precludes the perpetuating or condoning of suffering.

O_1 = Suffering does not exist.

Now H_1 & A_1 is taken to imply that suffering does not exist, since a God who is omnipotent is capable of preventing it if he does not want it to exist, and he cannot want it to exist since he is omnibenevolent. But suffering does exist, that is O_1 is false. Thus

$$((H_1 \& A_1) \rightarrow O_1) \& \sim O_1 \& A_1$$

has been established to be true. Therefore it logically follows that $\sim H_1$ – in the face of all the suffering that goes on in the world, God as conceived by almost all theists cannot be maintained to exist.

It is worth mentioning that Nelson Pike has argued in a well-known paper[2] that in fact H_1 & A_1 on their own do not imply O_1; it is only H_1 & A_1 & A_1' that logically imply O_1, where [A_1' = There are no morally sufficient reasons for God to permit suffering.] Without trying to suggest what these morally sufficient reasons might be, Pike goes on to say that we cannot be definitely certain that A_1' is true and thus we no longer have the necessary premises from which $\sim H_1$ would logically follow.

It seems not unfair to describe Pike's manoeuvre as a last ditch defence to be undertaken only after everything else has failed. A reasonable scientist, however anxious to defend a given hypothesis, would not resort to this kind of defence. For a brief illustration suppose

H_2 =   The earth is moving around the sun in an orbit of many thousands of miles.

A_2 =   When in motion one observes a parallax effect among distant objects.

O_2 =   From the earth we observe a parallax effect among the 'fixed stars'.

Clearly H_2 & A_2 $\rightarrow$ O_2. But before 1838 no astronomer was able to observe a parallax effect among the fixed stars. Thus we have

$$((H_2 \& A_2) \rightarrow O_2) \& \sim O_2 \& A_2$$

and therefore it follows that $\sim H_2$, i.e. Copernicus' description of the solar system is false. Now, not even at a time when scientific standards were somewhat looser than at present did it occur even to the most ardent followers of Copernicus to argue that H_2 & A_2 on their own do not imply O_2, only that H_2 & A_2 & A_2' do so, where

A_2' =   There is no scientifically sufficient cause to mask the parallax effect

without suggesting what this might be. What they did suggest was that A_2^* should be assumed to be true where

A_2^* =   The fixed stars are so far away that the radius of the earth's orbit relative to their distance from us is negligible.

On assuming A_2^*, of course, O_2 no longer follows. It is therefore not unreasonable to point out to Pike that A_1' is not an adequate defence of H_1 and we need a counterpart of A_2^*, namely A_1^*, which explicitly suggests the 'morally sufficient reason' alluded to in A_1'.

It would not appear to be of much help if Pike insisted that the forms of reasoning adopted by scientists do not necessarily apply everywhere else. We could still ask whether he suggests that outside science we might uphold the principle 'Adopt any belief which has not yet been conclusively proven to be false.' The suggestion is not plausible. Yet he could argue, as it has been argued before, that the situation of the theist is best compared to that of someone who deeply loves a person S, to whom he feels greatly indebted and for whom he has nothing but admiration and trust. Suppose that one day he is informed that there is solid evidence, which everyone takes as conclusive proof, that S is an entirely worthless person. He may well say: yes, what I have heard seems to indicate quite unmistakably that S is unworthy of my admiration, but my faith in him is so great that I believe S will be vindicated and his strange behaviour will be explained, even though at the moment I have no idea what this explanation is going to be.

This well-known line of defence is all right so far as it goes, but it removes the possibility of public discussion. It is a defence with which the believer can justify his own position to himself, but which would be of no use in a debate in which he was attempting to win over anyone who did not share his profound faith.

Is there too much suffering?

It is particularly important that some thinkers would be quite prepared to put up with a certain amount of misery but find the existing amount excessive. They hold that some of the events of the twentieth century render it no longer possible that an omnipotent, omnibenevolent ruler of the universe exists. For example the influential theologian Richard R. Rubinstein declared: 'After Auschwitz many Jews did not need Nietzsche to tell them that the old God of Jewish patriarchal monotheism was dead beyond all hope of resurrection.'[3] Another theologian, Eugene B. Borowitz, also refers to those who take this attitude:

Any God who could permit the Holocaust, who could remain silent during it, who could 'hide His face' while it dragged on, was not worth believing in. There might well be a limit to how much we could understand about Him, but

Auschwitz demanded an unreasonable suspension of understanding. In the face of such great evil, God, the good and the powerful, was too inexplicable, so men said 'God is dead'.[4]

Thus some people seem to find the atrocities perpetuated in previous centuries still reconcilable with a belief in a loving God while those of our own age are not.

The reason why we must take note of these views is because they seem to create a problem for our understanding of the nature of metaphysics. Few people would be prepared to deny that theism – whether credible or not – is a typical metaphysical doctrine. However, if these theologians are right theism has been essentially subject to the same process as, for instance, the flat-earth theory. As the centuries passed with their wars, famines, epidemics and so on it became increasingly difficult to maintain theism. After the unprecedented horrors of Nazism, all reasonable people honest enough to acknowledge obvious facts had to abandon it. In short, the set of evidence relevant to theism cannot be regarded as static. I hope to be able to show that there is no basis for this objection.

The solution we shall explore in some detail is a fairly solid one, and many will agree that it is quite unassailable in the theist's own terms. Admittedly someone who finds theism unreasonable to begin with will refuse to accept any of its implications and thus will be able to deny the validity of a solution which is based on them. But ultimately such an objection is not based on the empirical evidence provided by suffering but rather on a determination to deny the theist's basic belief any credibility in the first place.

Some unsuccessful solutions

A familiar way of trying to solve the problem of evil is by maintaining that all suffering is instrumental in achieving an important goal which it is logically impossible to attain without suffering. It is generally agreed that omnipotence implies the ability to do anything, no matter how hard it is or how many laws of nature have to be violated in the process. Yet an omnipotent being is incapable of doing what it is logically impossible for him to do. To assume the contrary is self-contradictory and would make a coherent discussion of such a being impossible.

I shall begin by discussing a solution that proceeds along these lines, the so-called free-will defence. This solution deserves attention not because it is a good solution – in fact none of the various versions of it seem to stand up even to a superficial scrutiny – but because it has probably been the solution most discussed in the past 20 years or so. According to the free will defence, a world in which creatures endowed with free will exist is a better world than one in which they do not. It is, however, logically necessary to admit that a creature who has free will may commit acts which cause others suffering. The existence of free agents is such a good thing that it is worth paying for it by having widespread suffering. Assuming that the world is governed by an omnibenevolent being who sees to it that the world is as good as logically possible, it follows that the world will contain free agents and hence suffering.

I shall not query the value judgement which places such high importance on having free-willed agents. But I shall present two objections, each of which is sufficient to render the free will defence untenable.

The first question that immediately arises is: what about natural evil? It might perhaps be claimed that the worst forms of torments have been devised by sentient beings, but there is still undeniably a great deal of human misfortune brought about by forces of nature such as earthquakes, floods, tornadoes and diseases. The free will defence does not seem to account for these.

Clearly then some additional proviso is required. A fairly well-known attempt to supply one is cited by McCloskey.[5] It involves the suggestion that the non-occurrence of various natural evils would involve either the constant intervention of God in a miraculous way, or the construction of a universe subject to different laws of nature. But why should either of these possibilities not be realized? As to the second, the boldest suggestion I know is that in order to allow a complex universe like ours to exist it is logically impossible to have any set of laws which will permit less suffering than do those actually operating. This is a far-reaching claim, but I shall not query it. Surely, however, we could keep the existing laws of nature and yet whenever a disaster threatens have God to intervene miraculously and prevent it? I have heard it said that this would leave us with the evil of a chaotic universe and unpredictable events, since we would never know when any given law might be suspended and hence would have to live a life of constant uncertainty. The weakness of this reply is not hard to find. It may be pointed out, for example, that in the present state of scientific knowledge earthquakes or tornadoes are not predictable very far in advance. Thus, if many of these events that work such havoc had not been permitted to occur, we would not even have noticed the divine intervention, and would be quite unaware that anything unnatural had taken place and live just as happily as we have hitherto in our assumption that nature is uniform.

A recent article[6] attempts to argue that even to interfere from time to time with the laws of nature would require God to do what is logically impossible for him to do. It is in the very essence of a law of nature, it is claimed, that it expresses a completely universal regularity. It is analytically false to say that a regularity which sometimes fails to be observed, which used to obtain but obtains no longer, or which has any kind of exception, constitutes a law of nature.

This approach is not very useful either. We can ask: why is the universe not governed by what are now *thought* to be the laws of nature, but which in reality, on occasions when they threaten the welfare of human beings, can be miraculously suspended? To the objection 'But these so-called laws of nature are not genuine laws of nature by virtue of the very meaning of the term' we can calmly reply that it would not seem to do any harm to anyone if we did not really have genuine laws of nature but only 'so-called' laws of nature.

Plantinga chooses an entirely different way to try to justify the existence of natural evil. He postulates the existence of free non-human spirits one of whom is Satan, who is very powerful; having chosen at some early stage in history to rebel against God, he has since wrought as much havoc as he could. Plantinga claims that just as the existence of free human agents is desirable even at the expense of moral evil, so is the existence of free non-human spirits, even if it gives rise to all the natural evil the world contains.[7]

Many readers may reject Plantinga's thesis outright as bizarre. For example, Flew called it 'a desperate *ad hoc* expedient of apologetic'.[8] I wish, however, to emphasize that there is nothing unacceptable about the notion of Satan as such. Angels and demons have of course no place in scientific discourse, where they perform no function whatever. But there can be no objection to references, in discussions about religion, to beings that typically feature in religious discourse.

What is objectionable is not Plantinga's belief in the existence of non-human spirits but his belief that their existence can be invoked in order to explain the occurrences of natural evil. First it may be objected that we are dealing with natural theology, which is supposed to be a common denominator among all major monotheistic religions; the notion of a free-willed Satan manipulating nature for evil ends may be acceptable in some theologies, but certainly not in all. According to Judaism, for instance, angels – good or bad – have no will of their own; they are merely divine agents. An angel may bring about destruction provided he has specifically been so instructed by God, as in the case of the angels who destroyed Sodom and Gomorrah; he may bring affliction upon a person, as Satan did upon Job for the explicit divine aim of providing

Job with an opportunity to demonstrate his unbreakable faith; but he cannot arbitrarily create evil.

There are also grave logical difficulties with Plantinga's suggestion. He surely does not mean to imply that Satan represents an independent force which God would be incapable of controlling even if he wanted to, since that would do away with divine omnipotence. Plantinga merely wishes to maintain that God has allowed the birth of free non-human spirits since their existence contributes to the goodness of the universe, and it was logically impossible for him to ensure that among these creatures there should not spring into being one with the evil disposition of Satan. Leaving aside Plantinga's controversial contention that it is indeed logically impossible for God to do what he claims it is logically impossible to do, he surely does not claim that it would be logically impossible for God to do away with Satan. After Satan has revealed his evil character and shown that he will use his freedom to bring about human misery, why did an omnibenevolent God not eliminate him or confine him to performing acts that can do no harm, and replace him with another angelic agent who is not known to have an evil disposition?

The second question concerns moral evils. The objection I wish to discuss is one that has been raised before, namely, why, given divine omniscience, did God not refrain from creating wicked people, and confine himself to creating only those who he knew would freely choose never to cause any suffering to others? Philosophers who have attempted to answer this objection fall into two classes: those who have assumed it would have been in the power of God to choose thus and those who have argued it would not. Paterson,[9] for instance, belongs to the first group, and argues that the existence of a creature who on balance contributes more good than evil to the world is morally justified. It is good that such a creature is allowed to exist as the world is on the whole a better place for having him than it would be without him. Paterson insists, somewhat strangely, that it is reasonable to maintain that God never permits a single human being to be born unless he is certain that on the whole that person will perform a sufficient number of good deeds to outweigh any evil he may cause. Paterson says:

we have excellent and indeed coercive grounds for believing that each several one of God's creatures – not excepting Hitlers and Amins – will in the fullness of time entirely justify his creation by making a moral contribution to the universe which will be predominantly good.[10]

Even if we went along with such a rosy view of wicked people, we would still have no solution. Let us grant that God has never created a man who did more evil than good. It is still the case that at any instant at which he created an 'imperfectly good' person (like Adolf Hitler!) he had a vast number of alternatives at his disposal, not merely the alternative of creating nothing (which may not have been preferable). He had the alternative of creating better people, and in particular a completely good person. The question remains then: why did God not do that?

Philosophers who belong to the second group have argued that it is logically impossible to create a genuinely free agent and at the same time predict with complete certainty all his actions. As we shall see, we need not examine any of their arguments, for even if we grant they are valid their conclusion does not provide a solution to the problem of evil.

Plantinga is a rather special case within this group as his argument is an unusual one leading to the conclusion 'Every actual free person performs at least one wrong action.' His intricate reasoning has prompted replies from quite a number of philosophers. These philosophers do not seem to agree on exactly what the argument is or even on the precise nature of the conclusion. The excitement his views have aroused may have been responsible for diverting everyone's attention from the fact that they are of no help in blunting the edge of the argument from evil.

It may well be feasible to show that it is logically impossible to predict with absolute certainty what any free agent will do or that it is logically impossible to create a perfectly good person. We need however no arguments to show that not only God, but also an average human being, is capable of predicting with high probability how an entirely free agent with whose character he is well acquainted will act in familiar situations. Any reasonably intelligent person who knew Albert Schweitzer or Adolf Hitler fairly well up the age of about 30 would have declared it highly probable that the former would perform morally better than most people and the latter would do more evil than most people. There is no reason to assume that both Schweitzer and Hitler were not free agents. So it would never be possible to predict what either would do on any given occasion with absolute certainty, only with high probability. For instance, all who were familiar with Schweitzer at some time during his stay in Africa would have predicted that it was highly probable that he would agree to treat the next sick person to come to him for help, but of course there was a small chance that he might use his free will to act out of character and callously refuse treatment. It is true that different people are endowed with different characters, partly determined by genetic make-up and partly by early childhood experiences, and that many of our actions are strongly influenced by our characters. People are free agents and are therefore capable of choosing to act in a manner that belies their characters at any time. Mostly, however, people act more or less as expected, that is, characteristically. Now as soon as God recognizes the character of a given person – and this he should do considerably earlier than that person's friends – and discovers it is morally inferior to that of, say, Albert Schweitzer, then he should prevent that person committing evil. This he may achieve in a variety of ways: by doing away with him; by not allowing him to carry out any of his evil designs; by interfering with his choices and forcing him to act in a morally desirable way. As a result this particular person may no longer be a free agent. Nevertheless, the world may contain many free agents, namely those who possess superior characters. Neither Plantinga nor anyone else who subscribes to the free will defence answers the question why an omnibenevolent God does not act in this way.

The 'virtuous response to suffering' solution

I should now like to discuss a solution to the problem of evil that is entirely effective and not only deprives the atheist of conclusive proof for the correctness of his position but allows the theist to maintain his belief without the least difficulty. This solution has a venerable history but is not generally accepted because of various objections raised against it, which, I shall argue, are all groundless.

The solution is sometimes referred to as the 'soul making' theodicy or the 'virtuous response to suffering' solution. It is based on the indisputable claim that certain noble human sentiments and acts exist which cannot be actualized unless cases of human suffering occur. Consider such admirable characteristics as fortitude, charity, compassion, courage or forgiveness. It is logically impossible for instances of fortitude to occur where there is no pain, since by definition fortitude is firmness of mind in meeting adversity and the readiness to endure hardship without complaint. It is logically impossible to have charity where there is no want; compassion where there is no suffering, and thus nothing to be compassionate about; courage where there is no danger; or forgiveness where no injury has been done. A world that contains instances of these desirable qualities – all of which may be described as virtuous responses to suffering – is a better world than one that does not. God, wanting to have a better world, was compelled to permit suffering. Now let us consider the various objections that some might think of as valid:

1 The objection often raised is that this seems to put the cart before the horse. Certainly we admire virtuous responses to suffering because they are instrumental in alleviating it; without them suffering would prevail unabated. But they have no purpose when no suffering exists, that is, in the absence of suffering, these responses have no value of their own; their value is solely functional, they are of use only when mitigating pain. It is absurd, it might be claimed, to create pain for no other reason than to render possible certain human acts whose sole virtue is the overcoming of pain.

This objection can be met by pointing out that to value these noble qualities only for their effectiveness as antidotes to suffering is a possible view, but by no means the most reasonable view. Another view, which many people hold, judges that these qualities constitute good in themselves. It can be claimed that a person who has exercised charity, for example, has done good not only because he has eliminated want, but also because he has enhanced his character by being charitable, as well as enriching the world by adding to the virtuous acts performed in it. Admittedly if there were no want we would not need an act of charity to eliminate it, but we would be missing chances for the giver to improve his character and contribute to the moral wealth of the world. Charity is valuable not merely because of its usefulness but also because of the moral beauty inherent in it. The theist ascribes this second view to God, who is therefore justified in permitting suffering which can bring forth virtuous responses of intrinsic value.

It would not do to object by saying that when it comes to the ennoblement of human beings surely God in his omnipotence is able simply to decree that a given individual should possess a character of any degree of exaltedness he desires. It is still obviously logically impossible to achieve by mere divine decree the particular ennoblement that comes of responding virtuously to human suffering, without first allowing such suffering to take place.

2 The second objection is invalid, but since confused arguments about it have appeared in print it may not be entirely superfluous to discuss it briefly. The objection is that the virtuous response to suffering solution does not require that all the great variety of suffering, which prompts different responses from many different people, should actually exist. It is sufficient that we merely *sincerely believe* that it exists. R. G. Swinburne raises this objection. He says:

One might reasonably claim that all that is necessary for some of these good acts (or acts as good as these) to be performed is belief in the existence of certain evils, not their actual existence. You can show compassion toward someone who appears to be suffering but is not really.[11]

Surprising though it may appear, Swinburne takes this objection quite seriously. He believes that the correct answer to it is to point out that it requires a world in which creatures are in general systematically deceived about the feelings of others, a world in which people's behaviour does not truly reflect the state of mind they are in. But then, following Descartes, Swinburne claims it would be morally wrong for God to create such a deceptive world. So God was morally obliged to create a world in which appearances are not misleading:

In that case, given a creator, then, without an immoral act on his part, for acts of courage, compassion, etc. to be acts open to men to perform, there have to be various evils. [12]

I believe that if the virtuous response to suffering solution really needed this kind of defence it would be in a bad way − not merely because not everyone necessarily agrees with Descartes that divine morality is incompatible with the creation of a deceptive world, nor even because Descartes himself said this only about a situation in which we are totally deceived about everything but may not object to our having a rather small number of false beliefs. The most telling objection is this: causing or condoning human suffering is universally acknowledged as the paradigm of moral evil. Yet according to the advocates of the virtuous response to suffering solution, acts designed to alleviate human suffering are so precious that we readily excuse God for doing what otherwise would be most objectionable − namely, creating human suffering. Surely we should be willing to exonerate him if he did something else instead that it would be absurd to regard as morally more objectionable − namely, placing his creatures in a world in which they are deceived about the inner states of their fellows.

But the objection is complete nonsense anyhow; Swinburne would have to agree that in order for him to perform genuinely felt virtuous acts in response to suffering, he would have to be thoroughly convinced about the genuineness of other people's suffering. We may then ask him how does he *know* that human suffering actually exists, and that he is not merely led to believe it does by the convincing evidence of a great deal of suffering in the world? He may conceivably complain 'But I know with certainty that my own sufferings are real.' This, we reply, is necessary for two reasons: first in order to create the opportunity for him to respond virtuously to his own suffering (by behaving with fortitude, patience and courage), and it would make no sense for him falsely to believe himself to be suffering; and second because he himself must genuinely be in pain when he exhibits pain, for otherwise he would not believe that others are actually in pain when they appear to be. Thus, Swinburne can, if he so wishes, hold that no one apart from him really suffers pain.

3 A far more convincing attack on the virtuous response to suffering solution has been made by J. L. Mackie in an often cited article.[13] He argues that, if we are to assume that charity, compassion and the like are such highly desirable qualities that we must secure their existence even at the expense of enduring devastating earthquakes, hurricanes and diseases, then the opposites of these qualities, such as meanness and cruelty, are of a comparable degree of undesirability. Just as we have said that the man who responds virtuously to suffering does far more good than simply lessening the amount of suffering in the world – for he also enhances his moral character and contributes to the world's moral wealth – so we would have to agree that a man who responds callously to suffering does more evil than merely failing to diminish human misery, for he also debases his own character and adds to the amount of morally despicable acts. If it is claimed that God has greatly improved the world by providing opportunities for virtuous responses, then it has to be admitted that he has impaired the world to no lesser degree by providing opportunities for vicious responses. Surely the world could not be worse off if it offered opportunities for neither?

To paraphrase Mackie, the world contains, among other things, first order good and evil. First order goods are food, shelter, good health and so on. First order evils are lack of food, shelter, good health and so on. Mackie takes the virtuous response to suffering solution to assert that the existence of first order evil is justified because it makes possible a higher order good, specifically second order good, which in essence comprises human qualities associated with the efforts to eliminate first order evil. But the world also contains second order evil which consists of parallel human qualities associated with the efforts to perpetuate first order evil, and the need for second order good does not explain this.

Mackie goes on to suggest a solution to his objection, only to reject it at once. He considers the possible defence that second order evil could be justified by the need for a yet higher good, third order good, which comprises human qualities associated with the efforts to combat second order evil, that is, efforts to curb those who are trying to perpetuate first order evil. It should be noted that third order good has all the merits of second order good as well as an extra merit which elevates it above the latter. Those who fight evil-doers contribute to the lessening of first order evil, enhance their own moral stature as well as enriching the moral content of the world, and in addition tend to decrease the amount of second order evil. The existence of third order good could perhaps be claimed to be important enough to justify the existence of second order evil. Mackie rejects this defence by arguing that it at once raises the question why there is also third order evil. This will presumably be explained by the need for fourth order good, and so on, leading to an infinite regress.

Elsewhere I have argued against this by pointing out that Mackie has not shown that the regress he has generated is a vicious regress.[14] A clear example of a vicious regress is the one generated by a statement such as 'No theorem is justified unless deduced from another justified theorem.' Suppose we derive logically T_1 from T_2; we have not yet done anything to justify T_1, since T_2 has not yet been justified. If we in turn derive T_2 from T_3, still nothing has been achieved; T_3 has not yet been justified, so that T_2 has been deduced from an unjustified theorem and is therefore itself not justified. Consequently T_1 remains unjustified. It makes no difference whether we take one more step, and derive T_3 from T_4, or many more steps: wherever we stop we are equally badly off – nothing has been justified.

But the case is quite different here. Admittedly we can look at the regress pessimistically and assume we cannot escape our difficulties. As soon as we have justified the existence of evil of level n by pointing out that it is a necessary prerequisite for the existence of good of level $(n + 1)$, the question arises: how do we justify evil of level $(n + 1)$? Every attempt to solve our problem is frustrated because there is evil of the same level as the good whose existence it was so desirable to secure. But there is also an optimistic perspective on the question. For as soon as the question why we have evil of level $(n + 1)$ is raised we are able to explain this as a necessary condition of having good of level $(n + 2)$. It is not clear that we have to feel frustrated because we are immediately confronted with a new problem after every solution; we could feel reassured that for every question we are at once provided with a solution. In the standard infinite regress, which all agree is vicious, it does not matter where we stop in the regress, for each step is as bad as another. Mackie's is a peculiar regress, however; in it we alternate between a step that lands us in a difficulty, and a step which resolves the previous difficulty. He would have to produce an argument to convince us that this kind of regress invalidates the virtuous response to suffering solution.

In *Religion and Scientific Method* I also pointed out that we are not actually faced with an infinite regress of any kind, vicious or benign. It would be absurd to assert that, in practice, there is evil of level 537 which is associated with the attempt to stop those who are trying to combat those who are endeavouring to curb those (and so on 537 times). . . who practise compassion. We may find third order evil in the world, perhaps even fifth order evil, but the theist could safely challenge anyone to produce an actual example of evil of an order much higher than that. Suppose an advocate of the virtuous response to suffering solution claimed to believe that the highest order of evil act permitted by God in practice was n where $5 < n < 10$, but good has been actually performed up to the level $(n + 1)$. Mackie would be exceedingly hard put to produce an observed counter-example and thus demolish the solution.

It has subsequently occurred to me that all this is unnecessary; a much simpler reply is available. Mackie's objection is based on his unquestioning assumption that the disvalue of second order evil is exactly equivalent in degree to the value of second order good. There is no reason why this should be granted; in fact there is a good argument for not granting it. A human being is physically an animal and hence represents a strongly self-seeking system whose very essence lies in constantly striving to satisfy a wide range of appetites. By virtue of his animality, it is quite natural for a human being to pursue his selfish goals at the expense of everybody else; to be insensitive to other organisms' needs which he does not feel; and to persist in trying to satisfy his voracity without regard to the effect on his fellow creatures. He has been created with an innate bent for callousness and meanness. Acts of the superego, such as charity and compassion, are results of exerting a special noble will to curb these natural drives. Thus the positive value of virtuous acts by far exceeds the negative value of immoral acts, 'for the imagination of the heart of man is evil from his youth' (Genesis 8: 21). It is far more remarkable for man to act virtuously, a non-animal-like spirituality transcending his selfish impulses, than it is for him to do what comes naturally.

4 In an interesting article Clement Dore[15] raises the objection that, though the virtuous response to suffering solution has provided an answer to the question why misery should exist in cases where it is redeemed by the virtuous responses it elicits, we have no explanation of why suffering to which no one responds virtuously is also permitted to exist. He claims that there have been cases of useless human wretchedness, those that were not instrumental in bringing forth noble actions or noble states of mind, and it has yet to be explained why God has allowed these to exist. He does attempt to provide answers to this question but his reply has shortcomings. First of all, it assumes that God is not able to predict how agents who possess free will are going to act, something not everyone will readily grant. Secondly, his answer explains at most why there are cases of suffering with respect to which everybody

refuses to respond virtuously; it does not account for cases where the failure to respond is simply due to lack of opportunity. An example of the latter might be an abandoned child who met with disaster when he was alone and nobody could learn of his plight. There is no scope for virtuous response here: the child himself is not yet of an age when he is capable of reacting with fortitude to his own sorrow, and others are oblivious that anything requiring a virtuous response has happened.

But the reply is quite simple once we realize that there is no time limit for virtuous responses: one may react nobly to human tragedies that took place many years ago, for one may sincerely lament them and be stirred to resolve to take humane action to prevent similar happenings in the future. Moral indignation is a response that is virtuous no matter how long after an evil occurrence it takes place. It should be clear that cases of suffering that are in principle unknowable to anyone, either at the time they happened or at any later time, can only be claimed to have happened at the expense of contradicting oneself by claiming to know the unknowable. All that we can know is that some human suffering has taken place to which *so far* everyone *seems* to have reacted indifferently. But once we realize that a misfortune may be justified by the benevolent responses it evokes at any time, not necessarily only when something can still be done to mitigate it, Dore's problem does not arise. It is not possible to have evidence that useless misery, that is, misery that never has and never will elicit a philanthropic response from anyone, has ever existed.

McCloskey, in the well-known article in which he argues that the problem of evil is insoluble, says:

Much pain and suffering, in fact much physical evil generally, for example, in children who die in infancy, animals and the insane passes unnoticed; it therefore has no morally uplifting effects upon others, and cannot by virtue of the examples chosen have such effects on the sufferers. [16]

This, of course, raises the question whether McCloskey really knows of such cases: if so, this in itself provides the opportunity for at least one person to respond by deploring them: if not, how can he be certain that they will never be known to anyone else who might be moved by them?

5 While most people will be ready to concede that noble sentiments and acts elicited by suffering are of positive value, they will disagree about its magnitude. Many will regard them as not sufficiently valuable to justify an unlimited amount of human misery. Admittedly, it is likely that the greater the human tragedy, the more intense the feelings of regret and the resolve to mitigate it, and the greater the lengths good

people will be prepared to go to in order to combat the forces of evil. Yet there are thinkers who are unable to reconcile themselves to some of the horrible catastrophes that have afflicted large numbers of people, which no amount of noble response can ever redeem in their judgement.

One could argue with such thinkers and point out that they are making a value judgement which happens to disagree with the judgement of God, who knows exactly how much positive response is generated by human misery and finds that the latter is justified by the former. However, it is impossible to claim that the ethical rule God observes makes no sense to humans at all and that the term 'good' is meaningless when applied to divine conduct. After all, we do not simply and piously claim that God's ways are ineffable and that divine benevolence is of a kind that is entirely beyond human comprehension. A clear description *has* been given of the ethical principle to which God subscribes and which permits him to create human suffering. It is a principle with which we may not quite agree when the amount of suffering seems excessive to us, but it is intelligible.

However, a much stronger reply is available to the theist. He may claim that in the afterlife, which is of infinite duration, there is unlimited scope to compensate the sufferer. In fact, he may receive so much recompense for his earlier sufferings that, in view of this and the important goals his travails have served, he will ultimately feel that he has no reason to complain.

It may be pointed out that the idea of the virtuous response to suffering solution and the idea of compensation of the victim go back as far as the Bible. It is explicitly stated there that the sufferings of Job were not due to any wrongdoing on his part. The accepted interpretation is that he was put through all his torment for the sake of spiritual enrichment, for it provided him with an opportunity to display his immense fortitude and unwavering faith in the ultimate justice of the Lord in the face of pressing adverse evidence. An opportunity was also provided for 'all his brothers and sisters and who have known him before' to show sympathy and to comfort him (Job 42: 11). The next verse says 'And the Lord blessed the latter days of Job more than his beginning', indicating that Job was abundantly compensated for the ordeal he had endured. The last verse of the book states 'And Job died . . . full of days', the Hebrew expression for which is usually understood to mean 'fully satisfied'. Thus it may be taken that in the end Job had no complaints. Ultimately, when he reached an understanding of the noble purpose of his suffering and was so richly compensated for it, he himself deemed his torment worthwhile. This of course does not happen to most sufferers, who will reach such a state of satisfaction only in the world to come.

Some readers may think that there is a major stumbling block here. The theist has to resort to the extraordinary measure of invoking a world of which we know nothing. He would find it exceedingly difficult to convince the sceptic of the reality of such a world. The notion of an afterlife is a large topic and I shall not attempt to tackle it here. Let it suffice to remind ourselves that the problem of evil has been raised in the atheist's endeavour to disprove theism conclusively. All the theist is called upon to do is to show that there is no convincing proof that atheism is true. The burden of the proof that an afterlife exists does not rest upon him. Before claiming victory, the atheist would have to show positively that such a life is non-existent; merely to deride the theist for his belief will not do. Nor can the theist be accused of ad hoc argument, since he has not postulated the world to come simply to provide a reply to the specific objection we are discussing – on the contrary, it is deeply embedded in a theistic world view. The typical attitude of a real believer is illustrated by the famous Hassidic leader who is reported to have said 'I have heard that some people doubt the reality of the world to come. I can understand if someone doubts the reality of this world, but not the world to come!'

6 The last objection is based on the assumption that ethical rules which apply to human beings are also the rules whereby we judge the goodness of divine actions. C. Dore[17] points out that a human being who claims he should not be condemned for having caused unnecessary suffering, since by his acts he has created the opportunity for others to respond virtuously, would certainly not be exonerated; so why should God? Madden and Hare put it the other way round: if God is allowed to create suffering for the sake of the virtuous responses it may evoke, why are not humans? They say:

If courage, endurance, charity, sympathy, and the like are so spiritually significant, then the evil conditions which foster them should not be mitigated. Social and political reforms designed to achieve social security, peace, plenty and harmony automatically become pernicious. We do not really believe this, of course, and thereby reflect the fact that we have spiritual values which we place above those negative ones fostered by extremely trying conditions.[18]

McCloskey argues in a similar vein:

Theists usually hold that we are obliged to reduce the physical evil in the universe; but in maintaining this, the theist is, in terms of his account of physical evil, maintaining that it is his duty to reduce the total amount of real good in the universe, and thereby to make the universe worse. Conversely, if by eliminating the physical evil he is not making the universe worse, then the amount of evil which he eliminates was unnecessary and in need of justification.[19]

One may go even further: it is not merely that it happens to be the case that we would give no consideration to a criminal's plea to be excused from punishment because his assault on a victim has provided opportunities for noble responses to human suffering, but that we are compelled to reject such an excuse. For suppose A injures a person, and we exonerate him on the grounds that he has provided opportunities for virtuous responses. Then we should also excuse B, who comes along and kicks A's victim when he is down instead of helping him, thereby providing even more opportunities for positive response. Further, C and all who follow after should also be excused for further aggravating the victim's plight. Then for whose virtuous response did we excuse A's actions in the first place?

A brief and entirely sufficient answer is that the moral rules according to which we judge human and divine conduct are in fact the same, but men and God act under different circumstances. It may be maintained that A is permitted to cause another person suffering with the view of providing opportunities for others' noble responses only if A is absolutely certain that he is capable of compensating the victim fully for his suffering. By 'fully compensate' I mean that the victim will eventually agree that the experience of suffering which A had subjected him to in the pursuit of his stated goal, together with the subsequent compensation, is no less preferable to having had neither experience. It is obvious that only God is in the position to be able to guarantee this.

Divine omnipotence

It is worth noting that divine omnipotence has usually been taken as the factor which clinches the atheist's argument: we could excuse a less than infinitely powerful creator for the imperfections of the world. He may well have done his best, we could say; to create a universe as complex as ours requires enormous powers and to create a universe free of blemish may require infinite powers. But God is supposed to have infinite powers, and so the argument from evil seems conclusive. The replies to the two objections above show that divine omnipotence is in fact crucial in ensuring the elimination of the problem of evil. It provides infinite scope for the compensation of the victim, and thus may justify his suffering in the service of the divine goal of increasing the moral wealth of the universe.

The virtuous response to suffering defence was designed to show not that there is no strong disconfirmation of theism, but that the existence of suffering, which is instrumental in increasing the scope for altruism, does not disconfirm theism to any degree. Any theodicy may be regarded as inadequate to the extent that it relies on ad hoc hypotheses. However, the supporters of the virtuous response to suffering defence would argue that all the claims it presupposes are claims the theist would want to make in any case, even if no one had raised the problem of evil. Many people agree, for instance, that God should be regarded as having created the best of all possible worlds. But surely a thoughtful theist would have maintained all along that the goodness of the universe is not measured solely by the extent to which its creatures have all the comforts they need and the degree to which they all enjoy themselves. He would take it for granted that a genuinely good universe contains a large number of moral and religious values.

Neither would it be correct to characterize the introduction of an afterlife as an ad hoc hypothesis. Many theologians – of the old school at least – would insist that theism makes no sense without it, and actually entails its existence. It is of course this part of the virtuous response to suffering solution that the atheist is expected to object to most resolutely. To him life after death is highly improbable and he may even find the very idea repugnant. But it is crucial to realize that for the present purpose the believer need not try to make the idea of the soul's survival palatable to the non-believer. We may take it as a fact that, to the theist, the denial of the soul's survival is a denial of everything he believes in, whereas to the atheist, its affirmation is the height of absurdity. The point is, however, that to claim that the existence of evil provides any positive evidence against theism in addition to any prior objections one may have had is a mistake. If we admit the notion of an afterlife the problem of evil disappears; if we do not, the argument for theism is not even begun and we do not need the existence of evil to challenge it.

Let us return to the problem raised at the beginning of this chapter, that the amount of evidence relevant to theism may change with time and hence its metaphysical status may be questioned (or my characterization of metaphysics is wrong). The simple answer is that the amount of suffering in the world has no effect on the problem of evil. In the absence of a solution, even a very small amount of human suffering should disconfirm theism. It would not make any difference if, instead of the way things are, everyone's life was continual bliss except that a single individual had to endure a slight inconvenience for a brief moment, and even this turned out to be instrumental in bringing about great material benefit to himself and others. The problem would not be felt so acutely, or perhaps would not be noticed at all, but logically it would exist no less than it exists now. In a perfect world, it seems, nobody should be allowed to suffer at all, and an omnipotent being should be able to bring about everything that is desirable in an entirely painless manner.

On the other hand, if we have a genuine solution to the problem of evil, such as the virtuous response to suffering solution, then the problem disappears, irrespective of how much suffering goes on. I cannot believe that theologians like Rubinstein and Borowitz[20] would want to claim that the virtuous response to suffering solution is quite effective in accounting for all the human suffering prior to World War II, but is unable to accommodate the horrible events which occurred subsequently.

Theism and verifiability

Now we come to the question whether there is positive evidence in support of theism. Some contemporary philosophers, instead of claiming merely that theism is not well founded and that therefore there is no good reason to believe it to be true, have raised a more fundamental objection, denying it to have any meaning at all. According to this line of attack, which has been associated with A. Flew, not only is there nothing in our experience which confirms theism, but it is in principle impossible that we should ever have such experience. It is wrong, therefore, to assume that the theistic claim is a factual claim when, being unconfirmable, it is actually devoid of any cognitive significance.

Flew's attack has been remarkably successful: a number of defenders of the faith hastened to surrender, abandoning some of the most traditional positions. R. M. Hare, finding Flew's thrust irresistible, conceded 'on the grounds marked out by Flew he seems to be completely victorious'.[21] He goes on to advance the startling claim that theism is indeed meaningless and that it would be pointless to assert theism if it intended to make any factual claims concerning the existence of anything. But enlightened theists make no such claims. They merely recommend a way of life to us. When a theist states 'God exists', this is merely his peculiar way of urging us to be humble, charitable and compassionate. It must be admitted that Hare has been successful in retreating into a practically impregnable position. He need not fear that he might be forced to concede any further ground, since by now he has nothing left to concede.

There are, however, other philosophers not yet prepared to surrender everything of religious significance. For example, John Hick, a highly respected thinker, advanced the view that though in this world there can be no evidence for the existence of God, so that theism is presumably unverifiable in the here and now, we need not exclude the possibility of eschatological verification. In other words, when our earthly existence ends and we arrive in the world to come, we could be confronted with the divine and thus obtain clear evidence of his existence. (Even Bertrand Russell seems to have conceded the possibility of this; he declared that should such a contingency arise, then instead of blaming himself for having led the life of an atheist, he would at once ask 'Sire, why did you not give better evidence of Your existence?') It is remarkable that all the objections to Hick are based on the complaint that he has resorted to such a bizarre notion as that of the world to come. This does not seem a well-justified criticism to me. After all, the survival of the soul is one of the most central features of most theistic beliefs, and I can see no reason why the theist should not be allowed to employ it to any purpose he wishes. To me the real difficulty in Hick's position is that it is entirely pointless to introduce the notion of the world to come in the present context. What we have to ask him is, what kind of experiences does he have in mind as leading to eschatological verification? Are those experiences such that they are at least coherently describable? Suppose not: then surely we must admit that although the world to come may legitimately be claimed to be a very strange world, nevertheless nothing takes place that is logically impossible even there. Hence, in that case, the notion of the world to come is of no help. On the other hand, if the relevant experiences are coherently describable then they are logically possible. But, if they are logically possible, then it is in principle possible that we could have them in the here and now, and theism is not unverifiable in the first place. Hence the notion of the world to come is superfluous to our present purposes.

Another important defender of theism, A. Plantinga, has no compunction in conceding that theism is indeed unverifiable in principle. He argues vigorously, however, that there is no obligation on the part of a rational person to accept the verification principle and that we are free to maintain that a sentence is meaningful and capable of making an empirical claim even if it is unverifiable. He arrives at his conclusion after demolishing the basis of the verificationists' theory of meaning by claiming that their criterion has not been and cannot be clearly stated and thus no one knows what it amounts to.

I must confess that I have no idea why these leading philosophers were in such a rush to concede that their religious beliefs were in principle unverifiable. I take it of course that by 'verifiable' we do not mean conclusive verification, which after all is not granted us in any domain, but the possibility of an event which would increase the credibility of a hypothesis. I also assume that there is no reason to think that miraculous events are logically impossible. But then even on the crudest understanding of the nature of a miracle it would seem obvious that a miracle is the kind of occurrence that could in principle provide empirical evidence for theism. What has been questioned by philosophers, beginning with Hume, is that there is any good reason to believe that such events have ever taken place. But virtually anyone who has given the matter any thought has conceded the power of miracles to confirm religious beliefs. The following statement, for example, reflects a typical position:

However in this world the gods do not appear in a publicly verifiable form high in the sky, giving loud predictions and performing miracles in accordance with those predictions, hence religious belief-claims cannot be established by scientific criteria.[22]

In other words, something often ruefully expressed by those who are not quite sure what to believe is taken for granted: that we should be very lucky if we lived in a world in which miracles took place that were announced in advance by some divine agency. We would no longer need to live with nagging doubts, for then theism would be firmly established.

I shall devote the last parts of this chapter to more detailed discussions of miracles. This serves a number of purposes. First, there are widely different views as to what constitutes a miracle and it would be useful to try to find out which, if any, is likely to lead to the correct description. Then, of course, we should like to identify the crucial feature of a miracle that is responsible for virtually everyone conceding its confirmatory powers. We shall want to investigate the question whether there is good enough justification for this general attitude. Lastly, I have a special reason for wanting to discuss this topic since, as we shall see, the possibility of miraculous events may seem to constitute proof that my basic claim concerning the nature of metaphysics is wrong! But first let me examine one of the most elementary principles used in science, one which may most profitably be employed in evaluating the credibility of theistic claims.

The argument from design

The argument from design is undoubtedly the most widely debated argument for the existence of God. It is not easy therefore to account for the fact that the basic structure of the argument is quite frequently misunderstood. The most common error is aptly illustrated by the arguments advanced by Wesley C. Salmon, one of the leading experts in confirmation theory at present, who wrote in 1978 and again in 1979[23] claiming that the argument from design is unsound.

Part of Salmon's efforts are directed at establishing the thesis that given 'the standard model' of our universe, according to which it came into being approximately 10^{17} seconds ago as a result of a 'big bang', the evolution of life was quite probable. Salmon maintains that the elementary particles that are supposed to have constituted the universe at the beginning were quite likely on their own, without the benefit of divine intervention, to give rise to the kind of universe we have today. Before indicating why Salmon's approach is based on an elementary mistake, I should mention that his detailed arguments involving probabilities in support of his contention are in any case utterly pointless. Surely it would not matter if the chance of life emerging in our universe was a trillion times smaller than he claimed it to be. If our universe is infinite in time or space, or both, then anything that is merely possible, no matter how immensely improbable, is bound with absolute certainty to happen at some time. Many maintain that our universe is infinite in time. Even if the big bang occurred 10^{17} seconds ago, that was one stage in a chain of cycles which reaches infinitely far back into the past. Then, of course, space, if not infinite, is immensely large. It is therefore reasonable for the naturalist to claim that we need no help from a divine designer since the event of life emerging somewhere at some time is virtually certain anyway.

It would be quite useless to try to argue that Salmon cannot permit the chance of life developing to be too small because our solar system is only n years old and is confined to a relatively small space, so that the probability of such development taking place may not be high enough. Clearly in a universe with an infinite space – time anything possible is bound to happen somewhere at some time. Thus, in such a universe, the emergence of life in one of its short-lived solar systems is bound to happen.

But the existence of any number of arguments showing that the evolution of life from elementary particles is highly probable is entirely irrelevant to the question of the validity of the argument from design.

This is evident from the fact that the argument from design was proposed long before scientists entertained the hypothesis that the universe consisted in the beginning of nothing but elementary particles. Those who found the argument convincing found it so irrespective of what they believed about the initial stages in the universe's history. Consider for a moment the extreme example of someone who believes that the universe has contained all the forms of life we know today from the first moment of its existence. Would such a person be prevented from making use of the argument from design? Certainly not. He, like everyone else, would point out that the universe could have been very different, devoid of any form of life now and for ever. Significantly, however, the actual universe does have living things and this should be interpreted as an indication of a Creator.

In other words, the existence of design was not inferred from the fact that the emergence of life in our universe would have otherwise been unlikely. The whole issue of what is likely to happen because we have the universe we have is utterly without any relevance. What we are called upon to contemplate is this question: given that there are infinitely many universes in which conditions are such as to ensure with certainty that no life will ever evolve in them, was it absolutely necessary that a world like ours should be actualized? Those who subscribe to naturalism are compelled to admit that this is not required by any principle of logic, and we do not know with certainty any necessary premiss that entails our world being one of those in which life could evolve. On the other hand, the theist, whose thesis we shall describe more precisely below, can derive logically that the laws of nature and the initial conditions had to be such as to make it possible for human-like creatures to emerge at some time in some place.

Thus the general idea implicit in most versions of the argument from design may be put more accurately as follows: it is obvious that among all the possible worlds there are infinitely many in which the prevailing laws and initial conditions are such as to ensure that no form of life ever evolves. For example, a world in which there exist exactly three elementary particles is logically possible. There are infinitely many possible laws that could govern the relative motions of these particles, there being for each a separate possible world. In none of these worlds is the emergence of human-like creatures possible. Given that there is only one actual world, certainly no one would want to insist that it *had* to be our world or even that it *had* to be a world in which human-like creatures may eventually emerge. Thus let

N = Naturalism (i.e. the thesis that there is no supernatural power behind nature) is true.

L = The laws of nature and initial conditions in the actual world are such that it is possible for human-like creatures to emerge at some time in some place.

It seems then that

$$p \text{ (L/N)} < 1$$

which means that the probability p that L is true, given only N (plus, of course, the set of statements describing all the logically possible worlds), is less than 1. This seems obvious because naturalism is compatible with the actualization of any world, including those in which either the laws of nature or the initial conditions preclude the possibility of human-like creatures ever emerging. Now let

T = An omnipotent being interested in human-like creatures exists.

Critics of the argument from design, including Salmon, do not seem to query the assumption that the being referred to in T is interested in seeing the world contain human-like creatures. But it follows from the definition of 'omnipotence' that if an omnipotent being wants a statement S to be true, then as long as S is logically possible it is absolutely certain that S will be true. Consequently, $p(L/T) = 1$. L, of course, is known to be true. There is, however, a well known rule of confirmation which we may denote as (C*) which says

(C*) = If $p(L/T) > p(L/N)$
    then L confirms T more than it confirms N.

This, in a nutshell, is the form of the argument from design. It makes no reference to the likelihood of life emerging *given* the initial conditions and the laws of our universe. It is essentially based on the judgement that in the absence of a supernatural guiding force the prior probability that L will hold in the one world that is to be actualized is less than one.

An argument using only the actual world

A more promising line of attack on the argument from design would focus on a crucial facet of the argument, namely that it does not treat the actual world as given and it relies on assessing the probabilities that various non-existent, but logically possible, worlds would have been actualized instead of our world. One could make out a sound case that this is indeed the argument's most vulnerable aspect. For example, it could be claimed that in flipping coins or throwing dice, as well as dealing with molecules or sub-atomic particles – all physical entities whose nature we are through experience to some extent familiar with – we have empirical bases on which to make probability judgements concerning events that involve them. But we have had absolutely no experiences that relate to unactualized universes. Thus we are treading on far too unfamiliar ground to be able to advance probability arguments with any confidence. In particular, we have no experience that might be said to indicate that all logically possible worlds, no matter how different, can equiprobably be actualized.

An objection could be raised even to the assumption that we are entitled to assign the same probability of actualization to all possible worlds. No one will dispute that there are infinitely many possible worlds in which human-like creatures do not exist. However, obviously there are also infinitely many possible worlds in which such creatures do exist. Given the peculiarities of sets with infinitely many members, unless we are provided with more arguments about how the relevant sets compare to one another, we cannot assert with full assurance that p (L/N)<1.

Others may go further and deny that it makes sense to say that a logically possible world other than ours had such and such a chance of being the actual world. If they believe that this world had no beginning in time, they may well ask: *when* did that other universe have such a chance? Furthermore, it is a fact that there are processes whereby a die may be thrown and fall this or that way and whereby molecules acquire various velocities or an atom disintegrates and loses a certain number of its constituent particles. It therefore makes good sense to assign a certain probability to the truth of the prediction that a well-defined physical process is going to take place. But can we also claim the existence of a physical process whereby various non-existent worlds turn into actual worlds? Does it make any sense to assign a value to the likelihood of such a process taking place?

Finally, it may also be mentioned that probabilities are always assigned in the context of some physical situation, for example, given such and such an experimental set-up, the probability that an electron will pass through a given slit is n. Can we, however, talk about a physical situation in the context of which the probability of a certain world becoming actual is such and such?

I propose to introduce a stronger argument for theism, employing the same principle of confirmation (C*) but making no reference to worlds other than ours. We begin by pointing out that to the theist, what is special about human-like creatures and makes their existence so valued is their capacity to respond to the divine. They are able to engage in a variety of religious activities and they are moral agents who may freely perform acts of love, compassion, generosity and so on. It is clear, however, that in a world in which we were incapable of knowing any laws of nature and of making any correct predictions at all, and in which any given event might be followed by any of infinitely many different events, we could not be expected to accomplish anything, and it would be entirely pointless to attempt to do so. Any action of mine might have any one of indefinitely many results quite unrelated to my intentions. I might see a blind person walking into the path of a speeding car. If I attempt to pull him back, this might result in his falling forwards, sinking into the river a mile away or bursting into flames. On the other hand, if I attempt to throw him in front of the car perhaps this could result in the car suddenly going sideways, rising into the air or evaporating.

It follows therefore that if T is true, in which case human beings are expected to accomplish as many morally and religiously desirable goals as possible, then we cannot be ignorant of all the laws of nature and must be able to make quite a large number of correct predictions.

People generally assume that they are capable of accomplishing a vast number of tasks by doing what they have learned through experience is the appropriate act for accomplishing such tasks. The method whereby people learn from experience has been called the inductive method by most philosophers. It is the method that was used by prehistoric man, and later by people of widely different civilizations, before it ever occurred to anyone to entertain sceptical thoughts and wonder why it is bound to produce the right results. Let us denote

> V = My virtuous act A, designed to bring about result R_1 that serves some divinely approved purpose, is going to succeed in producing R_1.

It will have to be admitted that $p(V/N)$ is considerably less than one. There are a variety of reasons for this. Even if we ignore the major philosophical source of doubt, and assume for a moment that we have a sound basis for regarding predictions made through correctly applied scientific method as completely reliable, there are still grounds for regarding $p(V/N)$ as being less than one. There are at least two sources of uncertainty following from the fact that we are never sure that we have applied the correct scientific method. The famous story of Russell's chicken is one of the many possible illustrations of one source of doubt. That hapless bird is said to have argued that since the farmer had hitherto fed her every day, he was bound to continue to do so for ever, only to find herself on the farmer's dinner table the next day. Of course, her case does not invalidate the inductive method; her failure was due to an incorrect application of it, not using a wide enough sample class. But such mishandling of what may well be a perfect method has occurred in human history as well; the history of science provides any number of examples of people arriving at false predictions by inductive reasoning. A famous illustration is presented by the case of the colour of swans. For thousands of years only white swans were observed in the northern hemisphere, leading to the universal conclusion that only white swans would be observed in the future too; of course, this turned out to be false with the discovery of Australia, where many black swans were found.

Yet another important source of uncertainty is generated by the fact that we are never sure about the truth of the empirical premises on which any given inductive argument is based. As is well known, in the middle of the last century it was predicted, on the basis of laws of nature that had been established inductively, and of the initial conditions astronomers assumed to be in force, that the planet Uranus would be situated at a given spot in the sky at a given time, and yet it was observed to be situated somewhere else. The reason was that the astronomers' assumptions about the initial conditions were false; they failed to take into account the still undiscovered planet Neptune, which interfered with the motion of Uranus.

But of course the most profound reason for doubt was provided by Hume, who argued that no amount of past experience can render any future event probable to any degree. I shall have to be exceedingly brief about this vast issue. I should mention however that nowadays the majority of philosophers of science are not engaged in attempting to solve Hume's problem. They believe that philosophers should devote their time to investigating exactly *what* are the rules of induction rather than *why* these rules are to be regarded as reliable. But this is definitely not because they are all satisfied that the latter question has already been adequately answered. No, there are a variety of other reasons. Some believe that the rigorous explication or reconstruction of scientific method is an important task in itself and that we are now in a good position to accomplish it. Others have maintained that every inquiry has to start with some unquestioned presuppositions if it is to start at all, and philosophy of science begins with the presupposition that the observed may serve as evidence concerning the nature of the unobserved. It has also been pointed out that surely we cannot be expected to sit and wait and make no predictions until a solution to the problem of induction is found. Hence in the absence of any other proven reliable method we shall go on using induction and investigate its nature.

An additional important point is that even among those philosophers who claim to have provided a justification for induction, few if any would go so far as to insist that their arguments are strong enough to establish with anything near certainty the uniformity of nature, that is, that the world is such that predictions based on the correct application of induction are bound to be true. Indeed, many of these justifications do not claim to offer any guarantee at all for the success of inductive reasoning. What they do attempt is to show that even in the absence of such guarantees, rationality requires, for this or that reason, the use of the inductive method.

There are clearly infinitely many ways in which V may turn out to be false. It is possible that instead of R_1, my actions will produce R_2 or R_3 or R_4 etc., that is, one of infinitely many results other than the desired one. Now any reason that a naturalist may cite to justify our inclination to rely on induction, and thus to regard it likely that V is true, is available to the theist as well. However, if I am a theist then I have a strong extra reason for believing that V is true: God expects me to bring about R_1. I know of no other way of accomplishing this but by performing A on the assumption that V is true. It would be difficult therefore to deny that $p(V/T) > p(V/N)$. Principle (C) therefore implies that V confirms T relative to N. It should be noted that as time goes on there is a continual accumulation of evidence to support T: every time we observe a V-like proposition turning out to be true we have additional evidence to support T against N!

Reasoning from predictability

Our argument was based on the following points:

First, there are at least three reasons why $p(V/N)$ is considerably less than one:

1 The premisses of every inductive argument contain assumptions concerning the prevailing physical conditions. We can never be certain of the truth of these assumptions.

2 Even if the inductive method has been proved absolutely reliable, we could never be sure that we have applied it correctly, that is, that we have made all the relevant observations and have an adequate sample class.

3 The greatest source of uncertainty is our continued inability to show that events of the past are capable of providing any support for hypotheses about the future. Many philosophers are pessimistic about

the prospects of attempts to justify induction. But even among those who have offered such justification, most have not claimed to have provided reasons for regarding the conclusions of inductive arguments as highly probable.

Secondly, among the various attempts that have been made to justify our use of the inductive method there does not seem to be even one that is based on the assumption of the non-existence of God. It is safe therefore to assert that there are no arguments with some prima facie valid claim to defend the reasonableness of our confidence in induction that may work for a naturalist but not if we assume that theism is true. In other words, an argument with any degree of plausibility that a naturalist may want to use to support the reliability of inductive reasoning is also available to the theist. Thus $p(V/T)$ is at least as great as $p(V/N)$.

Thirdly, however, the theist has an important additional reason to believe that V is true. He holds that God wants him to behave in certain ways, in particular to alleviate suffering, promote the welfare of others and engage in religious activities such as attending a place of worship. This implies that he is in the possession of the means to achieve these goals. Consequently $p(V/T) > p(V/N)$

It might seem for a moment that the objection could be raised that if the preceding argument were sound it could be employed to support the validity of induction! For let

Φ = Predictions based on induction can be relied upon.

Then surely $p(V/\Phi) > p(V/\sim\Phi)$, and when V turns out to be true we obtain a confirmation of Φ. But it is universally agreed that there exists no such simple and straightforward way of empirically establishing the validity of induction, and hence it could be claimed that something must be wrong with this type of argument.

But of course the answer is that this argument form is of no use in helping to raise the credibility of Φ, since there are indefinitely many rules which stand to V in exactly the same relation as Φ stands to V. For let

Φ' = Predictions based on induction can be relied upon till tomorrow

Φ'' = Predictions based on induction can be relied upon till the day after tomorrow

and so on. Then obviously $p(V/\Phi) = p(V/\Phi') = p(V/\Phi'')$ . . . and Φ is not confirmed by V relative to any of these hypotheses.

I should point out that we are not ignoring the fact that V-like predictions have been known to fail from time to time. Such failures do of course constitute disconfirming instances. But the ratio of successes to failures is enormous and the net result is therefore a strong confirmation of T.

I trust the reader will readily agree that the fact that those who set out to perform evil acts do not as a rule succeed less often than those who desire to act virtuously provides no objection to the present line of argument. Theists have always maintained that only in a world in which it is as easy to act sinfully as righteously is there good reason to assign to virtuous acts the high religious value generally assigned to them.

The problem of alternative hypotheses

There is another, rarely considered, objection that points to a weakness in our solution as well as in every one of the different versions of the argument from design. It is that even if all the assumptions of the theists are granted, these arguments do not specifically point towards theism. What we have done is to compare T to N only, failing to take into consideration the possibility of other hypotheses. A sceptic could ask, for instance: what about D, the hypothesis that a powerful, evil demon rules the world and for some peculiar, perverted reason is interested in ensuring that certain states of affairs expected also on the basis of T come about? Since it is clear from our description of D that $p(L/T) = p(L/D)$, our rule of confirmation is not capable of adjudicating between T and D.

Let me give a brief indication of what would be a rather ambitious answer to this objection. It might be claimed that once N is sufficiently disconfirmed, and we examine the hypotheses postulating that, in addition to the physical world and the laws governing it, there is some being who possesses intelligence and power and who wills what happens in the universe, then theism is superior to all other available hypotheses. One argument that comes readily to mind is that theism, which amounts to claiming that the being in question is perfect, is unique among all the possible hypotheses. 'Perfection' is a single attribute which, some would claim, at once determines all the other attributes its possessor must have:* a perfect being must have maximum power, maximum intelligence, maximum benevolence and so on. Anyone who wants to postulate that the being assumed responsible for everything that exists is not perfect is obliged to make indefinitely many arbitrary

---

* 'Absolutely imperfect' may also have this special feature, but of course the creator and ruler of the universe cannot have this attribute for, among other things, he cannot have minimum power.

decisions about whether this or that property should be assigned to this being independently of all the other properties already assigned to him. After having ascribed n properties to the powerful ruler of the universe, no matter how large n may be, the question will always remain whether some property P, not included among these and unrelated to them, belongs or does not belong to him. The theist, on the other hand, would claim that all he has to do is ask himself whether P or not-P contributes more to perfection, a question he would insist always has a clear answer.

A more modest contention would be to maintain that it is reasonable for us to confine our attention to 'plausible' hypotheses, that is, those that have actually been entertained by an appreciable number of people who were genuinely concerned with an ultimate account of reality. As we know, the argument from design, which has been recognised as potentially the most persuasive argument in support of theism, contains no element by virtue of which theism compares favourably with a belief in some other being as the designer of the universe – a being powerful but not omnipotent, intelligent but not omniscient, morally imperfect, entirely amoral or even highly malevolent. Yet, while the argument has been continually under attack since Hume, this apparent weakness has not received much criticism. The explanation is that it has been recognized that the great majority of people concerned with theological questions are usually torn between a very limited number of alternatives. It is hardly ever the case that any one of a dozen different answers to the question of the existence and nature of a creator appears equally likely. It is by far the most common occurrence for a person to be attracted to naturalism because of the success of secular science and because of its economy in not postulating anything beyond familiar physical particulars, but at the same time to find that one given version of theism has some emotional appeal to him. Virtually no other account enters his mind as a viable alternative. Basically, such a person faces a competition between N and a particular version of T, for he regards them alone as plausible candidates for the ultimate explanation of the origin of the universe and its laws. The argument from design, in tilting the scale against naturalism, may be of considerable help to a person in such a frame of mind.

I shall not go on to elaborate upon this or any related point as I am anxious not to be sidetracked from my central thesis. This thesis is that the present argument must be regarded as clearly superior to the celebrated argument from design. I do not claim that no plausible objection can possibly be raised against it, but I do think that any such objection will be seen to apply equally to the traditional argument from design. On the other hand, quite a number of objections of varying force that have been or could be raised against the traditional argument are clearly irrelevant to the new thesis.

As mentioned before, the most vulnerable aspect of the classical argument from design is that it is based on an attempt to assess the probabilities that various non-existent, possible worlds will be actualized. Some of the charges, as we have seen, amount not merely to denying that such an assessment can be made with reliable precision, but to something more fundamental, namely, that it is based on incoherent or meaningless presuppositions. In addition to the various objections described above (p. 74), there are other quite well-known ones that, though not entirely explicit on this point, may also easily be shown to have been directed against this particular weak spot.

Consider, for example, what is probably Hume's most famous objection, in which he contends that the argument from design is based on an illegitimate analogy. He points out that, while there is evidence that within our universe systems that are adapted to some purpose and have useful and orderly organizations do not as a rule spring into being as a result of random processes, there is no justification for extrapolating from this evidence and applying it to the question whether the universe itself is designed. There is no support for the claim that universes like ours are normally designed by sentient beings.

What Hume claims is that experience may be said to have taught us that our universe is such that processes unguided by intelligent action produce a certain kind of system only. Hence we are entitled to hypothesize about the origins of systems with certain characteristics that we find in this world. But surely we cannot do the same with respect to that all-inclusive system which is our universe. We cannot maintain that on the basis of experience (or indeed on the basis of anything else) we may assume that there is some X, where X is of such a nature that it precludes the production of certain kinds of universe. In a complete void, in which it is assumed that no universe exists, there is nothing to which we can ascribe this or that characteristic; nothing may be said to be capable of permitting or precluding the occurrence of this or that event.

The argument I have outlined in this and the previous two sections is fully immune to all objections of this kind. It makes no reference to any but the actual world. It is pivoted on our inability to find in our universe any guarantee that even the simplest of our acts will produce the desired result rather than any one of infinitely many possible different results, as well as on the fact that theism *does* provide us with reason to expect the desired result.

A different kind of advantage may also be claimed for our argument. Anyone prepared to admit that it provides some support for theism will have to admit that its support is cumulative. If the argument is valid then thousands of new instances are produced every moment which confirm T relative to N.

The definition of a miracle

In the concluding parts of this chapter we turn to a discussion of the concept of a miracle, which many would agree is of considerable philosophical interest, reaching beyond the concerns of this book. The concept of a miracle is basically a religious one and we should be inclined therefore to think that a description of its nature is to be sought in religious literature and nowhere else. Once theologians have stated the conditions that are necessary and sufficient for an event to qualify as miraculous, there is wide scope for philosophers to subject their statements to analysis in order to discover the presuppositions upon which they rest and their various implications. One would want to maintain that, just as philosophers of science allow scientists to employ whatever terms they find useful for the construction of their theories, and confine themselves to the study of the logical features of the statements employing these terms, so must philosophers of religion grant freedom to theologians to use whatever term they find useful for their purposes. It is not reasonable to expect significant results if philosophers follow their own fancy in defining religious terms and then subject these to analysis.

There are numerous instances in which philosophers have, to different degrees, deviated from the practice I believe they should adhere to. Hume's treatment of our topic may be an important case in point. There is a famous Humean argument that it is unreasonable for anyone to believe in any miracle he has not himself witnessed. This argument has caused consternation among theists, who greatly cherish the traditional stories about miraculous events, and they have strived to find fault with it. As we shall see, however, given Hume's presuppositions, his argument may be quite unassailable. But what we must ask is: need we grant Hume his presuppositions? It is not necessary to be a Biblical scholar in order to see that, for instance, Hume's description of a miracle and the description in the Old Testament, even if not entirely unrelated, are certainly not equivalent. On the Biblical notion of a miracle, however, his arguments do not work, as I hope to show here.

It would be unfair not to mention that the case for philosophers keeping out of theologians' business, just as they keep out of scientists', could be claimed to be weaker than I have suggested. First of all, it may be said that the scientific concepts subject to this rule have no role to play outside science. 'Entropy' may be such a concept. If entropy had no use in thermodynamics and the word 'entropy' appeared in no physics textbooks it would not be listed in any dictionary or be part of the language. In contrast, many religious terms, and in particular the word 'miracle', also have an established, independent secular use. Even if the term 'miracle' had never occurred in the Scriptures, people – even wholly unreligious people – would talk about miracles that had occurred, or seemed to have occurred, or failed to occur in their own lives. The investigation of the notion of a 'miracle', unlike that of the notion of 'entropy', may be of interest to someone interested in finding out how it functions in ordinary discourse.

Secondly, if a philosopher is told that when trying to understand a scientific term he should confine his attention to the official version of that term provided by scientific authorities, he at least knows for sure what he is supposed to do. There is no difficulty in ascertaining from various textbooks what the exact definition of a given scientific term is. But the case of religious terms is quite different. Different sources, and even different interpretations of the same source, may assign quite different senses to the same term. There is simply no such thing as *the* description of the nature of a given concept; different religious authorities offer any number of different descriptions.

These objections need to be qualified, however, as follows. First, even if the notion of a miracle is a fully fledged secular notion in its own right we cannot hope to gain much from examining its use in common discourse when our purpose is to find out whether certain believers' claims involving that notion are correct or not. Secondly, in spite of the high degree of disagreement, the situation in religion is not entirely chaotic. We distinguish between versions from different sources that are more or less authoritative, as well as between versions that are widely accepted and those that are not.

The Biblical notion of a miracle

The first step towards evaluating philosophically the degree to which the religious function of miracles may be fulfilled is to make sure that we have an adequate definition of a miraculous event. However, the first step towards achieving this aim is, I believe, to realize that at least two fundamentally different notions of a miracle exist and that we have to keep them apart. It should be quite obvious that the term 'miracle' stands for one idea in an everyday context and another in a religious context. Everyone is likely to understand me if I say 'The biggest miracle that has happened to me was when I was granted a PhD in economics even though the thesis I handed in was nothing but two chapters from Milton Friedman's book.' I will have expressed myself in correct English. At the same time, the success of my fraud by no means qualifies as a miracle in a religious sense. For one thing, the story of the PhD committee's amazing oversight is unlikely to generate religious statements or pious acts. Whether it is part of the actual definition or not, few will disagree that an essential feature of a genuine miracle is that it is a source of religious inspiration.

The reader may recall that Hume wrote 'a miracle may be accurately defined a transgression of a law of nature by a particular volition of the Deity, or by the interposition of some invisible agent'.[24] We find a similar definition in Webster, who says that a miracle is 'an event or action that apparently contradicts known scientific laws'. The latter does not speak about the volition of a deity, which in any case does not add much to the definition since to the theist everything that happens is in accordance with divine will. Both seems to have captured fairly well the popular notion of a miracle.

On the other hand, a cursory reading of, for instance, the first 15 chapters of Exodus, which mainly report various miracles, reveals that a miracle is always denoted by a word which also means 'sign' or 'evidence'; that on many occasions when a miracle is predicted, the prediction is followed by 'so that you will know that I am the Lord'; and that nowhere is there any indication that a miracle is either a real or an apparent violation of a law of nature. The conclusion that seems to be indicated is that the purpose of a miracle is to serve as a sign of God's existence, power and providence, in consequence of which people will tend to acknowledge a divine order in the world. The question whether miraculous events are necessarily a violation of nature does not seem to carry significant weight. Thus if we want to gain a better understanding of the nature of a miracle what we need to inquire into is the question: what are the characteristics of an event whose occurrence will contribute to the confirmation of religious belief?

Religiously significant events

It should be pointed out that there have been philosophers since Hume who have realized his definition leaves something to be desired and have suggested an amendment to it. A number of authors have claimed that it is not necessary that an event should violate a law of nature in order for it to qualify as a miracle; it is sufficient if it is extraordinary and therefore unexpected. The motives for such a suggestion have been varied. Perhaps the most obvious is the thought that there may be no such thing as an event that violates a law of nature. The very fact of its occurrence constitutes full proof that there is no law prohibiting such an occurrence. There are, however, ways of dealing with this difficulty. Hume's definition could simply be loosened so that it states that a miracle is an *apparent* transgression of a law of nature, or that it violates what hitherto has been thought of as a law of nature. A more sophisticated attempt might be to claim that only events that are found to occur invariably under identical circumstances occur in accordance with a law. Thus when a law L is repeatedly 'violated' under circumstances C, then we conclude that the correct law is 'L, except under circumstances C'. However if L is violated under C once but not again, then we say that the law is L but it has been violated once. For we shall insist that an event which happens once and fails to occur at another time when the relevant physical conditions are identical occurs unlawfully. Accordingly it is not by definition impossible for an event to constitute a violation of a law of nature.

However, a simple reason for wanting to extend miracles beyond those events which violate laws of nature is that an occurrence compatible with the actual and even known laws of nature may well be a wondrous event. It is in keeping with common usage to equate a miracle with an event that causes surprise and fills people with wonder.

Other people have added the requirement that a miraculous event should have religious significance. This is unquestionably a vital point. However, the notion of 'religious significance' is broad, and we need a more specific statement of the particular kind of religious significance a miraculous event is supposed to have. Not all attempts to provide such a statement have been helpful. Let us consider a story that has been quoted several times before, a story that originates with R. F. Holland:

A child riding his toy motor-car strays on to an unguarded railway crossing near his house and a wheel of his car gets stuck down the side of one of the rails. An express train is due to pass with the signals in its favor and a curve in the track makes it impossible for the driver to stop his train in time to avoid any obstruction he might encounter on the crossing. The mother coming out of the house to look for her child sees him on the crossing and hears the train approaching. She runs forward shouting and waving. The little boy remains seated in his car looking downward, engrossed in the task of pedalling it free. The brakes of the train are applied and it comes to rest a few feet from the child. The mother thanks God for the miracle; which she never ceases to think of as such although, as she in due course learns, there was nothing supernatural about the manner in which the brakes of the train came to be applied. The driver had fainted, for a reason that had nothing to do with the presence of the child on the line, and the brakes were applied automatically as his hand ceased to exert pressure on the control lever. [25]

The main point, of course, is to illustrate that an event does not cease to be miraculous once it is accounted for by natural factors. The story succeeds in showing this. But there is also supposed to be another point. Richard Swinburne tries to explain:

On a wide understanding of 'religious significance' an event will have religious significance if it is a good event and a contribution to or foretaste of the ultimate destiny of the world. Thus the healing of a sick person will, on the Christian view, be of religious significance, since the world's ultimate destiny is, on the Christian view, a state where evil, including sickness, is no more. Or the train stopping, in Holland's example quoted earlier, will be of religious significance on the Christian view since a separation by death of mother and child is an evil to be abolished in the last state of the world. [26]

This may momentarily appear to have some authenticity: one is attracted to the idea that 'religious significance' is to be ascribed to an occurrence that is a clear manifestation of God at work, and one would readily agree that this is the case when an intrinsically divine, desirable event takes place. But then one is bound to remember that as often as not people in mortal danger fail to be rescued at the last moment and that sick persons are not always healed; a variety of disasters befall all sorts of people all the time. This, of course, is what gives rise to the problem of evil, a problem the theist cannot afford to leave unsolved, but the solution of which compels him to maintain that human suffering is an indispensable means for attaining certain vital aims in the overall divine plan. In brief, a believer is forced to acknowledge that hurtful events are no less divinely ordained than pleasant ones. Thus the train coming to a sudden halt cannot be said to have religious significance in the substantial sense of something we could know beforehand God was bound to make happen and whose failure to happen would have left the theist at a loss to explain it. According to Swinburne's explanation of the notion of 'religious significance', an event having such a significance is just as likely to take place whether God exists or doesn't exist.

It may also be pointed out that theists, at any rate those belonging to the Judaeo-Christian tradition, would regard the story of the spectacular punishment of Pharaoh and the Egyptians related in Exodus as constituting the paradigm of miracle stories. The eighth plague caused everyone in Egypt to fall sick, the tenth plague killed all the first born, and finally the miracle at the Red Sea resulted in the drowning of the whole Egyptian army; but since sickness and death are evils to be abolished at the end of the world, these events must therefore be lacking religious significance as defined by Swinburne. Would he deny therefore that these were genuine miracles?

I shall not continue to explore the crucial notion of 'religious significance'. Nor shall I review any additional suggestions that have been made concerning the precise explication of a miracle. But I would like to point out that in all the fairly extensive literature I have not found anyone expressing the view that a miracle not only is not a violation, real or apparent, of nature's laws, but that it need not even be an extraordinary or highly improbable event. The reader may perhaps find this strange at first, but I shall argue that a miracle need not be improbable and even may be an event that was more likely to take place than not.

Hume on miracles

Let me devote this section to a discussion of what has been perhaps the most celebrated argument on the subject of miracles, Hume's argument that it is irrational to believe any of the stories we have heard concerning miracles. Robert Hambourger, in a recent article, has usefully paraphrased Hume's argument thus:

As I understand Hume's argument, it rests on two principles: . . .
(1) Suppose that someone or, perhaps, a group of people testify to the truth of a proposition P that, considered by itself, is improbable. Then to evaluate the testimony, one must weigh the probability that P is true against the probability that the informants are lying or mistaken. If it is more likely that P is true than that the informants are lying or mistaken, then, on balance, the testimony renders P more likely than not, and it may be reasonable for one to believe that P. However, if it is as likely, or even more likely, that the informants are lying or mistaken than it is that P is true, then, on balance, the testimony does not render P more likely true than false, and it would not be reasonable for one to believe that P.
The second principle on which I think Hume's argument rests is this:
(2) An event properly could be judged to be a miracle, if it occurred, only if there were a proof against it, 'as entire as any argument from experience can possibly be imagined,' and therefore the probability that such an event does

not occur is as great as the probability of any proposition based on inference from experience.

Principles (1) and (2), if true, are sufficient to prove that it is never reasonable to believe that a miracle has occurred on the basis of the testimony of others. [27]

Hume's major premisses are clearly stated here and the argument based on them seems powerful. It does contain one weak element but, as we shall see, this is something Hambourger slipped in, not a part of Hume's original argument. Everyone is likely to agree that if we think of one of the most truthful people we know and assign n to the value of the probability that he might be lying, then even though n is very small it is surely not as small as the probability that a well-established law of nature has been violated. However, when there are two such persons the probability that both are lying is far less, namely n^2, while if we are given a report by m such trustworthy people then the probability that the report is false is no more than n^m. It should seem quite absurd to claim that no matter how large m might be, n^m will always remain greater than the probability that a violation of a well-confirmed law has taken place. How can one therefore claim that it is *never* reasonable to believe that a miracle has occurred on the basis of the testimony of others?

One might attempt to reply, for instance, that it is not true that the probability that a report given by two truthful witnesses should be false is as small as n^2. It may be that both $p(L_1) = n$ and $p(L_2) = n$ but it is false that $p(L_1 \& L_2) = p(L_1) \times p(L_2)$ since the two probabilities are not independent. What is the case is that $p(L_1 \& L_2) = p(L_1) \times p(L_2/L_1)$ where $p(L_2/L_1) > n$. If the first witness is lying this may be ascribed to the presence of some special factors that induced him to do so, and the same factors are likely to influence the other witness too. Nevertheless it is out of the question for us to claim that $p(L_2/L_1)$ is as high as one. Consequently it must be admitted that the probability that two witnesses should be lying is less than n, and that three witnesses should be lying is even less. It follows therefore that there is bound to be a number m large enough for the probability that m witnesses are all lying to be lower than the probability of a miracle. It seems wrong to maintain therefore that in principle it is never reasonable to believe the testimony of others concerning a miracle.

But in fact Hume is more cautious than one would have expected from Hambourger's paper. He seems to have denied proving that in principle it can never be rational to believe that a miracle has occurred on the testimony of others. All he claims – and this is sufficient for his purpose, which is to combat the religious beliefs held by his contemporaries – is that under the prevailing circumstances it may be said to be unreasonable to believe that any of the miracles cited by religious people as part of their tradition have indeed taken place. Hume states clearly:

The plain consequence is (and it is a general maxim worthy of our attention) that no testimony is sufficient to establish a miracle unless the testimony be of such a kind that its falsehood would be more miraculous than the fact which it endeavours to establish. [28]

This of course is compatible with what I have said, namely, that there must be a sufficiently large number m such that when there are m reliable witnesses the falsehood of their testimony would be more miraculous than the fact it endeavours to establish. Hume, however, maintains that this has never been the case. Hambourger seems to have overlooked this point; otherwise he would not have written some of the things that appear later in his paper. For example, after a good deal of argument he concludes his paper with the sentence 'Thus I believe that, at least in principle, testimony could give one adequate reason to believe in a miracle.' In view of what I have just said his efforts to establish this conclusion, which was supposed to refute Hume, were quite superfluous since Hume agrees with it.

The most remarkable part of Hambourger's paper contains an argument that should be regarded as quite devastating by anyone ready to accept it. He claims that we should reject Hume's conclusion since, among others, premiss (1), or what may be called the principle of relative likelihood, is false. He advances the following somewhat startling argument to show that this is so. Let us assume that there is a lottery in which there are a million participants and a single large prize. Following the draw a highly reliable newspaper like the *New York Times* reports that Smith was the winner. We shall unquestionably accept the report as true. But the probability that a paper like the *New York Times* should print an erroneous report, even though small, is not smaller than say $1/10,000$. On the other hand, the probability that Smith is the winner is no more than $1/1,000,000$. If Hume's principle were correct we would have to say that the reliability of the *New York Times* was not high enough to make us want to believe such a highly improbable story. But as we have said we will not hesitate in accepting the newspaper's report. It should follow then that it is reasonable to believe the reports of reliable witnesses even if they concern the most improbable events.

Even with virtually no knowledge of probability theory one should be able to see that the lottery case cannot be compared to reports of miraculous events. Consider, for example, the report that Jericho was captured because of the spectacular collapse of the walls surrounding the city at the sound of the Israelites' trumpets. According to Hume, reason requires that we should refuse to believe this report. It is clear that Hume is not asking us to say: we refuse to accept this report as authentic and prefer to believe that Jericho was actually captured as a result of some other, equally improbable miracle. This would be an absurd demand – why prefer one unlikely story to another? Obviously what Hume wants us to say is that we refuse to accept the traditional story and prefer to believe that Jericho was captured in some natural and not improbable way, or perhaps that Jericho was not captured at all. What Hume urges us to do, then, is very sensible, namely, to regard it as much more probable that something that happened was actually likely to happen in the first place, rather than highly improbable. Supposing we accept his advice, how are we to apply it to the case of the lottery? Are we to say that we refuse to accept that Smith is the winner and prefer to believe that someone else, more likely to win, was the actual winner? But every ticket has exactly the same chance of winning. From the established fact that there is a lottery with one million tickets and that a draw has taken place, it follows as a certainty that one ticket whose probability of being drawn was no more than $1/1,000,000$ *was* actually drawn, and the only question is which it was. In the case of the lottery we do not have the option of assuming that some other ticket more likely to be drawn than Smith's won the prize. I may confidently add that if it were established beyond doubt that on a particular occasion some miracle must have happened Hume would not urge us to reject a report specifying the nature of the miracle.

The truth seems to be that Hume is quite correct in arriving at his conclusion on the basis of his own assumptions. It is his assumptions that should be questioned.

Miracles as testimony

We have already seen that the essence of a miracle in the religious sense is that its occurrence contributes to the confirmation of religious belief. Now, as we have explained before, whenever

$$p(E/T) > p(E/N) \ldots (C)$$

obtains, the observation that E is true (that is, that the event E asserted would happen has actually happened) confirms the hypothesis T relative to the hypothesis N.

I should advance it as a definition of a miracle that it is a special kind of event whose occurrence is deemed to confirm, dramatically, religious belief. It would seem that this is always the case when the occurrence is significantly more probable on the assumption that T is true than on the assumption that N is true. This again is so whenever it is vividly evident that the value of $p(E/T)$ is considerably higher than the value of $p(E/N)$.

Consider the story of the deliverance of the Jewish people as reported in the book of Esther. Haman is determined to destroy all the Jews in the kingdom of Achashverus, which contains all the Jewish people in the world. Will the Jews escape extinction? It is reasonable under the circumstances for naturalists to conclude this is not very likely. Haman is obsessed with his plan; the King has already given his approval; in Persia a royal decree cannot be revoked even by the King himself; Persia has the mightiest army in the world, and so on. Thus it must be deemed more likely that the Jews will perish than that they will not. On the other hand, a believer could have argued under the same circumstances that the Jewish people are the people of God who proclaim his name; is it possible that he should permit them to disappear from the face of the earth? Is it possible that the forces of evil will have absolute victory and that no believer will remain to spread the word of God? No, it is more likely that some combination of events is going to foil Haman's plan. But that is what has actually happened. Thus let

S = A combination of events takes place which radically changes the King's attitude and the Jewish people are saved

then, as we have said, $p(S/T^*) > p(S/N)$ where T^* stands for theism, or rather for that particular version of theism according to which the annihilation of the Jewish people is likely to be contrary to the divine plan for the history of mankind. The fact that the inequality of the form (C) obtains implies that the truth of S confirms T^*.

The following points are to be noted:

1 The Talmud regards S to have been one of the most important miracles ever to have taken place. It has been widely celebrated as such every year for many centuries. Significantly, there is not a single sentence in the book of Esther which would suggest that anything supernatural took place. What did occur, we are told, was a combination of a number of happy events, such as the King's becoming favourably disposed toward the Jews after their leader warned him of a plot against his life, and so on.

2 I emphasized above that to a theist whatever happens happens with God's approval and, therefore, when people perish it can be no more

against his will than when people flourish. It might occur to some to ask: how can I claim that S is more in accordance with the divine will than ∼ S? It might also be asked: what should we have said if ∼ S had turned out to be true?

Let me begin by stating clearly that if ∼ S had turned out to be true we would have witnessed a serious disconfirmation of T*. It would be implausible, as well as pointless, to maintain that theism, in any version, is completely immune from disconfirmation. It may not be conclusively falsifiable (since $p(S/T^*)$ is not one, for instance), but then very few hypotheses are. There is, however, scope for any number of disconfirming events to take place which result eventually in many people abandoning T*. Admittedly, as we have said before, disasters that ordinarily befall individuals or groups of people are not seen by the believer as evidence hostile to his belief. But decisive events with unique implications would be seen as such; for example, the destruction of a whole people who proclaim the validity of T*, or the failure of a prediction of a momentous event which could benefit all believers and which was announced by a universally acknowledged religious leader of the stature of Moses.

3 It is crucial to realize that S does not refer to an event that is exceedingly improbable. But now we can see clearly that for an event to qualify as miraculous it is not necessary that its probability be of low absolute value. In fact, its value can be anything between zero and one. All that is required is that its probability under N be lower than its probability under T. For example, an event that was quite likely to happen since it had a probability greater than 50 per cent could in principle qualify as a miracle, provided its occurrence was appreciably more probable on assuming T to be true than on assuming it to be false.

It should be quite obvious that Hume's objection to the acceptance of reports concerning miraculous events has no relevance to the present interpretation. According to my definition, a miracle is an event with religious significance in the precise sense that it possesses some unique feature by virtue of which it is assigned a higher probability under the assumptions of a believer than under those of a non-believer. It therefore has religious significance simply because it confirms the believer's assumptions by satisfying relationship (C). Low probability is not a part of the definition of a miracle, nor is it implied by it. Thus Hume's objection does not get off the ground so far as reports of miracles that do not involve low probabilities are concerned.

4 I should like to stress that I am not trying to prove that it is no longer rational to deny, for example, the authenticity of the story told in the book of Esther. All I wish to argue is that Hume's reason for denying

it is not valid. The events reported in that book are by no means so highly improbable that even if we were inclined to hold its authors in high regard we would here think them unworthy of trust. But of course there may be other bases for a person's refusal to believe the story of Esther. Historical research may provide all sorts of reasons to doubt its veracity.

Nor do I wish to claim that if we accept the story as true then it is no longer rational to refuse to subscribe to T*. The fact that S confirms, even strongly confirms, T* does not on its own decide the question whether T* is to be accepted. There is, first of all, the issue of the prior probability of T*. Those who ascribe a very low value to it will require a large number of confirming instances before they are prepared to entertain T*. In addition a person will have to consider whether history does not also contain events which are to be construed as disconfirming instances of T*, and evaluate the relative strength of the evidence for and against this hypothesis.

5 It would be unfair not to mention that it does not follow from all this that the deeply entrenched view that a miraculous event must be an anomalous event, perhaps even to the extent that it should remain unaccountable forever in terms of established laws of nature, is completely groundless. The present account regards the testimonial function of a miracle as its primary feature. Such an event will of course fail in its purpose if those witnessing it overlook what it is supposed to be a sign of. Obviously, the greater the difference between $p(E/T)$ and $p(E/N)$, the greater will be the impact of E's turning out to be true, and the more certainly will people feel impelled to apply (C), with the desired result. If $p(E/N)$ is itself of considerable value then there is no scope for $p(E/T)$ being dramatically larger, and the realization of E will have no stunning effect. Ideally, therefore, E should be 'inexplicable and accountable only as a result of divine intervention', which translated into more prosaic language means that E is exceedingly improbable on the assumption that N is true, but vastly more probable on the assumption that T is true. But while I have admitted that a low prior probability of an event may contribute to its effectiveness as a miracle, it should be clear that what is desirable is not simply a low prior probability. We should want it to have a low prior probability on the assumption that T is not true, but it need not have a low probability at all on the assumption that T is true.

In the course of our earlier discussion of the argument from design I have attempted to outline some replies to the complaint that we have only compared T to N, and have failed to take into account the possibility of other hypotheses. Similarly, it might well be objected again in connection with our present topic: what about D, the hypothesis that a powerful evil demon rules the world and it is he who has brought about certain improbable events which may appear to promote the welfare of the pious and the chastisement of the wicked for some peculiar, perverted reason of his own which may not be too difficult to invent?

It seems to me that we should now be better able to meet this kind of objection than earlier. It is sufficient to remember that a miracle occurs in the context of a specific situation to which alone it need be relevant. At any point in a given society, different parties hold different concrete beliefs, and the miraculous event that then takes place is supposed to adjudicate between them. It may have no bearing – and need not – on a hypothesis which is logically quite respectable but which is not actually held by anyone. For example, Moses came along to proclaim the veracity of theism, which the Egyptians denied, subscribing to some other, pagan, view of the world. Although we are not given a detailed description of the hypothesis Moses was bent upon defeating, it is clear that the particular non-theistic view held by the Egyptians did not contain anything that required the materialization of the awesome catastrophes predicted by Moses. On the other hand, those who placed their trust in the kind of divinity of which Moses claimed to be the spokesman tended to believe that the predictions, which were to result in God's deliverance of his people, setting them free so as to reveal himself to them, were likely to be true. The wondrous events that occurred subsequently had the function of adjudicating between these two specific hypotheses. They were efficacious to the extent that even Pharaoh, despite his enormous interest in doing otherwise, exclaimed after the seventh plague 'The Lord is in the right and I and my people are in the wrong' (Exodus 9: 27). The Egyptians may have done nothing to discredit some other esoteric hypothesis that also happened to imply the fulfilment of Moses' prophesies. However, for whatever reason, such hypotheses were in any case not entertained by anyone.

Theism and metaphysics

The thoughtful reader is quite likely by now to suspect that the subject of miracles provides a strong reason for denying the soundness of my account of the central characteristics of metaphysics and of why it is so fundamentally distinct from the various other more down-to-earth empirical enterprises.

In particular, my claim that the case depends on the same principle of confirmation that is most commonly used in the physical sciences gives rise to the objection that the controversy between the believer and the non-believer no longer bears the distinguishing mark I have assigned to metaphysical controversies. It no longer appears to belong to a basically different category of enterprises from the one to which typical scientific controversies belong; just like, for instance, the debate concerning the shape of the earth, it too is subject to an indefinitely long process in which emerges more and more prima facie evidence for the belief of one side, which makes it increasingly harder for the other to defend its position. How are we to explain that by an almost universal consensus the foundations of religion are a part of metaphysics, when in principle any number of miracles could supply firmer and firmer grounds for the position of the believer?

But of course there is still a great difference between science and metaphysics. In the case of the belief that the earth is flat, for example, it is an ordinary empirical belief and so we were *bound* to encounter an indefinitely large number of experiences that seem to clash with this false belief. The shape of the earth is an actual fact among millions of other facts with which it is intertwined and any one of which may provide relevant clues about it. Miracles, on the other hand, are not a necessary part of the physical world, and it is not inevitable that sooner or later we shall experience them.

Thus an important revision has to be introduced into the characterization offered in the first chapter of the feature of metaphysics which plays the major role in distinguishing it from other disciplines. It is not that metaphysical hypotheses cannot in principle be subject to the dynamic confirmatory process typical of scientific hypotheses. However the hypotheses which we regard at the moment as belonging to metaphysics (a) have not so far been subject to this confirmatory process and (b) on the basis of what we know about the physical universe, are seemingly not *bound* to become subject to this process.

We have thus far dealt in some detail with the first in the set of metaphysical beliefs to be studied in this book. We have also examined one of the special techniques employed in metaphysics, one which makes use of the tools scientists also employ in their work. The particular rule under discussion was the most elementary confirmation rule involving the inequality (C). Later, in chapter 7, when dealing with the metaphysical belief that other people besides oneself have minds, we shall come across this technique once more. In that chapter we shall discuss the question whether and how enumerative induction might be employed in order to achieve the result we are seeking. Finally, I advance the suggestion that we apply the scientific rule of confirmation, according to which the hypothesis which best explains our observations is taken to be most highly confirmed by those observations.

I should like to emphasize that I am not an adherent of scientism and do not believe that scientific methodology is a panacea for all problems. The methodology of the physicist cannot be indiscriminately applied to every problem that confronts human beings. In fact we have seen the limitation of the scientific method here in its application to the theistic hypothesis. In the question of the existence of other minds this limitation also becomes vividly apparent. An explanation is deemed 'best' in a sense unique to the specific metaphysical belief in question, and nothing of the kind is to be found in science. In the next chapter, where once more we shall see the use of one of the techniques of the scientist, the great difference in the way it is applied in the two disciplines again becomes evident.

4

Thought experiments and the flow of time

Thought experiments in science and metaphysics

In this chapter we shall look at another important metaphysical issue, namely temporal becoming, in the context of which an opportunity arises for the philosopher to employ a technique also used in science. The technique in question is the conducting of thought experiments. One significant difference between such practices as the use of the confirmation rule involving the relation (C), which we encountered in the previous chapter, and the use of thought experiments, is that the latter is much more frequently applied in metaphysics than in science.

Yet thought experiments have played an important role in science, a role that is not yet well understood, for philosophers of science have not devoted much time to studying their function, which incidentally, is more complicated in science than in metaphysics. The complication is due to the constraints placed on this specific methodological device in science, constraints that are not required in metaphysics. Fortunately, however, Thomas Kuhn, probably the most famous living philosopher of science, has published an essay[1] which makes a first step towards a better understanding of this topic.

Kuhn's conclusion in this paper is that while thought experiments, unlike laboratory experiments, cannot provide new empirical data, they nevertheless have basically the same function. He claims that the two can have similar roles because 'thought experiments give the scientist access to information which is simultaneously at hand and yet somehow inaccessible to him'.[2] He explains that, although no experimental results can possibly be obtained through thought experiments, the scientist may discover the hidden implications of what he already knows. Such a discovery plays a central role in the process of reconceptualization, which constitutes scientific revolution where it is clearly the case that the 'data requisite for revolution have existed before at the fringe of scientific consciousness; the emergence of crisis brings them to the centre of attention; and the revolutionary reconceptualization permits them to be seen in a new way'.[3]

Admittedly, Kuhn, who discusses only two experiments in detail, concedes that there are also others of different types. Nevertheless, it should not be unfair to assume that his examples were meant to be treated as quite typical. In fact, however, there is a vast range of entirely disparate types of thought experiment which differ greatly in function, scope and method. But his article contains much more explicit distortions as well. Let me mention just one example. Kuhn poses the question as to what conditions of verisimilitude thought experiments are subject to. The answer he implies right until the last sentences of his paper is that the conditions are those imposed by the actual laws of nature, and in the two experiments he discusses the laws of nature are taken for granted. He seems completely to overlook the fact that there are many thought experiments whose very point is to find out what would happen if the laws of nature were different from what they are. In such cases the experiment may be set up in a strange situation unobtainable in practice, or even in principle; the only constraint imposed upon the imagination is that there should be no contradiction within the story told.

It is rather a pity that Kuhn happens to be wrong, for had he been right we would have been in a position to state at once a straightforward basic difference between science and metaphysics in the use of this methodological device: in science thought experiments must be confined to conditions under which all the laws of nature are observed, while no such restrictions apply in metaphysics. In metaphysics we can make uninhibited use of our imaginations. We may set up our experiments in the weirdest situations we can think of as long as we are not contradicting ourselves in describing them.

However, only the second half of what I have just said is the case and consequently matters are considerably more complicated. In the last page of his paper Kuhn does concede that in the unique case in which a thought experiment is directed to uncovering a logical contradiction or a confusion no condition of physical verisimilitude is required. He does not go so far as to state clearly what conditions are required. No matter. It is clear, in any case that, contrary to Kuhn, scientists may range far beyond the boundaries of physical verisimilitude even when their purpose is not to reveal logical contradictions. For instance, in a widely known and brief thought experiment using Minkowsky's diagram representing the world-lines of space travellers, it is posited that a traveller's speed is faster than light. It is consequently shown that a negative interval would be required to complete his journey. The notion of a negative amount of time is by no means self-contradictory; it could be given a variety of interpretations. So far, however, negative intervals have no applications in physics. The result of the experiment is consequently taken as suggesting the impossibility of travellers moving at speeds greater than the speed of light, contrary to what had been assumed at the outset of the experiment.

Incidentally this same result was obtained by Einstein by using the contraction formula $(c - v)^{1/2}$. In an exceedingly simple thought experiment in which something travels faster than light, it is immediately seen that $v > c$ and the expression $(c - v)$ is negative and hence $(c - v)^{1/2}$ represents an imaginary number. The conclusion that a certain quantity is represented by an imaginary number does not by any means amount to a contradiction. Imaginary numbers find a very useful application in, for instance, the theory of alternating currents. However, in the absence of compelling contrary reasons it is more rational to assume that imaginary contraction factors do not correspond to reality. Thus the result was taken by Einstein to indicate the impossibility of speeds faster than light. Yet the possibility of this was assumed at the start of his experiment.

In many cases thought experiments in science are performed not in order to discover anything new but rather to convey a new idea in a manner likely to make an impact. A famous case is the experiment involving the demon described by J. C. Maxwell to illustrate his contention that the second law of thermodynamics must be understood not as telling us that such and such will definitely not happen, but only that it is highly improbable that it will happen. His demon is a device that allegedly shows that the law in question could in principle be violated. It is an exceedingly small creature, which can see individual molecules, and it is placed at a small window in a partition that separates two gas chambers. When the demon sees a fast molecule heading towards the window it opens it for a split second to let it pass into the other chamber, but it does not allow a slow molecule through the window. Gradually fewer and fewer fast molecules will be left in the demon's chamber as increasingly more of them will have been transferred to the other chamber. Consequently, the demon's chamber becomes colder and the other hotter. Heat will thus be flowing in the wrong direction, opposite to that required by the second law of thermodynamics.

But the belief that the second law of thermodynamics is ultimately only a statistical law is not based solely on the experiment. If Maxwell had had no reason to arrive at his conclusion other than this experiment he would not have been justified in holding it. His demon is after all required to do all sorts of things that are physically impossible. For example, it has to slide a window's shutter that is absolutely without friction and also without mass and thus without momentum. However, since Maxwell's conclusion follows from the postulates of his kinetic theory, which had already been accepted by most scientists, he employed his demon mainly for its dramatic effect.

I shall say no more about the role of thought experiments in science and shall conclude this section with one reason for their importance in metaphysics. In metaphysics, often the very meaning of utterances is being queried, sometimes because it is claimed that a given utterance is in principle unverifiable. Those who wish to defend the meaningfulness of sentences that have come under attack will want to describe circumstances under which the required verification would be forthcoming. The scope of thought experiments is of course infinite.

The common-sense view of time *

Human beings in widely different cultural settings and in all periods of history have regarded it as one of the most central features of existence that time moves, so that events are carried from the future towards us and then recede further and further into the past. Thus we hear Job complaining 'My days are swifter than a weaver's shuttle', Chaucer declaring 'Ay fleets the time it will no man abide' and Sir Walter Scott observing that 'Time rolls his ceaseless course.'

Yet the majority of analytic philosophers today hold with Russell that the transient view of time is hopelessly flawed. They have characterized all attributions to time of such properties as flying, passing or rolling on, whether swiftly or relentlessly, as involving misleading metaphors, since in reality all events and moments stay for ever fixed in the position in which they occur. There is no such entity as the moving NOW; time remains still, and all temporal relations are permanent.

This remarkable situation is, I venture to suggest, due to a number of factors. First of all, Russell's suggestion, that we can achieve great ontological economy by eliminating all reference to any transient feature of time and still be able to say about our temporal experiences most of the things we want to say, is singularly ingenious. Secondly, the physical sciences, whose prestige has been high in this century, seem to provide support for Russell's position. In books on physics, chemistry or

---

* The subject of the rest of this chapter was discussed in my book *Aspects of Time* (Indianapolis, 1980). However, the arguments presented here are new.

astronomy, we usually do not find what McTaggart called A-statements, for example, 'E is in the *future*' or 'E is in the *past*' (except, perhaps, in the Preface). There are of course indefinitely many natural processes that are functionally related to time, yet they can all be fully described by using only so-called B-statements, for example, 'E_1 is *before* (or *after*, or *simultaneous with*) E_2'. Thirdly, the Russellian view has been vigorously defended by some of the most outstanding philosophers of this century. And finally, the alternative view – the transient view – has not for some reason been argued to any comparable degree.

In this chapter I shall attempt to show that even at this advanced stage of the debate quite a number of things have not yet been said. I shall present some arguments that seem to show that the Russellian attack on the transient view of time is unwarranted, and others demonstrating the positive advantage of the transient view.

Common-sense impressions versus philosophical analysis

Let us begin by briefly reminding ourselves of the two accounts of the basic nature of time. The first account is associated with McTaggart, who articulated the deeply entrenched common-sense view according to which temporal points from the future, together with events that occur at those points, keep approaching the NOW and, after momentarily coinciding with it, keep on receding into the past. The NOW is not conceived as some sort of object, but rather as a point in time which any temporally extended individual experiences as being in the present and which has, so to speak, the spotlight of time focused momentarily on it.

According to Russell and his followers this is a completely false picture. To begin with, no event has the monadic property of being in the future. Consequently, it can never shed this property to assume the property of 'presentness' and subsequently of 'pastness'. An event E_1 may occur earlier than some other event E_2, but if this is so, then it is true for ever that E_1 occurs earlier than E_2. E_1 has the unchanging relationship of being either before or after or simultaneous with every other temporal entity. Apart from moments and the events that occur at them, there is no extra particular such as the NOW to which E_1 may have a changing relationship. Also, E_1 is really occurring at t_1 just as E_2 is occurring at t_2; there are no privileged moments in time and events do not momentarily become more real as they are embraced by the NOW.

Russell's supporters have advanced a number of arguments to demonstrate not merely that their view is adequate but that the transient view of time is downright incoherent. They have claimed that regardless of how uncomfortable we may feel – and they have anticipated correctly that many of us are made to feel uneasy – logic forces us to adopt the static view of time.

Before examining these arguments, let us look briefly at a claim an adherent of the dynamic view may advance, that he is entitled to ignore all the arguments that have been marshalled against his position. He might claim that he is justified in continuing to hold his view without replying to any of the charges that they are untenable. Admittedly, he might say, it is of some philosophical interest to discover what the fallacy is in the Russellian arguments, but it is not a necessary precondition for holding on to the traditional view. The situation is, after all, not much different from the one faced by philosophers when Zeno claimed to have proved that spatial movement is impossible. Most philosophers were greatly impressed with the ingenuity of Zeno's arguments, but they were not shaken in their belief in the possibility of motion. They regarded it philosophically worthwhile to try and locate the error in Zeno's reasoning; however, they did not make their support of the view that motion is possible conditional on the success of the effort to refute Zeno. As is well known, for many hundreds of years the precise solution to Zeno's paradoxes was beyond the mathematical tools available. Philosophers, however, were not prepared to give up their conviction that physical objects are capable of movement, since it was too obviously true. Any philosophical argument designed to prove that something that is clearly observable does not exist amounts at most to clever sophistry. Hence, followers of McTaggart may claim that the passage of time is a given, everyone at all times has been distinctly aware of it, and therefore Russellian arguments, while they may provide some scope for the intellectual exercise required in order to locate their fallacy, cannot affect our firm view concerning the status of temporal becoming.

In reply to this, Russellians may argue that the two cases differ greatly. Suppose everyone observed that a given object was at point p_1 in space at time t_1. Zeno would, of course, not want to deny that the object in question was at p_1 at t_1. Suppose again that at t_2 everyone reports observing the same object situated at p_2. Once again Zeno would not insist that everyone must have been mistaken in what they think they have observed. But then if a given object is said to be at p_1 at t_1, and at p_2 at t_2, then that amounts precisely to saying that the object in question has moved from p_1 to p_2. Zeno does not offer any new interpretation of our observation that would entail no movement having taken place, in consequence of which the paradox he has generated would disappear. On the contrary, it is his intention to assert that we are facing an unresolvable difficulty, in that logic forces us to renounce the possibility of a spatial movement which so distinctly seems to us to be going on all the time. Russell, on the other hand, is doing something quite different. He resolutely denies that it is a fact that the NOW is at t_1 and subsequently at t_2. There is simply no such particular as the NOW and hence it can occupy no temporal position. Thus Russell's arguments do not constrain him to assert anything contrary to the results of experience. He categorically denies that we actually observe such a thing as a moving NOW. That entity has been fabricated by McTaggart's peculiar interpretation imposed upon experience. Russell was not worried that his analysis of temporal becoming clashed with what went on in McTaggart's imagination.

Later we shall probe somewhat further into the question to what extent, if at all, Russell's logical analysis results in the negation of what might be said to be given or implied by experience.

Objections to the transient view

The most vigorous and sustained attacks on the transient view of time are probably those of J. J. C. Smart. I propose to examine his major arguments.

1 In a celebrated article[4] Smart declares that changes themselves do not change. He claims that while it makes good sense to speak of the traffic light changing colour it is a mistake to attribute change to that change itself. Unfortunately he does not explain why this must be so. I can see quite clearly that it would be absurd to maintain that, just as the traffic light changed colour from red to green, the event of this change also changed its colour. But this is by no means accounted for by saying that attributing changes to events as such is to commit a category mistake. An event cannot change colour for the simple reason that it has no colour at all to begin with. But there is no reason to think that it cannot change with respect to a property it does have. Every event is related in a specific way to the NOW (i.e. to begin with it is *after* the NOW, etc.) and is capable of undergoing changes in this relationship; an event is typically the kind of particular which may turn from being in the future into being in the present.

2 Another argument of Smart is based on the contention that it is only a temporally extended process, such as a journey, that may undergo changes. It can, for instance, as he points out, become more pleasant or more tedious. A journey has an early part which may be tedious and may have many other properties as well, all of which may be absent from

a later temporal part. But an event of merely momentary duration has no temporal parts and therefore lacks the room to accommodate different properties. And yet supporters of the transient view of time insist on assigning changes to events of infinitesimal duration by claiming that such events may lose their futurity and acquire presentness.

It might seem that Smart's objection can easily be met. One's immediate reaction is likely to be that Smart is right so far as some properties are concerned. It is correct to say, as he does, that a momentary event like an arrival – unlike a journey – cannot become more pleasant or more tedious. But there are other properties with respect to which even an instantaneous event like an arrival could undergo changes. For example, the same arrival may be remembered as a pleasant occurrence a week later and an unpleasant one a month later. Thus any momentary event may at a time t_1 possess the property of 'being remembered as a pleasant event' and lose this property by time t_2. There is no reason therefore why it should not also have the property of being in the future at t_1 and lose this property at t_2.

However, Smart's argument may go deeper than this. It is not necessary to assume that he forgot that momentary events may undergo changes with respect to properties that can easily be exhibited as relational properties, for example, that the same event may be related to t_1 in being remembered as pleasant at that time, while it is differently related to t_2. This however is not much help to an adherent of the transient view. Are we to interpret his insistence that a momentary event E may change as amounting to no more than a claim that the same E may be in the future at t_1 while it may also be in the past at t_2? Surely not, since

E is in the future at t_1 . . . . (a_1)

as well as

E is in the past at t_2 . . . . (b_1)

are B-statements, that is, statements with unchanging truth values. To see the failure of such an argument we may point out that (a_1) is equivalent to

E is after t_1 . . . (a_2)

while (b_1) is equivalent to

E is before t_2 . . . (b_2)

and the fact that both (a_2) and (b_2) may be true does not in any way indicate that E may undergo changes. The same particular may have a specific *dyadic* property with respect to another particular [i.e. a property that is essentially a relationship between two particulars], and at the same time lack it with respect to a third particular. Thus, for McTaggart to be able to maintain that moments and instantaneous events may undergo genuine changes with respect to their temporal properties, he would have to be referring to monadic properties and show that a statement like 'E is in the future', which assigns a non-relational property to E, may turn from true to false unlike 'E is bright yellow', where E denotes an instantaneous flash, which is either true and thus cannot turn false, or is false and thus cannot become true.

If this is indeed what Smart intended to say, then it should be pointed out that this objection has been anticipated by McTaggart's famous argument which leads to his conclusion that the transient view ultimately harbours a contradiction. In order to remove this objection it is necessary to argue that the monadic predicates 'future', 'present' and 'past' are unique in the way in which instantaneous events may change with respect to them. This argument will also account for the fact that there exist A-statements which assign monadic temporal properties to particulars and are unique in that they are the only kind of statements which may undergo changes in truth-value. In the last section of this chapter I propose to discuss this argument.

3 Professor Smart has recently put forward a brand-new argument designed to have the most devastating effect. According to this no subtle analysis is needed to see that any talk about time's flow is complete nonsense, for we cannot engage in such talk without obviously contradicting ourselves. He says:

The notion of pure becoming is connected with that of events receding into the past and of events in the future coming back from the future to meet us. This notion seems to me unintelligible. What is the 'us' or 'me'? It is not the whole person from birth to death, the total space – time entity. Nor is it any particular temporal stage of the person. A temporal stage for which an event E is future is a different temporal stage from one for which event E is present or past.[5]

Smart is of course right that if we say that a person was born at t_1 and died at t_2 we cannot say, without contradicting ourselves, that there is some point of time earlier than t_1 or later than t_2 which he also occupies. Such a person is confined permanently and unchangingly to the interval $t_1 - t_2$. Smart is also correct in claiming that we cannot assign temporal motion to any given temporal part of a person without contradicting ourselves, since any temporal part of a person which is at t is at t and never anywhere else.

Yet this objection is based on a complete misunderstanding of McTaggart's view. Surely when I say that a given event E is approaching us, the 'us' is meant to refer not to a particular temporal stage of ourselves but to that constantly varying temporal part which momentarily coincides with the NOW. A person who stretches from t_1 (the time of his birth) to t_2 (the time of his death) will have the NOW moving across the whole interval $t_1 - t_2$. When the NOW is at some point t, between the extremities t_1 and t_2, then that person's temporal part at t constitutes a momentarily privileged part that is directly experienced in contrast to all other parts which are either remembered or anticipated. Thus when I say 'event E is approaching us' this is to be construed as saying that our variable temporal part at which the NOW momentarily resides keeps moving closer and closer to E.

The rate of flow of time

Probably the most famous argument against the idea of temporal becoming, an argument that has been advanced by several philosophers, consists in the claim that if there really was a relative movement between the NOW and the series of moments, it would have to make sense to ask how fast this movement took place. A moment's reflection, however, reveals that it is not because we lack this or that information that we are prevented from providing an answer to this question, but that it is in principle impossible to measure the speed of this 'movement'. Consequently, it is clear that it does not exist. It may also be pointed out that a movement always essentially involves two series, so that points in one may be correlated with points in the other. For example, when a car is moving along the road, its motion is embodied in the fact that one position of the car in the series of spatial points corresponds to a given point in the series of temporal moments while a second position of the car in the same series of spatial points corresponds to another point in the series of temporal positions. But what other series is there in which two different points correspond to any two positions the NOW occupies along the time series? It has been claimed that only by postulating a hyper-time, with reference to which our advance through our time could be defined, would the definition make sense.

The eminent philosopher C. D. Broad, who has devoted himself perhaps more than anyone else during this century to the problem of temporal becoming, was among the first to introduce the possibility of saving the notion of time's flow by introducing a second order time series. But then, he says that in order to assign motion to the second order time we need yet a higher order time. And so he claims: 'It is easy to see that the argument is quite general, and there is no stage at which one could consistently stop in postulating further time-dimensions and events of a higher order.'[6] It is to be noted that Broad says nothing to show that the regress is a vicious regress. That is, he does not attempt to show that the given logical inconsistency cannot be removed because as soon as it is removed it arises again. But of course Broad was not obliged to show this, since even without it the regress is highly objectionable from the point of view of ontological wastage: it is absurd that in order to save a particular view concerning the nature of time in our world we should have to postulate an infinite number of higher orders of time.

I hope to provide an adequate rebuttal to this objection in the last section of this chapter. I should like to make a few other points now. P. J. Zwart, in discussing the flow of time, says:

It is by no means a forgone conclusion that the concept of 'the rate of flow of time' is meaningless. However what is certain is that its meaning (if it has one) will differ widely from the ordinary meaning of 'the rate of flow' when this term is applied to a gas or a liquid.[7]

A few pages later he writes 'To be more specific: one suggestion is that the rate of the flow of time is the ratio of the total number of events in the whole universe in unit time.'[8] In support of Zwart it may be pointed out that indeed the flow of gas need not be taken as the sole paradigm on which we need to model every other case we wish to describe as representing a flow. A given process may advance at a certain speed even though it does not involve the covering of a specific amount of something per unit time. Tom may be playing poker in one group and Dick in another and it may be possible to assert truly that Tom is losing money at a faster rate than Dick and mean by it not that Tom is losing more money per minute than Dick, which may be false, but that Tom is losing more money per game than Dick. Thus a broad term like 'flow' may cover a variety of processes which include water flowing under the bridge as well as money flowing from the pocket of Tom per game.

Nevertheless, Zwart's suggestion seems quite unsatisfactory. We would certainly not find it meaningful if someone referred to the speed of a moving car as being 1000 metres per kilometre. Nor would it be much better if, when the car travelled along a tree-lined road, someone asserted that its speed was 200 trees per kilometre. Two hundred trees per kilometre signifies the average distance between every two trees or the density of trees along the road. Similarly to say that time flows at the rate of one minute per minute does not seem to convey any information about the speed of time. It is not much better when we talk about the number of events per unit time, which could denote nothing else but the density of events along the series of moments.

I shall conclude this series of Russellian objections with a simple objection I have not seen raised elsewhere. On page 106 above, attempting to reply to Smart's objection to the transient view of time, I wrote 'When the NOW is at some point t . . . then that person's temporal part at t constitutes a momentarily privileged part that is directly experienced . . . .' This sentence would I believe be used by a philosopher defending the transient view to express a central feature of that position. It could, however, be objected that this sentence is ill-formed and that there does not seem to be available any meaningful sentence to which it could be reduced and still represent adequately the idea the philosopher is trying to convey. The difficulty lies with the term 'when'. Referring to a moving car one can say 'when the car is at p_1 . . .', which is a brief way of saying 'at the time when the car is at p_1 . . .', but it makes no sense to say 'at the time when the NOW is at t_1'. To put it differently, somebody could ask me 'Please find out the time when the car is at p_1' and I would of course understand what he wanted me to do; but I should be very puzzled if I were asked 'Please find out the time when the NOW is at t_1.'

I hope to offer a satisfactory reply to this objection too in the final section of the chapter.

Objections to Russell

I should like to show that adherents of the transient view of time need not remain for ever on the defensive as we have seem them in the last two sections; they might launch a counter-offensive against the Russellians. The strategy underlying the first such attack I shall describe will be to show that Russellians exhibit behaviour which distinctly presupposes movement through time. For clarity's sake, let me point out that Russellians readily admit that there are strong psychological reasons for thinking of time as moving inexorably into the past. They do not claim to be exempt from the psychological constraints that determine the way all people tend to think of time. What they do claim, however, is that in view of the results of their dispassionate conceptual analysis they have become firmly convinced that the way we feel about time is not imposed upon us by external reality; time does not actually flow. Now suppose I am under the impression that I am trapped in an air raid and have no shelter. It would be quite understandable if I were to shake with fear. After some investigation I declare that I was mistaken; the explosions I heard came from a nearby mine in which workers are trying to widen an underground passage. If in spite of this I go on trembling with terror, people would be entitled to conclude that I myself do not believe in the conclusion I claimed to have arrived at – that there is no bombardment going on. I shall attempt to describe one argument showing that Russellians may be said to be in a similar situation.

Let us imagine that Solzhenitsyn's character Ivan Denisovich is reliably informed a week after his arrival in the Gulag that he will be set free in 15 years' time. Naturally he is profoundly distressed at the thought that he has to endure 15 years of inhuman hardship before regaining his freedom. We would all sympathize with him and certainly admit that he has genuine reason to be unhappy. But suppose someone raises the following question: is it not true that he is so distant from freedom in one temporal direction only and that in the opposite direction freedom is no farther than a week away? The obvious answer is that admittedly Ivan's period of captivity has two ends, beyond each of which there is freedom; however, the end that is back in the past is of no help to him since he is not *moving* in that direction. The fact that the end in the past is so near provides no comfort since he is moving away from that end towards the other end, which he will reach only after enduring many years of suffering. One end marks the point of *entrance* into a state of servitude; the other represents the point of exit. Naturally, what determines his mood is the distance between him and the exit through which he will eventually pass, *leaving* behind the sorrowful times he is now enduring.

I have little doubt that everyone will grant that my interpretation is a correct one and therefore that Ivan Denisovich has good reason to be concerned, and will have our sympathy. Only someone wanting to make a cruel joke would tell him that he should not be depressed since there is an end to his incarceration that is no more than a week away.

But an opponent of Russell may well say: every part of our explanation was formulated in a language that presupposes a moving NOW, in which the past is receding and the future is approaching. According to Russell, there is absolutely no movement across the series of moments; the future is no more coming closer to us than is the past; the time of Ivan's arrest is merely a dividing point to one side of which lies a period of freedom, and to the other a period of imprisonment, but it is definitely not a point at which he enters an unpleasant period any more than it is a point at which he leaves it, since he is not crossing that point; there is no movement across any point in time. Russellians, although they too have the natural impulse to assign motion to time, claim to have become convinced that there is no such motion. Surely then they ought to realize that there is absolutely no reason for despair. Yet all the evidence shows that the behaviour or attitude of Russellians does not differ one iota from that of non-Russellians under circumstances similar to those just discussed. Does this not clearly show that they themselves do not believe in the result of their analysis?

I have heard some Russellians replying that there may be an objective basis for our dissimilar treatment of time and space which would explain why our attitude towards events situated in one direction in time is different from our attitude towards those situated in the opposite direction, while we do not distinguish between events that are placed to our right or to our left. The objective basis is provided by the fact that time does, while space does not, have a direction. But I cannot see the relevance of this. After all, it could well turn out that space too has a direction, that for example the density of a certain type of elementary particle increases in a given direction. This does not seem to have any bearing on the way we view events situated in different parts of space.

A better reply for Russellians might be to say that it is perfectly true they would be just as depressed as Ivan Denisovich if they found themselves in his situation. They would admit that this is simply a psychological fact which they are incapable of showing to be 'reasonable'. However, they may also argue that it is no more than an illusion to think that opponents of Russell can more successfully explain Ivan's attitude. What is so illuminating, they may ask, about being told that a certain unpleasant period of time is contemplated with apprehension because it has yet to be endured or because one is approaching it and has to pass through it? This so-called explanation amounts to no more than saying that one is unhappy at t because the period of suffering is later than t. Just as Russellians have to accept it as a fact about human nature which they are incapable of explaining any further that a person worries at t about suffering that is later than t, and not about suffering that is earlier than t, so their opponents too are incapable of really explaining why a period one has to go through should be of greater concern than a period already over.

I leave it to the reader to decide whether Russell and McTaggart are exactly in the same position with regard to explaining or failing to explain all our attitudes toward events of the future and the past, and shall consider another objection that might be raised against Russell's position. Suppose a person P says on January 1 1982, which is his 50th birthday, 'How I wish I was ten years younger' and explicitly denies that what he means is that he wishes he had been born ten years later so that in 1982 he would be only 40 years old. No, he does not wish to change the date of his birth and is fully satisfied in being 50 years old in 1982. What he would like is that the NOW should shift back to 1972. P is also aware that one well-known Russellian translation of the statement 'Now it is New Year 1972' is 'New Year 1972 is simultaneous with this utterance', but he would emphatically reject the suggestion that all that he is wishing is that some utterance be simultaneous with New Year 1972. What S is concerned with is his ageing self; he would very much like to be ten years younger. In McTaggart's view P's wish makes full sense and the fact that it has no chance of being fulfilled does not diminish it. In Russell's view, however, it makes no sense at all. This seems to create a difficulty for him, especially when it is pointed out that we are not dealing with some fancy too ludicrous to be given a second thought. This kind of wish is expressed by millions of people every day and, I would suspect, by Russellians no less than by others.

A defender of Russell's position might perhaps want to say that regardless of how frequently people have made such wishes, when it comes to human desires it sometimes happen that one is yearning earnestly without really knowing what one is yearning for, since the object of one's desire cannot be described coherently. The wish to be someone other than oneself, for example, is also quite a common wish. For instance, I may most intensely wish to be Prince Charles, yet many philosophers will tell me that not only is it certain that my wish will not be fulfilled, but that it does not even make any sense. I must be conceptually confused to entertain such a wish. It makes no sense for anyone but Prince Charles to be Prince Charles. The intensity or frequency of a wish is no guarantee that it is coherent. Similarly the wish to roll back time to 1972 is incoherent.

It might, however, be objected that the two cases are not similar. If I can find no logical fault with the view of personal identity that rules out the logical possibility of my becoming someone else, I would certainly not be able to protest that I definitely know from experience that I could be Prince Charles. But it seems that I am right in claiming that I do know for sure that I am capable of being 40 years old, since I have had that experience. How could it be incoherent to ask for a state of affairs which I have actually experienced, and which I am now merely asking to experience again?

However, Russellians will resolutely reject this argument. P's experience of being 40 years old occurred in 1972. It is definitely not the case that P experienced in 1982 – the year when he is making the wish – the occurrence of 1972. Nor could P claim ever to have experienced the NOW as being in 1972, since the NOW does not exist at all.

However, what P can do is to reformulate his wish in a manner that everyone will be compelled to admit is clearly coherent. Suppose that the state of the universe on January 1 1972 is fully described by $p_1, p_2,$ $\ldots p_n$. P may explain that what he wishes is that in the next instant the state of the universe should be such that it is fully described by $p_1,$ $p_2, \ldots p_n$. The day following this he would like the state of the universe to be fully described by a set of propositions $q_1, q_2, \ldots q_n$ which is a set of propositions fully describing the state of the universe that prevailed on January 2 1972. It is no longer possible to dismiss P's talk as meaningless.

I believe that Russellians would indeed be compelled to agree that P's wish as just set out is completely intelligible and consequently is in principle capable of fulfilment. However, they would interpret the situation differently if P's wish were indeed fulfilled. Russellians would say that what happened was not that the NOW leaped back from the beginning of 1982 to the beginning of 1972. Instead they would claim that December 31 1981 is followed by a day in which the state of the universe is an exact duplicate of the state it was in ten years ago and consequently, although none of its inhabitants would know this, it is actually January 1 1982 today. The calendar, of course, would say that it is January 1 1972 today and everyone would clearly 'remember' that yesterday was December 31 1971 and so on; nevertheless, in actual fact, Russellians would say 'It is the beginning of 1982 today.'

Not wishing to spend more time over this issue, I shall conclude by indicating that it would not be unreasonable to claim that Russell's account of what would happen if P's wish came true is inferior to McTaggart's account. Consider just one point: according to Russell, at the moment the universe abruptly assumes a state characterized by $(p_1,$ $p_2, \ldots p_n)$ infinitely many events occur which were not supposed to happen in the natural sequence of occurrences and none of which can be accounted for. According to McTaggart, however, there is only one event which would require explanation: the sudden shift of the NOW from 1982 to 1972.

How much can science and philosophy change our views?

I would like to touch upon an issue whose proper treatment would require a much more extensive study but which I feel we cannot completely ignore. Russellians admit that they too have the strong impression that time moves. For example, Smart says 'Certainly we feel that time flows, but I want to say. . . that this feeling arises out of a metaphysical confusion.'[9] It might also be added that this feeling is not some insignificant part of our experience but rather a central one which is with us all the time. Our thoughts are constantly occupied with what the future is going to bring us, opportunities that are passing us by and time going by too fast. Can such a crucial feature of experience be dismissed? Is it not an important rule that our account of the universe should be based as much as possible on experience? Admittedly, as pointed out in the first section of the chapter, our feeling that time flows is not quite as indestructible as our experience of spatial motion, and yet it is an ever present and important feature of our existence.

Russellians may reply that there are many examples where common sense impressions have to yield to whatever experts in a given field tell us to be really the case. They may remind me that my impression of the desk I am writing on is that it is a continuous solid body at complete rest. Physicists will tell me, however, that it is actually a swarming collection of particles rapidly moving in all directions with large gaps separating them, so that the solid body I am talking about contains a much higher volume of empty space than matter. If I am a sensible person then I shall admit that the physicist, whose description of the desk is different from my own but who is an acknowledged expert on the properties of matter, must be right. Thus a common-sense interpretation of experience has to give way to the account of those who are authorities on a given subject.

After some reflection it becomes evident that nothing can be inferred from this example that is relevant to the problem of time. It was not correct to describe the case of the desk as one in which common sense and professional opinion clash. It is very much part of common sense to realize that in order to determine the ultimate structure of solid bodies we need the technically advanced methods of modern science. When physicists tell me about elementary particles that are obviously inaccessible to any of my senses I do not feel that his results clash with my own impressions at all. Provided it is explained to me clearly, I am bound to realize that he is not claiming that reality is hugely different from appearances. After all, he is referring to happenings in a domain of magnitude that is far beyond the limits of appearances, a domain of which I will acknowledge that I have formed no impressions.

No such thing has happened in the context of our feeling that time moves. Philosophers who have denied the movement of time have not shown us that our impressions are due merely to our unthinkingly extrapolating from our experiences in a domain to which we have access into a domain beyond our reach. They have not shown that their thesis and what distinctly appears to us to be directly experienced do not really clash. The denial of temporal becoming continues to strike us as a total rejection of what we feel to be a central feature of our temporal existence.

One more example might be suggested from among the claims of philosophy. I have from early childhood always taken it to be an indubitable fact that all people around me have a mind just as I do. Not until adulthood did I become acquainted with the philosophical problem of other minds and discover that many philosophers hold the view that what I took to be my observations of other people's inner experiences were nothing of the kind. I was told that the mental events of other people are in principle completely beyond the reach of my observations. Only their physical behaviour can be observed. And physical behaviour is logically irrelevant to the question of what goes on in the minds of other people, or indeed whether anything goes on there at all.

Now this philosophical contention is quite different from the news that solid objects are really discontinuous. The general public has calmly accepted the latter. However, most people refuse to accept the claim that there is room to be sceptical about the mindedness of others, which they take to be one of the primary data of their experience. Quite frequently they declare that the arguments philosophers offer in order to convince them of the possibility of solipsism amount to clever sophistry, which, due to their lack of training, they are unable to refute. Nevertheless, those who take philosophy seriously and approach the matter dispassionately learn to appreciate that from a logical point of view their conviction of the mindedness of others may not have been firmly grounded. Thus a Russellian might suggest that here we have an indication that it is sensible to give up beliefs, no matter how fond we may be of them or how firmly we regard them as being rooted in experience, and try to adjust mentally to the results of dispassionate logical analysis.

It is not hard to see, however, that this is not an appropriate example either. The great initial resistance we all have to solipsism is not due to the overwhelming evidence we feel we have for the mindedness of others. It is rather due to the fact that solipsism implies a vast change in our attitude; it would rob us of most that gives meaning to our lives; it would destroy the basis of all the many sentiments we have towards our fellows. Nevertheless, once I assume a disinterested stance, and it is explained to me that what I thought I had observed I have not really observed, and that I merely extrapolated unthinkingly from the behaviour of others (my account of which I am not required to renounce) to their inner experiences, then I am bound to admit that I have no access to these experiences. Thus as soon as I give myself a chance to understand the philosophical problem of other minds, I realize that the position of the sceptic is not based on a denial of what I think I know on the basis of direct observation.

There is no need to look at any further examples, for by now it should be clear how each side of the debate will simply disarm any seemingly hostile example. There are indefinitely many instances of a scientific or philosophical account of something replacing the common-sense account. The explanation in these cases is always that the experts have demonstrated that we have placed an unwarrantable interpretation on our experience. It may be said, however, that they never demand that we should change our account of our experiences themselves, which are in no way an extrapolation. In the case of the temporal debate the very issue between the disputants is: which of the two situations are we facing? According to McTaggart, Russell is simply asking us to fly in the face of our experiences, describing the basic nature of time differently from what it distinctly seems to us to be. No examples are available to show that this could ever be a legitimate demand. According to Russell, however, the moving NOW is not something we directly experience. It is merely our interpretation of our experience, an interpretation we are justifiably asked to renounce after logical analysis has shown it to be untenable. The decisive question, to be investigated, therefore, is: does logical analysis indeed show that the notion of time's flow is incoherent?

A *thought experiment*

In this section I would like us to consider briefly an imaginary situation. Let us suppose that our knowledge of physics and astronomy is considerably greater than it actually is, and that on the basis of our observations of the radiation received from the sun and so on, we have established that our solar system is *n* years old. Let us assume that this year we discover the existence of another solar system, X, many billions of light years away, where the same initial conditions prevail as in our system and which is subject to the same laws of nature. We cannot interact with X except for communicating with it via some strange medium which transmits signals instantaneously. We are told by the people of X that the age of their solar system, which they have carefully established by using the kind of methods we ourselves have been using, is at the moment *n* − 300 years. They give us a full report of the state of their planet and the state of their whole solar system, and we find that their description fits the states of our own planet and the rest of our solar system in the year 1681. The most remarkable feature of X turns out to be that its time seems to be passing twice as quickly as ours and thus next year, when we celebrate the beginning of 1982, they will have already reached 1683, and when we are commemorating the tenth anniversary of our first verbal contact with X they are celebrating the 20th anniversary of the same event.

What many of us will want to say under these circumstances seems to be that our solar system and X resemble each other with respect to their geological, oceanographical, planetary and other features but there is one major difference: the two solar systems did not come into existence at the same time, but when X was born our solar system was already of considerable age and that time flows twice as fast in it as in our solar system. This explanation would also fully account for the following: m years after 2281 (the year when X 'overtakes' us), which according to the inhabitants of X is already $2m$ years after our 'temporal meeting', the X people give us a detailed description of the values of several physical parameters that are functionally related to the age of their solar system, and these are very similar to the ones we obtain when we repeat the measurements $2m$ years after 2281.

Russellians will be able to give an account of the physical situation in their own language. However, the point of our story is to help us see how the remaining difficulties with the transient view of time may be resolved.

1 As we have said, several authors have claimed that one of the major difficulties with the transient view is that it can be made sense of only if we postulate the existence of infinitely many hierarchies of time systems. I believe we can now clearly see that this is false. The only other time system that we would need is a system like X's (and it seems wrong to characterize this as hyper-time). The time system that prevailed in X could also be attributed motion without having to speak about a third system. Our own NOW is perfectly adequate for that purpose.

But not only would it make full sense to speak of time as moving, we could also assign a definite value to the speed with which it is moving. We could take the speed of time in X as the unit of temporal speed, in which case our time would be moving at the rate of ½. This would have a parallel in the practice of physicists, who when dealing with rockets and fast aeroplanes designate the speed of sound as the unit of speed and call it Mach, and may then find that a given plane travels at the speed of ½ Mach.

2 It was also claimed that temporal becoming is beyond the reach of the instruments and theories of the physical scientist. Some philosophers went so far as to state that this must be interpreted as a sign

that temporal becoming is not an actual feature of reality. Something that is for ever inaccessible to the physicist cannot be a genuine fact. In the situation we have considered, however, the movement of time would lend itself to the investigations of the empirical scientist. Since that situation is clearly not logically impossible it is false that time's flow, or even the magnitude of the rate of its flow, is in principle inaccessible to scientific study.

3 Our example also seems to indicate what we have suspected right from the beginning – that the speed of time's flow is not a function of the number of events per unit time. In the particular example we have considered, for instance, it is quite clear that the relative speed of time's motion in the two solar systems does not depend on the rate at which events occurred in either. The two systems in question were said to be very similar; consequently the number of events in each system during a given time interval in that system are more or less equal; and yet the speed of the NOW in X is twice as great as in our system.

4 The expression 'when the NOW is at t_1' would of course make sense under the circumstances described. If t_1 denotes a given point in time in our solar system which corresponds to t_1^* in X then obviously we could assert meaningfully 'at t_1^* when the NOW is at t_1 . . .'.

5 One might still wonder, however, whether it is possible to talk about time's flow under existing circumstances when the situation we have described does not in fact obtain. Admittedly the mere possibility of such a situation is enough to demonstrate that the talk about time's motion is not incoherent. But surely, in order to be able to claim more, namely that time is actually moving, mere possibility is not enough.

Followers of McTaggart may argue that we claim that time flows on the basis of unmediated experience; we apprehend directly how we are relentlessly moving into the future. However, we may be questioned as to whether we can regard our experience as authentically reflecting reality, since no notion which must be judged nonsensical is capable of representing a genuine object in reality. To reply to this, we refer to a possible situation as described in this section to show that the concept of 'movement', when applied to time itself, makes straightforward sense.

The notion of spatial flow

The point of the last section would be blunted if it turned out that a parallel story could be concocted to lend sense to the notion of a space flow that corresponded to the notion of time flow. As we know, temporal statements or sets of temporal statements have their spatial counterparts. The latter are obtained simply by substituting all the temporal terms in the former with spatial terms, and vice versa. If the spatial counterpart of the story we have employed to explicate the notion of time flow should be unable to contribute at all to the illumination of the parallel notion of a space flow, then the point made in the last section becomes sharper. After all, we feel very differently about the idea of passage of space and of time: time appears to us to be moving relentlessly, but we have no experiences implying anything similar in the case of space. The fact that the story which gave meaning to the concept of the motion of the NOW fails, when transformed into its spatial counterpart, to do anything similar for space, should provide objective grounds for the basically different ways we think of these two manifolds.

The quickest way to see that this is so is by the use of space–time diagrams. Figure 1 represents the story told in the previous section.

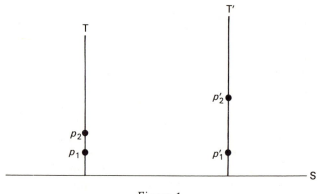

Figure 1

The essential feature of that story was that point p_1 in time system T was found to correspond to point p_1' in system T$'$ while p_2 in T corresponded to p_2' in T$'$. The temporal distance $p_1 - p_2$ was half of the distance $p_1' - p_2'$. The spatial counterpart of this situation is represented in figure 2.

It seems quite irrelevant how we fill in the details of the story, that is, it makes no difference what is taken to be travelling from q_1 to q_2 and from q_1' to q_2', and so it is not important to know the nature of the link which connects q_1 to q_1' and q_2 to q_2'. Nothing emerges here that is parallel to what resulted from figure 1. It is sufficient to note one of the decisive factors responsible for this difference. In the context of the first story it makes sense to say 'the NOW is at p_1 at p_1'', that is, it makes sense to claim that a given event which occurs at p_1 in system T occurs when in system T′ 'the time is p_1''. But we can make nothing of the phrase 'something is at q_1 at q_1'', that is, a given event takes place at point q_1 in system S where in system S′ the place is q_1'. Thus at the root of the fact that there is nothing similar in space to temporal becoming is that it makes sense to ask 'What time is it in T′ when it is t in T?' but not at all to ask 'What place is it in S′ where it is s in S?'

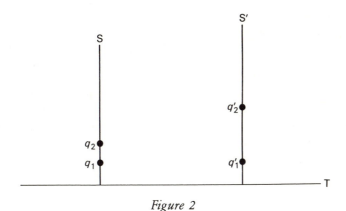

Figure 2

Finally it will be instructive to mention an important point made by Professor Smart in correspondence. I have claimed earlier that P's wish to be ten years younger makes straightforward sense and could simply be fulfilled according to the dynamic view by the NOW returning to January 1 1972. Professor Smart has raised the question how if at all could P's world-line be represented on a space–time diagram.

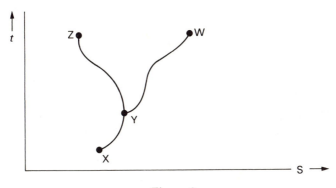

Figure 3

In figure 3, if we claim that YZ and YW stand for P's world-line, that would not give us an adequate representation. For one thing, there is no clue in the diagram as to which of the two lines represents P's progression from 1971 to 1981 the first time and which the second time. But worse still, for ten years there were two distinct P's side by side, which is contrary to our assumptions.

The answer, of course, is that a space–time diagram with a single time coordinate representing a single time system is incapable of portraying our story. This, however, is as it should be; for it is built into our story that within that framework there exists no observable difference between the case in which P's wish is not fulfilled and he lives from 1971 to 1981 once only, and the case in which his wish is fulfilled and he lives through the same period twice. But it is obvious that if we were looking at the matter from another time system, one which could be employed to explicate the motion of the NOW in T, the difference becomes evident. One way of doing this is with the aid of a TT' diagram (figure 4). When P's wish is fulfilled he covers the period 1971–81 twice, as seen in the diagram.

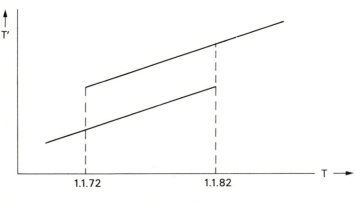

Figure 4

It is essential to realize that according to the dynamic view of time there are two distinct senses in which P may, in 1982, be wishing that it were 1972. First, he may be asking that it be 1972 *once again*. His request implies that the NOW having reached 1982 should return to 1972. The resulting situation is represented by figure 4. However, it is also possible to ask that the last ten years should not yet have taken place at all, and that 'we' should *still* be at the year 1972. According to the static view, of course, the second wish makes no sense either. According to the dynamic view, the situation wished for is easily described and a TT′ diagram is not required to represent it. It can be depicted on an ordinary space–time diagram with a single time co-ordinate on which everyone's world-lines, instead of stretching as far as 1982, have 1972 as their furthest point.

Further support for the transient view

Let me conclude with an example of the actual use that can be made in philosophical analysis of the notion of the NOW's return to a point in the past. As is known, the concept of universal determinism plays an important role in the philosophy of science, especially with respect to a question like that of human freedom. There have been various attempts to define it. An interesting suggestion has been advanced by Peter Van Inwagen, who departs from the usual practice of providing a definition in terms of 'predictability in principle'. He says 'Determinism is the thesis that if time could be "rolled back" to any past instant, and then allowed to "go forward again" then history would "repeat" itself.'[10] The point of citing this example is as follows. When a philosopher is committed to a view that implies that certain talk is inadmissible because it makes some unwarranted presuppositions, he will often declare that talk to be devoid of meaning. It is not an easy task for an opponent to demonstrate that what has thus been dismissed is in fact meaningful. Sometimes, however, it is possible at least to show that the charge of meaninglessness is implausible. In the present case, Professor Smart would have us regard talk of time being rolled back to the past as bereft of meaning, since he denies the existence of certain temporal features presupposed by such a discussion. Yet everyone can easily understand the definition of determinism just given. There is reason therefore to hesitate before denouncing as meaningless a definition that seems to make full sense and succeeds in elucidating a highly significant philosophical concept. Adherents of the dynamic view are in the advantageous position of not having to deny the meaningfulness of such a useful definition and of other statements that convey information.

5

The method of counter-examples, possible worlds and the mystery of existence

Counter-examples: some drawbacks

In this chapter, I should like to look at a far-reaching or, as some would say, even a startling metaphysical claim that some philosophers have espoused, namely, that all the infinitely many logically possible worlds exist and are no less real than our own world. At the same time, I would also like to discuss a widely employed philosophical technique, the technique of counter-examples. This particular technique may well be said to stand more in need of elucidation than any other. Let me indicate why.

If a philosopher was asked to name some of the major argument forms characteristically employed by the practitioners of his discipline, he is likely to mention Occam's razor or the transcendental argument, but not the method of counter-examples. This in spite of the fact that the latter has been employed by more philosophers on more occasions than probably any other. I do not think there is any great mystery about why it is overlooked. It has simply not occurred to many people that the technique of counter-examples presents any problems requiring close study. Most philosophers agree, for example, that the transcendental argument constitutes a profound issue. It is by no means easy to state, and in fact there are quite different versions of the argument none of which seems to have full logical force. There is a need to discover the precise structure of the argument and why it may be binding upon us.

But surely the method of counter-examples amounts to little more than producing an example e of which $\sim Fe$ is evidently true and thus providing conclusive proof that the generalization $(x)(Fx)$ must be false? This is a fully effective, unproblematic and therefore safe method, hardly requiring a second thought.

It is only after we have studied a large sample of examples of this method's application that its faults become apparent. It is rarely the case that we encounter an obvious fallacious step in the reasoning associated with the method. The drawbacks are more subtle and, perhaps as a result, capable of having wider and more lasting effects. Thus I would like the reader to take into account the following justification for my somewhat over-long treatment of this subject: the method has had wider use than any other; it has hardly been discussed elsewhere; and its misuse has had a considerable impact on recent philosophizing.

The method could be described as an essentially destructive tool, used in general to demonstrate a flaw in a thesis. Briefly, when a philosopher advances a given thesis T, then to someone who wishes to oppose it the most readily accessible weapon is to construct an example whose non-availability is claimed to be implied by T, and hence whose existence may be said to provide evidence for the inadequacy of T.

There are then three possible responses for those who wish to defend T:

1 Admit that T is untenable and withdraw it.
2 Reformulate T or add some qualifications to it so that in its revised form it escapes the force of the counter-example.
3 Show that the counter-example has actually missed its target, for on a proper understanding it is compatible with T.

What I shall attempt to demonstrate is that the widespread and indiscriminate use of the method of counter-examples has not always produced happy results. To appreciate the various ways in which we can go astray with this method we shall look at the different circumstances in which it has been employed.

The first is where the counter-example is used merely to confirm or illustrate a point we wish to make. In these cases we know what is wrong with T and are capable of articulating our objection to it without the aid of a counter-example, which serves as no more than a means of confirming and demonstrating in a concrete fashion the point we are trying to put across. Under these circumstances there is hardly anything that could go wrong with the use of counter-examples.

In the second case we do not know what is wrong with T; however, the fact that we are able to produce a counter-example shows that something must be wrong with it. In this case we could not articulate the nature of the fault T is supposed to have independently of the counter-example; indeed our objection amounts to no more than pointing out the existence of the counter-example. This case may arise in one of two ways:
1 Sometimes T is such that there is no room for manoeuvre; that is,

either T as it stands is correct or it has to be abandoned altogether, with no scope for revisions and qualifications. In cases like this, if we are unable to fault the counter-example then we have sufficient evidence that T is erroneous and has to be withdrawn. There does not seem to be much room for error here.

2 There are cases where T permits various alternative formulations in which different qualifications are added to it while part of the original content is preserved. These are the cases we need to look into, for it is here that it is possible to go astray in a variety of ways. I shall mention three:

(a) Since neither the opponent nor the defender of T has any idea what is wrong with it except that it clashes with a given example, which is clearly the symptom and not the root of T's malady, it is most natural for those who want to save T to introduce a qualification especially designed to protect it from this particular example. There is no guarantee at all that this kind of revision will bring us nearer to a genuinely sound formulation of T. The situation may be compared to one in which I notice blue smoke issuing from an opening in the back of my television set and I seal the hole so that no smoke can escape. Not only have I failed to repair the set but I have most probably made the situation worse.

But the problem is more complicated than this. The production of a counter-example, followed by the revision of T, is usually only the first step in an extended process with which the reader is surely familiar: a second counter-example is produced, and this is followed by further revisions, and so on. In the course of this process, it is quite often the case, and understandably so, that each revision produces a reformulated thesis that is one step further away from the correct thesis than was the previous thesis. It also follows quite naturally that at each successive stage it becomes more and more difficult to recognize the sound formulation of the thesis we were originally seeking, since we are getting farther and farther away from it. In addition, it is quite natural for a philosopher to seek the ultimate answer to the question of how to formulate his thesis in more or less this very direction. No one likes to admit that a complicated chain of arguments which has been generated by the process of counter-example followed by reformulation and has brought us to our present position, may be devoid of all validity, and that not a single step of the many we have taken so far is of any use because the actual solution lies in a quite different direction.

The end result of this process is often that we settle for a formulation which we have arrived at after we seem to have run out of further counter-examples, and a formulation whose defects we have managed to paper over for a while. The version of T we end up with is considerably more encumbered than the one we started out with, as well as containing more inadequacies than the simpler original version.

(b) But the supply of counter-examples does not always dry up. When they continue to arise philosophers sometimes conclude that, in view of the much repeated failure of attempts to formulate an acceptable version of T, the whole enterprise was misconceived. Thus, instead of looking further for the solution, they conclude that no solution exists.

(c) There have been cases in which the idea behind T was unsound or devoid of interest, but the successive presentation of counter-examples followed by reformulations of T has given rise to a growing edifice which then itself becomes the focus of interest. A great deal of intellectual effort may be spent on debating various elements of this artificial edifice which does not serve any good purpose.

I shall illustrate these three points by three examples taken from contemporary writings. I would like first however to describe what everyone is likely to agree is the safest and most profitable way of employing counter-examples. We must endeavour *not* to use them merely as a means of highlighting some problem of whose nature, scope and causes we are ignorant. It is desirable rather to use them to subject T to close scrutiny and discover what exactly is wrong with it. For example, it may be possible that T, which has been designed to characterize a category C, states that anything which belongs to C must possess the feature F. After careful examination of the meaning of C we arrive at the conclusion that it is not F but rather F′ that is the crucial feature which anything belonging to C must have. We may even realize that it is because a particular entity that has F often also has F′ that those who advanced T have committed the error we ascribe to them. In order to convey the nature of the problem we have detected, and, even more importantly, to convince the reader of the correctness of our analysis, an effective move is to produce a concrete example of an individual *i* which is commonly acknowledged to belong to C and which clearly does not have F but rather F′. I shall conclude our survey of this widely practised philosophical technique with a few examples of the doubtlessly profitable use to which it may be put.

The nature of explanation

I shall begin by discussing 2 (a). The long debate around the notion of scientific explanation may serve as a singularly dramatic illustration of my point. In this case the process of suggesting counter-examples to an account of scientific explanation, followed by a revised account, lasted over 30 years and has resulted in over a hundred articles. The notion of explanation is, of course, not specifically a metaphysical notion, for the techniques of metaphysicians are employed in all areas of philosophy. It will however play a crucial role in our discussion of the possible way of establishing the existence of other minds.

Probably the most famous account of explanation is the one associated with C. G. Hempel. He said:

(T,C) constitutes a potential explanans [the sentences that do the explaining] for a singular sentence E only if

(1) T is essentially generalized and C is singular
(2) E is derivable . . . from T and C jointly, but not from C alone.

. . . (T,C) constitutes an explanans for . . . E if and only if

(1) (T,C) is a potential explanans for E
(2) T is a theory and C is true[1]

This amounts roughly to saying that E (the statement that a certain event has taken place) is explained when it is shown that the description of the relevant laws of nature and the initial conditions logically imply E. In other words, E is explained when it is shown that E has to be true, for the nature of the universe is such that it is inevitable that the event referred to by E should occur.

It would take too long to cite all the counter-examples that have been produced to this account, but I shall cite some of them. The result of these counter-examples has been to enlarge Hempel's simple criterion by adding several extra conditions to it. For example Ackerman and Stenner[2] suggest the adoption of a criterion with seven conditions, some quite elaborate. Each of these conditions seems to have been formulated in response to a particular kind of counter-example. It is no longer easy to evaluate how far their criterion embodies the notion of explanation, as it is so complex that it is difficult to see what it amounts to.

The important point, however, is that if we cease to worry about these counter-examples and instead just ask ourselves exactly what an explanation is for and what it is supposed to achieve, then it is not hard to see what aspect of explanation Hempel has failed to capture in his account. Once Hempel's account is supplemented in a way that acknowledges this aspect, all the different objections disappear.

Let us then first look at some of the counter-examples:

Counter-example 1. This objection is raised by Hempel himself. He asks us to suppose:

E = Mt Everest is snowcapped

T = All metals are good conductors of heat.

T_s = If the Eiffel Tower is metal, it is a good conductor of heat

where T, and therefore T_s, which is an instance of T, is true. Let

$$C = T_s \supset E$$

then since E is true so is C. But T and C logically imply E, while C alone does not; thus all the conditions for a good explanation are present. Yet we feel it is absurd that T, which has no bearing whatever on E, should form an essential part in the explanation of E.

To this difficulty Hempel proposes a solution. He suggests that a third condition be added to his other two:

(3) T is compatible with at least one class of basic sentences which has C but not E as a consequence.

Hempel does advance an argument to show that (3) is reasonable and most philosophers will have no quarrel with him. However, I shall show in the next section how in the view of principle P_1, a principle all sensible people are bound to find compelling, the difficulty does not arise in the first place so that there is no reason to postulate especially any third condition such as (3).

Counter-example 2. This too is raised by Hempel. Let

$$T_1 = (x)(Px \supset Qx), \quad C_1 = Pa \,\&\, Rab, \quad \text{and} \quad E_1 = Qa \,\&\, Rab.$$

Then if T_1 and C_1 are true, they fulfil the conditions which render them a legitimate explanans. We feel however that there is no full explanation here: while we have explained successfully why Qa, the fact that Rab is true seems to be explained by saying: because Rab is true.

This problem may seem easy to solve to some. All we have to do is postulate that C and E must not have a common consequent. This will rule out the explanans as illegitimate since C_1 and E_1 have the common consequent Rab.

It is easy to show, however, that this innocent-looking postulate is far too strong, since it leaves us without a single admissible explanation. For suppose it were suggested that T_2 and C_2 explain E_2. Then, no matter what these stand for, by the law of addition:

$$C_2 \rightarrow C_2 \vee E_2$$
$$E_2 \rightarrow C_2 \vee E_2$$

Thus of necessity C and E always have a common consequent.

Hempel concludes that it is evident that while some partial self-explanations are inadmissible, such as the would-be explanation of E_1 by T_1 and C_1, we cannot disallow all partial self-explanations, since then we could never explain anything. He admits he does not know how to distinguish between legitimate and illegitimate self-explanations.[3] This difficulty alone would be enough to render his whole account quite useless.

Counter-example 3. Eberle, Kaplan and Montague have claimed that on Hempel's criterion any theory yields an explanation to any explanandum whatever, implying that the criterion is useless. For let

$$T = (x)\, Fx$$
$$E = Ha$$

where F and H stand for anything you fancy as long as they render T and E true. Clearly

$$T' = (x)\,(y)\,(Fx \vee \sim Gy \vee Hy)$$

is implied by T and is therefore true. Clearly also

$$C = (\sim Fb\ \&\ Ga) \vee Ha$$

which is implied by E is true. But $T'\ \&\ C \rightarrow E$ and therefore T' and C explain E, which is absurd.

Solutions of different degrees of complexity have been suggested. We shall see that on the Principle P_1 an obvious solution follows at once.

Counter-example 4. Hempel has restricted his account to the explanation of singular sentences. He acknowledges that it would be of the utmost importance to provide a clear account of the way in which general regularities embodied in laws of nature are explained. It seems to him that a law of nature is explained if it is shown to follow logically from a more comprehensive law of nature. But he finds himself confronted with a difficulty to which he confesses he cannot offer a solution. He says:

The core of the difficulty can be indicated briefly by reference to an example: Kepler's laws, K, may be conjoined with Boyle's law, B, to a stronger law K & B; but derivation of K from the latter would not be considered as an explanation of the regularities stated in Kepler's laws; rather, it would be viewed as representing, in effect, a pointless 'explanation' of Kepler's laws by themselves. The derivation of Kepler's laws from Newton's laws of motion and of gravitation, on the other hand, would be recognized as a genuine explanation in terms of more comprehensive regularities, or so-called higher-level laws.[4]

Hempel is at a loss as to how to set up a general criterion whereby these two cases may properly be distinguished. As a result, he believes that he cannot account for the ways laws are being explained. This, of course, would amount to a crucial defect in his explication. After all, the explanation of events by subsuming them under generalizations is only the beginning of science. To explain why this raven is black by citing the generalization that all ravens are black is not to engage in sophisticated scientific work. The interest begins when we go deeper and manage to show what it is in the constitution of ravens that requires that they all be black. The really important matter is the explanation of instantiable generalizations, which, incidentally, also results in a more illuminating explanation of the observed instances of those generalizations.

Counter-example 5. An ingenious example has been constructed by J. Kim[5] and discussed by C. G. Morgan[6] to show that the received account of explanation is inadequate. Given that there are no mermaids,

$$T = (x)\,(Mx \supset Cx)$$

that is, 'All mermaids are good conductors of heat' must be true simply because its antecedent is false. Similarly

$$C = \sim Me \supset Ce$$

that is, 'If the Eiffel Tower is not a mermaid then it is a good conductor of heat' must also be true, since Ce is true. Now suppose we attempt to explain $E = Ce$; then T and C could legitimately be suggested as explanans, since T and C entail E where C alone does not. But surely the fact that the Eiffel Tower is not a mermaid cannot be relevant to the fact that the Eiffel Tower is a good conductor of heat.

Let us however ignore these counter-examples and pause for a moment to ask ourselves: what is the basic function of an explanation? What is it supposed to accomplish? Surely, when we are confronted with an explanandum E and want it to be explained, what we are seeking is information concerning facts that render it inevitable that E is true rather than that it is false. The relevant facts – whose description is the explanans – are such that anyone who was not informed that E is the case could on the basis of the facts anticipate that E, rather than its denial, is true. Suppose, however, that when the explanans T & C yields E, none the less, under different conditions in which everything remains the same except that E´, a contrary of E, is true, then automatically T´ & C´ becomes available, where T´ & C´ is true and its relation to E´ is parallel to that of T & C to E. It is obvious that the explanans T & C is inadmissible.

A part of the assertion that we can explain E is the claim that anyone knowing the prevailing circumstances is not at all surprised that E, and not E′, is true. An act of explanation essentially consists in pointing out the unique conditions that exist and that unequivocally require that E be true. These conditions are such that if we were told that, instead of E, E′ was true, we would regard this as inexplicable in the intolerably strong sense that we would be driven to disbelieve the report that E′ was true, since the description of the prevailing circumstances logically implied E, that is, the falsity of E′.

It immediately follows that if we should find that a putative explanation lacks this vital feature since the conditions described by the explanans do not specially demand that E should be true any more than that E′ should be true,* then we have no genuine explanation. Thus a very simple and compelling principle suggests itself, which I shall formulate immediately after the following definitions:

1   p logically implies q in a parallel fashion to the way in which $p′$ implies $q′$ = p yields q by the application of the sequence of logical rules R_1, R_2, . . . R_n and $p′$ yields $q′$ by exactly the same sequence of rules.

2   The explanans T & C is the counterpart of T′ & C′ = T & C logically implies E in a parallel fashion to the way in which T′ & C′ implies E′.

3   T & C tend to explain E = T & C satisfies the set of conditions that T & C may reasonably be expected to fulfil in order to qualify as legitimate explanans of E (e.g., Hempel's original set without adding to it any one of the many complicated extra conditions that were devised to neutralize the numerous counter-examples concocted by various philosophers).

The following is an essential principle restricting the validity of explanations:

(P_1) = If T & C tends to explain E, then we have to ask: what would the situation be like if instead of E its contrary, E′

---

* The reader might wonder for a moment how this is possible. Surely the same explanans cannot imply both E and E′ which are inconsistent statements. But the answer is that the relevant conditions are describable by p_1 & p_2 . . . p_i which entails neither E nor E′. However if we add p_j to p_1 & p_2 . . . p_i then the enlarged conjunction entails E, whereas if instead we add p_k to it then the resulting conjunction entails E′. It is also to be assumed that $E \rightarrow p_j$ and $E′ \rightarrow p_k$. It clearly follows that if E is given then we have a set of statements p_1 & p_2 . . . & p_i & p_j which may serve as explanans in its explanation while if E′ is true we shall have a suitable explanans explaining it.

(and of course everything logically implied by E′), were true but otherwise nothing else changed? If in that case a counterpart of T & C, namely T′ & C′, inevitably becomes available which implies E′ in a fashion exactly parallel to the way in which T & C implies E, then T & C does not actually explain E.

An important aspect of (P₁) is that it is effective enough alone to block a large number of counter-examples against the received account of explanation which previously required a number of disparate conditions. Another important aspect is that (P₁) is by no means an ad hoc condition, but on the contrary expresses a most fundamental feature of explanation. This cannot be said about all the other conditions that have been suggested by various philosophers.

I would go so far as to claim that (P₁) is so fundamental that all intelligent people who are neither scientists nor philosophers subscribe to it. As we know, explanations occur not only in science but also in everyday life. Consider a murder case where everyone is fully convinced that the butler committed the crime but is still wondering why he chose to slay his victim with an axe when he is a champion marksman who owns several guns. One detective may attempt to explain this by saying that the gardener was working outside close to the window of the drawing room where the murder took place, and would have heard a shot if one had been fired, and for this reason the butler did not use a gun. It would be conceded that this seems to be an adequate explanation if true, and efforts should be made to ascertain the whereabouts of the gardener at the crucial moment. Suppose, however, that another detective advanced a suggestion which could be paraphrased thus:

T = The butler always does what he wants and wants what he does.

C = The butler did not want to use a gun.

Then T & C entails

E = The butler did not use a gun

and hence T & C should explain E. No detective, whether in real life or in fiction, would get away with such an explanation. Why?

Anyone with a little common sense will explain why: because if E were false, we could 'explain' that just as well. There is nothing in the situation, before we know whether E or its negation is true, that points more towards E than towards its denial. The putative explanation does not provide us with any real explanation why E is true rather than E′, where

E′ = The butler used a gun.

Surely if E′ had turned out to be true then instead of C we would obtain C′ from T & E′ where

C′ = The butler wanted to use a gun.

But T & C′ entails E′ exactly as T & C entails E. Principle (P_1) expresses nothing but plain common sense.

Now we shall see how with the application of (P_1) all the difficulties created by the previous counter-examples vanish at once.

1 The first difficulty (p. 126) is dealt with very easily. T & C does not actually explain E because of (P_1). For let it be given that

E′ = Mt Everest is *not* snowcapped

while everything in the universe remains the same. Then it follows that

C′ = $T_s \supset E′$

is true. But C′ is the exact counterpart of C since it differs from it only in that it has E′ as its consequent instead of E. But T & C′ tends to explain E′ in the same fashion as T & C tends to explain E. The two tendencies cancel one another out.

The reader may perhaps be wondering: would it be possible for everything in the universe to remain the same except that, instead of E, E′ was true? After all, if Mt Everest was not snowcapped this would imply a very different set of climatic conditions in that region, which naturally could not obtain unless appropriately different circumstances prevailed in many other places, so that there would be an indeterminate number of changes in current physical conditions in the world. But the whole point is that we need not be concerned at all with what is physically possible and what is not. The absurdity of attempting to explain what actually is the case, namely, that Mt Everest is snowcapped, with the aid of T and $T_s \supset E$ is brought out clearly by this fact: that we need do no more than merely postulate a (physically impossible but coherently statable) situation in which the world is not at all different from what it is now except that E′ is true instead of E, and we would automatically have exactly as good an explanation of E′ as we have of E under the prevailing circumstances.

Now, in order to illustrate the point of the assertion that our explanation of E is defective only if the explanation of E′, which would present itself if E′ was true, is the exact symmetrical counterpart of the first explanation, let us consider for a moment a situation in which

$$E_r = \text{Rod } r \text{ is a good conductor of heat}$$

and

$$C_r = \text{Rod } r \text{ is of metal}$$

are both true. Then unquestionably T & C_r which logically implies E_r explains the latter well and any principle which disqualifies this explanation must be invalid. But it might occur to some that (P_1) disqualifies it. For suppose

$$E_r' = \text{Rod } r \text{ is a bad conductor of heat}$$

were true. Then automatically

$$K' = T_s \supset E_r'$$

would become true. But T & K' logically implies E_r' and therefore tends to explain it. Should this tendency not be regarded as cancelling the tendency of T & C_r to explain the contrary of E_r', E_r? The answer, as we have said before, is 'No'. T & K' is not the symmetrical counterpart of T & C_r. T & K' is the symmetrical counterpart of T & K, where

$$K = T_s \supset E_r.$$

Consequently the tendency of T & K to explain E_r is exactly counterbalanced by the tendency of T & K' to explain E_r'. However, there is an additional explanans which tends to explain E_r, namely T & C_r. This explanans has no counterpart which tends to explain E_r'. Consequently T & C_r actually explains E_r.

  2 The second difficulty disappears as well. Suppose

$$E_1' = Qa \ \& \sim Rab$$

is true instead of E_1 but otherwise the universe is unchanged. It follows at once that

$$C_1' = Pa \ \& \sim Rab$$

rather than

$$C_1 = Pa \ \& \ Rab$$

is true. The relationship of E_1' to C_1' is of course mirrored exactly in the relationship of E_1 to C_1, and T_1 & C_1' logically implies E_1' just as T_1 & C_1 implies E_1, hence T_1 & C_1 does not actually explain E_1.

  Consider however for a moment a situation in which we wish to explain $E_2 = Bi$, that is, the true statement that an individual i is black.

To suggest that $C_2 = Ri$, which states the established fact that the individual i is a raven, together with the general law $T_2 = (x)(Rx \supset Bx)$, is to put forward what would be regarded by Hempel as a paradigm of a proper explanation. But suppose someone were to ask: do we not have here a violation of principle (P_1)? After all, consider what would happen if it turned out that $E'_2 = Wi$ (i.e. individual i is white) was true. Surely then we could explain *this* by using $T'_2 = (x)(Rx \supset Wx)$ and C_2 which entail E'_2 in a fashion that mirrors the way T_2 & C_2 entails E_2. In other words the logical rules we employ in the first case – Universal Instantiation plus Modus Ponens – are exactly replicated in the second case.

But of course the answer is that no violation of principle (P_1) has taken place, since if the universe changes in nothing else except that, instead of E_2, E'_2 is observed to be true, that by no means makes T'_2 at once available to us. T_2, which we used in explaining E_2, could legitimately be employed, since it is to be presumed that its credibility had been established earlier by a considerable number of observations – say, n observations – in which invariably ravens of different sizes and shapes were found to be black. Now we are asked to suppose we have come across i which instead of being black is white, and at the same time we are asked not to postulate any other changes in the universe. This means that we can still assume that in the past n ravens are found to be black. Thus not only is T'_2, which asserts that *all* ravens are white, unavailable to us as a sufficiently well-substantiated law of nature, but it is quite firmly established as false and thus we are certainly precluded from employing it as the legitimate theory which, together with C_2, could explain why this particular i was white.

3 Next, consider the third difficulty. Let us assume that

$$E' = \sim Ha$$

is true but otherwise everything remains as before. Then just as T implied T' it implies

$$T'' = (x)(y)(Fx \vee \sim Gy \vee \sim Hy).$$

We now of course find that

$$C' = (\sim Fb \,\&\, Ga) \vee \sim Ha$$

is true since it is implied by E'. That is, the relationship between E' & C' mirrors that between E & C. But T'' & C' logically implies E' in a fashion that mirrors exactly the way in which T' & C implies E, that is, the logical rules used in deriving E from the conjunction of T' & C are the same as those used in deriving E' from T'' & C'. Thus the tendency of T′ & C to explain E is exactly counter-balanced and by (P_1) it is disqualified from actually explaining E.

4 It is not hard to see the solution to the fourth difficulty. It was not necessary at all for Hempel to despair of ever giving an account of how laws of nature are explained. We may very well say that a law of nature is explained if it is shown to follow logically from a set of other laws not implied by it, with the proviso that principle (P_1) must be obeyed. It seems to me that no undesirable explanations will any longer be admissible. Newton's laws, which imply Kepler's laws but are not implied by them, form a legitimate explanans of the latter. But we are not permitted to explain Kepler's laws K, by the conjunction of it with Boyle's law, i.e., by K & B. The simple reason is that such an explanation would violate principle (P_1). It is clear that as soon as we were given that K′, a set of contraries of K, rather than K is true, we could produce K′ & B which is the exact counterpart of K & B and which tends to explain K′ just as well as K & B tends to explain K. K & B does not therefore actually explain K.

5 Once more there is no need for the relatively elaborate extra conditions that have been suggested by various authors in order to rule out this difficulty. Our simple principle (P_1) will do the job. For let us consider what would be the situation if, instead of Ce, E′ = $\sim$ Ce was true. Obviously

$$T' = (x)\,(Mx \supset \sim Cx)$$

would be available to us, since T′ must be true for the same reason as T is true, that is, because Mx is false for every x. $\sim$ Ce of course entails

$$C' = \sim Me \supset \sim Ce.$$

But T′ & C′ logically implies $\sim$ Ce by the following steps:

(a) Me $\supset \sim$ Ce   from T′ by Universal Instantiation.
(b) Ce $\supset$ Me   from C′ by Counter-position.
(c) Ce $\supset \sim$ Ce   from (b) & (a) by Hypothetical Syllogism.
(d) $\sim$ Ce

Thus T′ & C′ yields E′ by exactly the same four steps as T & C yields E. That is, T′ & C′ tends to explain E′ – the negation of E – in a fashion which is precisely parallel to the way that T & C tends to explain E. Consequently (P_1) disqualifies T & C from actually explaining E.

It would not be surprising if the reader has by this stage become rather sceptical and is starting to complain that all this sounds too good to be true. It is hard to accept – he might say – that a principle like (P_1), which hardly amounts to more than a plain truism and which is so much simpler than any of the various sets of conditions set up by others, should be so versatile in dealing with such a diverse collection of difficulties. After all, if (P_1) is really so useful, why is it that for all these years so many eminent philosophers have been kept busy erecting elaborate structures in the hope of being able to produce an adequate account of explanation, instead of simply advancing principle (P_1)?

But this is the crucial point I am trying to make concerning the strange power of the method of counter-examples. It has the capacity to draw the philosopher away from inquiring more into the nature of the concept whose explication is the declared purpose of his enterprise. It may lure him into building complex systems of statements at each stage of which the question he is concentrating on is: what extra elements must I add in order to neutralize the counter-example just raised? The longer this process goes on, the more philosophers are diverted from doing what is required, and the more absorbed they become in the task of further developing the artificial system they have erected in response to the series of counter-examples that has been posed.

'Verifiable in principle'

Now we shall discuss 2 (b) in which, after a needlessly generated process in the course of which successive proposals as to how to formulate a given thesis have repeatedly been defeated by counter-examples, what is actually an easily defensible idea is abandoned as useless. The history of verificationism provides an excellent illustration of this. However, it is also of considerable importance to discuss the verification principle for its own sake. It will make us realize that the commonly held view that the principle has been thoroughly discredited, since it is not possible to offer a coherent definition of the term 'verifiable', is entirely without basis. A completely unproblematic definition is easily produced, as is shown at the end of this section. In the last chapter, we shall have an opportunity to see a novel way of applying the principle in order to establish one of our most basic metaphysical beliefs.

The verification principle was advanced by philosophers calling themselves logical positivists. Their purpose was the complete overhaul of their discipline by the demonstration that many of the recalcitrant problems of philosophy are based on a misunderstanding of what can meaningfully be said and are not real problems at all. Much of the philosophical community's reaction to the call of logical positivists to approach traditional questions in an entirely new spirit was quite remarkable. After all, what we are confronted with here is a proposal to revolutionize philosophy; in consequence of their insistence that no sentence is meaningful unless it is verifiable in principle, logical positivists declared whole areas of philosophical discourse to be meaningless and whole sets of what had hitherto been regarded as the most puzzling problems to be pseudo-problems. Surely all attention ought to have been focused on the fundamental question: what features of the concepts of meaningfulness and of verifiable in principle are responsible for our judgement that there is an intrinsic connection between the two? In other words, what arguments exist to justify this restrictive view that what is unverifiable is devoid of meaning? But, as anyone acquainted with the literature knows, by far the most attention was focused on the seemingly much less pressing question as to how to define precisely the notion of verifiable in principle.

In response to the demand of the logical positivists A. J. Ayer suggested the criterion according to which S is empirically significant if and only if in conjunction with additional premisses S logically implies some observation statement O not implied by these additional premisses alone. This criterion was found faulty by Isaiah Berlin who pointed out that it confers meaningfulness on everything; since S may stand for anything, it together with $S \supset O$ will imply O.

There is no doubt that Berlin has conclusively demonstrated that the criterion proposed by Ayer cannot stand exactly as formulated. To remedy its fault, the most promising approach would seem to be one which started out to analyse the meaning and examine the various uses of 'verification'. Typically, though, instead of subjecting the notion of verification to a general scrutiny, attention is limited to the question of how to deal specifically with Berlin's counter-example, that is, to patch up the suggested criterion so as to strengthen it and rule out his example, without, however, losing anything significant.

As we know, Ayer has attempted this. However, A. Church, a leading logician, had no great difficulty, through the use of elementary formal logic, in deriving a more elaborate and obviously senseless sentence which qualifies as meaningful by Ayer's own criterion. Eventually, Nidditch came along determined to reformulate Ayer's revised criterion specifically so as to block Church's example. Later his version was found faulty as well, and so on.

After many years of ingenious but misguided efforts, hope of finding an adequate definition was abandoned. It was generally agreed that the persistent failure of the formal attempts to set up a satisfactory criterion was a sign that there is something basically wrong with the whole notion of verifiable in principle. It is remarkable that no one has attempted a frontal attack, by subjecting the notion of verification itself to direct analysis, to determine precisely what ails it. Not only does it strike us as a roundabout way to prove the intended point but also as a less secure one – since there are many legitimate concepts of which we do not have an adequate definition.

It is surprising, from a common-sense point of view, that a concept so innocuous as verifiable in principle is should ultimately turn out to be incoherent. After all, the notion of confirmation (or verification) is constantly used in every science from physics to demography as well as in everyday life. Also the distinction between 'actual' and merely 'possible' has been widely discussed in a great variety of examples. It would seem therefore that some convincing argument based on direct evidence would have to be given why 'in principle impossible to confirm' is somehow basically flawed. But the failure of successive attempts to provide a rigorous definition, was interpreted, even in the total absence of an understanding of the true causes of the failure, as fatal for the tenability of the concept. Consequently, it was concluded that meaningfulness cannot be tied to verifiability.

It should be clear, however, that the very first step along this treacherous path of formal manoeuvring, in the course of which the criterion of verifiability was reformulated with a view to eliminating a given counter-example, need not have been taken. An examination of the adequacy of the proposed criterion should have taken place, either in a context free of all concrete examples, by contemplating in the abstract the general nature of the concept of confirmation, or in the context of widely varying examples in which actual confirmation resulted from careful observation of common aspects of these examples. Instead of the severely limited view produced by merely concentrating on the problem of how to eliminate an artificially concocted counter-example, we would have seen the concept of confirmation in a proper light and discovered an elementary and basic aspect which can be ascertained as characteristic of it even before we have worked out in any detail in what the process of confirmation consists.

The aspect in question is briefly that whenever an observation sentence O has the particular relationship to S which constitutes a confirmation then O does not have the same relationship to $\sim$S. Suppose we have not yet discovered the relationship between an established observation sentence O and a given sentence S according to which the former can serve as evidential support for the latter. Let us denote this unknown relationship as R. It must then be obvious that, if in all those cases in which S has R to O we find that $\sim$ S too has precisely the same R to O, then it follows that since O is exactly symmetrically related to S and $\sim$ S it does not confirm one to a greater degree than the other. Hence we are in the position to formulate a very fundamental principle – (P$_2$) – concerning confirmation, even before we have started to work out what exactly constitutes confirmation:

(P$_2$) = If there is some logical relation R such that for every sentence S, if S is related by R to an established O, then O tends to confirm S, O actually confirms S only if it is not the case that ∼S too is related by R to O.

I believe that even someone who knew virtually nothing about what is confirmed when a statement is related to a hypothesis, and about how a statement is to be related to a hypothesis so as to serve as evidence for that hypothesis (except that the two must have *some* relation), would find principle (P$_2$) entirely compelling. When S has R to O and we find that ∼S too has precisely the same R to O, then O is completely symmetrically related to S and ∼ S and cannot therefore confirm one more than the other. (P$_1$) may have presupposed the principle of insufficient reason; (P$_2$) does not require even that. Plain arithmetic will do: if we provide S with n units of support as well as with $- n$ units of support (in consequence of providing ∼S with n units of support), the total amount of support S has received is surely zero. Thus I should be permitted to advance as an a priori rule, before examining any of the candidates for inclusion among the principles of confirmation we shall adopt, that *any* such principle must be understood to be qualified by the proviso expressed by (P$_2$). After all, (P$_2$) is based on nothing more than the a priori assumption that $n - n = O$.

We shall no longer find any reason why the first criterion suggested back in the 1930s by Ayer should not be accepted with the sole modification that it lays down merely the condition under which a sentence *tends* to be confirmable, and is shown to be actually confirmable if in addition it is seen not to violate (P$_2$). We recall that Ayer said that S is confirmed if and only if in conjunction with other premises it implies some established observation statement O that is not implied by those additional premises alone. All we need to do is to substitute for 'S is confirmed' the phrase 'S tends to be confirmed'. We can at once see how Berlin's attack becomes entirely irrelevant. Suppose S is nonsensical but O is an established observation statement then indeed S & (S ⊃ O)→O and we readily agree that O tends to confirm S. However, we see at once that exactly the same R which holds between S and O holds also between ∼S and O since clearly ∼S & (∼S ⊃ O)→O holds no less. Thus, because of principle (P$_2$), S is not actually confirmed by the established O and hence is not actually confirmable in principle by O.

But the truly amazing fact is that had philosophers discovered principle (P_2) not only could years of ingenious but futile reformulations of the criterion of verifiability have been saved, but there would have been no need even to enunciate principle (P_2) nor would Ayer have been obliged to offer any criterion in the first place. While the idea of tying meaningfulness to confirmability in principle was made familiar by logical positivists in the early 1930s, the connection between the credibility of a hypothesis and the degree to which it is actually confirmed has a very long history. Under precisely what circumstances a given hypothesis is confirmed is a question on which much work has been done by those who study confirmation theory. The fact that for the time being no comprehensive definition exists of what exactly constitutes confirmation has not prompted anyone to question the practice of tying credibility to being actually confirmed. We talk freely about one hypothesis being better confirmed than another, and about a third hypothesis not being confirmed at all, and about a fourth hypothesis being confirmed to a sufficient degree for it to be rational for us to accept it. Because of the entirely secure status of 'being confirmed', Ayer could have originally offered the following definition:

S is confirmable in principle if circumstances are coherently describable under which S would be confirmed in practice.

To the extent to which we recognize circumstances under which S is in practice confirmed, we shall recognize circumstances under which S is confirmable in principle. The lack of a complete definition of 'confirmed in practice' has not resulted in any attempt to rule out that concept as illegitimate. Hence the lack of a full definition of 'confirmable in principle' should not lead to the disqualification of that concept as illegitimate. We thus define 'confirmable' simply in terms of 'confirmed'. The legitimacy of the former is no less firmly established than that of the latter. It would be absurd to demand that 'confirmable' must be given a definition independent of 'confirmed'.

The definition of knowledge

Finally we come to the third kind of circumstance – 2(c) – under which the method of counter-examples may lead to undesirable consequences. An outstanding illustration is provided by the recent history of what has been called the Gettier problem. This problem concerns the traditional definition of the statement 'S knows that p.' Traditionally there are three conditions which are sufficient and necessary for the statement to be true: (1) p is true, (2) S believes that p, (3) S is justified in believing that p. It has, however, been objected that there are cases in which S satisfies all three conditions, yet cannot be said to know that p. As an illustration I may use a slightly modified example from Bertrand Russell which he produced in 1912 in his *The Problems of Philosophy*. Suppose that I believe that the last Prime Minister's name begins with the letter 'B' as a result of my justifiable, though mistaken, belief that Mr Balfour was that person when in fact it was Sir Henry Campbell-Bannerman. All three conditions have been satisfied, yet it does not seem appropriate to say that I actually know that the last Prime Minister's name begins with the letter 'B'.

It is quite astonishing to discover how many articles have been written about this relatively trival problem in the past 15 years. I shall briefly give two reasons why this problem is quite unimportant. First, the question whether S believes p is obviously of interest. Everybody's behaviour is largely determined by the beliefs he has. The question whether S is justified in believing p is also of importance. We all want to know the exact conditions under which we are justified in holding various beliefs so as to be able to select them on rational grounds. Finally, whether p, which is justifiably believed by S, is true is certainly of considerable significance. Much of our fate depends on the extent to which our beliefs are true. However, once it is given that p is a justifiably held true belief of S, any further question – namely, whether in addition S is legitimately described as knowing p – seems to be of no interest. It is impossible to find anything to which it would make a difference whether the answer to that question is 'Yes' or 'No'. Everything that is important in epistemology can be adequately studied if we concentrate solely on the notion of justified true belief.

Secondly, all those who have written on the Gettier problem seem to have assumed that in each individual case it is unambiguously clear whether S knows that p or not, and the only problem is to find a fourth condition which will provide a generalization whereby we can classify all cases into two sets, namely, the set of cases in which it is evident that S knows that p and the set of cases in which it is evident that he does not. But this is far from being true. In fact there are indefinitely many cases which are inherently doubtful, and no amount of clarification will help us to decide unequivocally that they do or do not represent cases of knowledge. No definition that classifies each case as the member of one of two sets – namely, the set of cases in which S knows that p, or the set of cases in which he does not – will be satisfactory, since a large number of cases are intrinsically undecidable. To see this we shall consider the following example of Gilbert Harman:

While I am watching him, Tom takes a library book from the shelf and conceals it beneath his coat. Since I am the library detective, I follow him as he walks brazenly past the guard at the front door. Outside I see him take out the book and smile. As I approach he notices me and suddenly runs away. But I am sure that it was Tom, for I know him well. I saw Tom steal a book from the library and that is the testimony I give before the University Judicial Council. After testifying, I leave the hearing room and return to my post in the library. Later that day, Tom's mother testifies that Tom has an identical twin, Buck. Tom, she says, was thousands of miles away at the time of the theft. She hopes that Buck did not do it; but she admits that he has a bad character.

Do I know that Tom stole the book? Let us suppose that I am right. It was Tom that took the book. His mother was lying when she said that Tom was thousands of miles away. I do not know that she was lying, of course, since I do not know anything about her, even that she exists. Nor does anyone at the hearing know that she is lying, although some may suspect that she is. In these circumstances I do not know that Tom stole the book. My knowledge is undermined by evidence I do not possess.[7]

Harman considers the suggestion that the reason why I cannot be said to know that Tom stole the book, in spite of the fact that the three traditional conditions for knowledge have been satisfied, is because there is also a fourth condition:

(4) One knows only if there is no evidence such that if one knew about the evidence one would not be justified in believing one's conclusion.[8]

He argues however that (4) cannot be correct since:

Suppose that Tom's mother was known to the Judicial Council as a pathological liar. Everyone at the hearing realizes that Buck, Tom's supposed twin, is a figment of her imagination. When she testifies no one believes her. Back at my post in the library, I still know nothing of Tom's mother or her testimony. In such a case, my knowledge would not be undermined by her testimony; but if I were told only that she had just testified that Tom has a twin brother and was himself thousands of miles away from the scene of the crime at the time the book was stolen, I would no longer be justified in believing as I now do that Tom stole the book. Here I know even though there is evidence which, if I know about it, would cause me not to be justified in believing my conclusion.[9]

So the problem, as Harman sees it, is how to devise a fourth condition which will disqualify me from knowing that Tom stole the book in the first case (in which the Council believed the testimony of Tom's mother), but will allow that in the second case (in which they did not believe her), I do have knowledge.

I am quite certain that not everyone will agree with Harman's judgements. There will be some who will deem it proper even in the first case to attribute knowledge to me, since after all it is true that Tom stole the book and I am fully justified in believing it. What does it matter, then, that evidence contradicting my belief was presented to the Council, when that evidence was false even though the Council happened to believe it? Then there might be others who would say that in both cases I fail to know that Tom stole the book. Yet others may maintain quite reasonably that it is just not clear whether I do or do not know and that there is no way of determining this. But Harman is not concerned with this, since his mind is firmly made up and he is sure that in the first case I do, and in the second case I do not, know that Tom stole the book. He is solely concerned with the problem of finding a single general condition which will fit all cases. But as to the more basic question whether he can decide in any case that may present itself whether it is a case of knowledge or not, his answer seems to be 'yes'.

Harman's position seems to be untenable. He happens to consider two cases, but between those two there is a whole spectrum consisting of indefinitely many cases. For instance, what if Tom's mother was not known to the Judicial Council as a pathological liar but (without my knowledge of course) Dick testifies (out of spite and without really knowing it) that Tom's mother was lying, and the Council accepts this testimony? Suppose Harman still retains his confidence and claims to be sure that my knowledge would not be undermined by the testimony of Tom's mother. Then we may ask: what if the Council accept Dick's testimony but later reverse it when they find out that it has violated some technicality by virtue of which it is inadmissible? Are we to say in that case that the testimony of Tom's mother does undermine my knowledge? Or perhaps we can say that prior to the Council's reversal the mother's testimony was counteracted and therefore did not undermine my knowledge, and thus I was to be regarded as knowing that Tom stole the book, but that I ceased to know this after the Council decided not to accept Dick's testimony. It should be amply clear by now that we could go on indefinitely and construct as many cases as we wish, in each one my knowledge being undermined to a slightly different degree. It is inconceivable that Harman could feel confident in every case that he knows whether it represents an instance of knowledge or not. Thus it is not true that all he is confronted with is the task of devising an adequate fourth condition that will exclude all cases which we want to exclude from qualifying as instances of knowledge, and only those cases. There is a more basic problem and that is that we simply do not know what we want and what we do not want to exclude. Nor shall we ever know. There are many situations with respect to which it is futile to look for a definition that will help us to decide whether or not they qualify as cases of knowledge, since there are intrinsically indeterminate cases. But, as I have already stated, this should cause us no concern. While it is important to know under exactly what circumstances S is entitled to believe that p, it is not at all important to be able to decide under what circumstances S qualifies as knowing that p.

And yet, as I have already pointed out, there is an inordinately large literature devoted to this subject. As anyone can see for himself by a cursory look at the relevant writings, the explanation is that this subject offers practically unlimited scope for producing and eliminating counter-examples. Typically a philosopher offers a fourth condition to be added to the three traditional conditions defining knowledge, and so a counter-example is presented. This may be one of two kinds. (1) A condition that the author is convinced represents a case where S knows that p, and yet the extra condition rules it out; hence that condition is too strong. A fifth condition to S is likely to follow. (2) A condition that the author is convinced represents a case where S does not know that p, and yet all the four conditions together do not rule it out. What is likely to follow is a fifth condition to strengthen the fourth. This is followed by the presenting of further counter-examples, and so on.

Soon we have a number of systems whose presuppositions, implications and other logical properties became a matter of interest in themselves. They may be discussed at great length and amended in various ways without regard to the question whether there is any good reason for having them, whether they serve any useful purpose or whether the discussions have much real philosophical interest.

I shall cite no more examples in this chapter to illustrate the undesirable consequences of the indiscriminating use of the method of counter-examples. But when we examine the issue of other minds we shall have the opportunity to look at a most remarkable example. There we shall see a noted philosopher produce what he takes to be a counter-example to the common belief concerning the way simple enumerative induction is to be applied. Consequently he lays down a principle which restricts the scope of inductive reasoning. He does this without giving a moment's thought to the question whether his principle satisfies a legitimate demand arising out of the nature of induction or whether there is any other argument in its favour except that it neutralizes his counter-example. It proves to be an entirely unwarranted and worthless principle. Elementary logic shows that the counter-example can be disposed of without any difficulty.

Possible worlds and conditionals

Now we shall discuss a situation where counter-examples are produced under circumstances that are wholly appropriate and in which no undesirable results are likely to arise, since we understand the nature of the problem these counter-examples are devised to illustrate. Let us return to the topic of possible worlds. The reason why there have been so many suggestions lately as to the status of these worlds, and in general such intense interest in the topic, is that a great number of uses have been found for them. Possible worlds have been employed to explicate the notions of 'essential' and 'accidental' properties, of logical modalities, of causality, and so on. Arguably the most interesting use they have been put to is the explication of conditional statements.

It is appropriate to begin by mentioning that the subject of counterfactual conditionals deserves special attention in this work, not merely for the sake of the illustrations it provides but also for its own sake. Counterfactual statements seem to occupy a unique position in the study of metaphysics. Normally when a statement is true, it is true because it corresponds to existing facts. A counterfactual statement, however, seems extraordinary in that if it is true it cannot be so for any such straightforward reason. As its name indicates a counterfactual does not refer to states of affairs that obtain in the real world; the scope of its assertion extends beyond actual facts. It refers to unrealized possibilities that are not subject to direct inspection. There seems to be a clear implication here that this species of statements is to be classified as one comprising typical metaphysical statements. Science may be dealing with all sorts of statements that purport to describe the world we inhabit, but statements that refer not to existing states of affairs but to unactualized potentialities, to facts which obtain not in any domain accessible to our senses but in unrealized and merely logically possible worlds, surely belong to the realm of metaphysics.

One of my aims here will be to challenge this view. First, however, let us have a look at a fairly novel approach to counterfactuals, the 'possible world' analysis, which has given rise to much interest and comment. The central notion required for this analysis is the three place relation:

World W_1 is closer to the actual world than is world W_2

where the term 'closer' is to be taken as an elementary term not requiring analysis. Now, many philosophers have expressed the opinion that even when we have in front of us three tables a, b and c which are accessible to direct inspection, it is not always easy to determine whether *b* or *c* more closely resembles *a*. Surely then, when we are dealing with entire universes of enormous complexity, universes that are merely logically possible and not actually available to direct examination, it must be immensely more difficult to judge their relative closeness with any assurance. I shall however ignore this difficulty and grant that David Lewis, the author of a famous book on counterfactuals,[10] can when he needs to determine whether W_1 or W_2 is closer to our world. We shall examine his suggestion that where A and C are two propositions and where A-worlds and C-worlds are worlds in which A and C respectively hold, then

> The proposition that if A were true, then C would be true, is true in our world iff either
> (1) there is no possible A-world, or
> (2) some A-world where C holds is closer to our world than is any A-world where C does not hold.

By now several conflicting arguments have been proposed as to how to apply possible world analysis to indicative and subjunctive conditionals. It will be best to concentrate on one account, one of the latest and one which seems to be a superior account. I shall confine my attention to Wayne A. Davis' paper 'Indicative and Subjunctive Conditionals',[11] in which he has certainly introduced some badly needed clarification to a thoroughly confused situation. Davis has, among other things, clearly stated what has not generally been recognized (and has in fact been explicitly denied by Stalnaker,[12] one of the chief originators of the idea under discussion) – that indicative and subjunctive conditionals cannot have the same truth condition. He has pointed out that we must distinguish between possible worlds which are over all fairly close to the actual world, and those which are very similar only up to the time at which the event referred to in the antecedent takes place, and that we must decide unequivocally which kind of closest world we want to associate with which kind of conditional. And he has compellingly argued, contrary to David Lewis, that a world in which Kennedy is not killed is vastly more different from the actual world than one in which not Oswald, but some other quite inconsequential person, killed Kennedy (since all our lives would be considerably different if Kennedy had lived, whereas whether Oswald or some other unimportant person assassinated Kennedy hardly affects any of our lives).

Davis considers the following three statements:

X = Oswald did not kill Kennedy (F).
Y = Someone else killed Kennedy (F).
Z = Kennedy was not killed (F).

and out of these he forms the following four conditionals:

Indicative	Subjunctive
X ⇒ Y (T)	X > Y (F)
X ⇒ Z (F)	X > Z (T)

'X ⇒ Y' reads, of course, 'If Oswald did not kill Kennedy someone else did' which common sense tells us is true since it is known that Kennedy was killed with virtually absolute certainty. Thus, if contrary to our very well-confirmed hypothesis it should turn out that it was not Oswald who was the assassin after all, then we are forced to conclude that someone else killed Kennedy. On the other hand, common sense tells us that 'X > Y', which reads 'If Oswald had not killed Kennedy someone else would have done', is false, since the evidence indicates that Oswald acted alone and thus if for some reason he should have failed in carrying out his intention, there is no reason at all to assume that someone else would have rushed in to take his place.

He then proposes the following two modified versions of Stalnaker's Principles:

SP (⇒)   The indicative conditional A ⇒ C is true iff C is true in $i(A)$ where $i(A)$ is the closest (in overall respect) of possible worlds in which A is true.

SP (>)   The subjunctive conditional A > C is true iff C is true in $s(A)$, where $s(A)$ is the A-world that is most similar to the actual world up to the time $t(A)$, the time reference of A.

On the basis of these principles we can account for the truth values of the four conditionals. For instance, we are to regard X ⇒ Y as true, since $i(X)$, the closest X-world, is a world where Y is true, as the history of that world is more similar to that of ours than that of a world in which Kennedy remained alive. On the other hand, it is X ⇒ Z that is false, because before $t(x)$ the closest world is that where Oswald misses by a couple of inches and there is no other person in reserve to take his place, just as in our world.

The following example shows, unmistakably I believe, that the Davis–Lewis–Stalnaker analysis of indicative conditionals is of no use.

Consider a situation in which there is strong and universally accepted evidence that Smith has killed an unimportant person Jones. The crime occurred in the mountain resort to which the Pope goes to rest from time to time, and it is absolutely certain that the Pope himself was in the vicinity when the crime occurred and that there was no other human being within a radius of five miles. We shall assume that the fact that

Jones was killed cannot be doubted, as thousands of people have seen his bullet-riddled body, whereas Smith's guilt has been established on the basis of the testimony of a handful of people and strong circumstantial evidence. In other words we assume that the probability of Jones' having been killed is virtually one, while the probability of the truth of the proposition that it was Smith who killed him is merely high enough to place it beyond legally reasonable doubt, but not practically one. We also stipulate that the facts are established in such a way that if it is after all false that Smith killed Jones, then no one but the Pope could have done it. (If the circumstances I have described should be found inadequate I am sure no one would wish to deny that it *is* logically possible to have circumstances under which the inevitable conclusion to be drawn, in the case of Smith not killing Jones, is that no one else but the Pope could have killed him.)

Needless to say, the sensational news that the Pope has committed the major crime of killing another human being would arouse the greatest astonishment and moral indignation of the century. We may well imagine that as a result of such an outrage thousands of priests and nuns would abandon their vocation, millions of Catholics would lose their faith, and the American Internal Revenue Service might even cease to recognize Catholicism as a religion for tax purposes. The death of Jones, who may be supposed to be the least influential person in Italy, makes hardly any difference to anybody. Now consider the following two indicative conditionals:

S_1 =   If Smith did not kill Jones, the Pope did $(U \Rightarrow V)$.
S_2 =   If Smith did not kill Jones, Jones was not killed $(U \Rightarrow W)$.

There seems little doubt that, given circumstances under which it is not possible to deny that W is false as it is virtually certain that Jones was killed, and given that U & $\sim$W practically implies V, which though very surprising is not certainly false, everyone would have to agree that S_1 is true. According to the Davis–Lewis–Stalnaker analysis, however, it seems clear that S_2 would have to be regarded as true, since a world in which U as well as W is true is much closer to ours than one in which V is true.

Although it is sufficient to cite a counter-example in order to refute a thesis, it is much more illuminating if we clearly state *why* it is that we are able to produce a counter-example – that is, why it is that a common-sense attitude regards a different proposition to be true than would the Davis–Stalnaker analysis. What seems entirely clear is that, in trying to decide whether S_1 or S_2 is true, we do not at all bring into consideration the relative similarities of $i(U \& V)$ and $i(U \& W)$ to the actual world. Our story was so concocted that i(U & W) is vastly more similar to the actual world than is i(U & V), since had it been that Jones was not killed this would have made little difference to the world, but a world in which V is true is fundamentally different from ours. We pay no attention whatever to this fact. In other words SP ($\Rightarrow$) plays no role at all when it comes to determining whether U $\Rightarrow$ V or U $\Rightarrow$ W is to be regarded as true. The fact that is of significance instead is that the evidence is such that W is to be regarded false and the falsity of W together with U implies V.

Here we have what is to my mind an instance of a wholly appropriate use of a counter-example, the reason being, of course, that the difficulty highlighted by our example is one that should be evident to any dispassionate person as soon as he is presented with Davis' analysis. It is a difficulty we can clearly articulate. When we embark upon the analysis of conditionals we must bear in mind that they are being uttered millions of times a day by non-philosophers and hardly ever raise a doubt in anybody's mind as to the truth conditions that apply to them. Surely the intention of these noted philosophers was not to invent a new language of conditionals but to examine their current usage and explicate the conditions universally assumed to determine the truth values of conditional expressions. It seems incredible that any philosopher should go ahead and produce a definition of these truth conditions, however clever, that is quite unrelated to what the rest of the population assumes applies. But we may ask: does anyone think about the question whether the world in which Kennedy remains alive differs more from the actual world than the one in which his assailant is someone other than Oswald? The answer is that no such thought enters anybody's mind who has determined that X $\Rightarrow$ Y, rather than X $\Rightarrow$ Z, is true. If we ask any fairly intelligent person why he regards X $\Rightarrow$ Y as true he might tell us something like this: it is virtually certain that Kennedy has been killed and the conditional does not postulate it to be otherwise. All that the antecedent asserts is that he was not killed by Oswald. But if we are asked to assume (a) Kennedy was not killed by Oswald and (b) Kennedy was killed, then the consequent follows that someone else killed him.

If we assume that the actual assignment of truth-values is performed roughly along the lines just indicated and definitely not in the way described by Davis, then it is entirely clear what kind of story we shall have to construct in order to produce a decisive counter-example. Our story should be similar to the Kennedy story in that the conditions that are commonly taken to be the relevant truth-conditions remain the same, that is, it should be assumed that the victim was killed and it is postulated only that his killer was someone other than the person everyone now suspects. On the other hand, we reverse what Davis took to be the relevant condition. In the Kennedy story, the world in which he remains alive is very different from our world, while the world in which someone other than the supposed killer shoots him hardly differs from ours. It is the other way round in our story: the world in which Jones remains alive is not much different from our world, while the world in which his killer was not Smith but the Pope is vastly different. The fact that everyone will still regard S_1 as true and S_2 as false without any doubt clearly shows that the reversal of the conditions Davis took to be decisive makes no difference at all. Any number of stories constructed along these lines could be told to serve as counter-examples to the possible world analysis of indicative conditionals.

Now let us look briefly at counterfactual conditionals. Suppose it is planned that precisely at noon a destroyer will launch a missile aimed at the enemy's most vital installation. The destruction that would result is estimated to cause at least a billion dollars' damage. Given the rigid rules governing the enemy's military establishment, it is virtually certain that the Commander-in-Chief of their combined armed forces will resign one hour – give or take at most one minute – after such a military disaster takes place. It has been agreed with the Captain of our destroyer that if the mission is successful they are going to hoist a red flag at exactly 12.05 to signal their success. Suppose that the mission, which had a high probability to go exactly as planned, happened to fail, and thus at 12.05 the flag has not been raised. Then surely the counterfactual asserted a few minutes after 1.00:

S_3 = If the flag had been raised at 12.05 then the enemy's C.-in-C. would have resigned by now

must be regarded as true. Let us assume that the flag could have been raised at 12.05 by mistake, that is, that though this was highly improbable, it was not entirely impossible for some unauthorized person to hoist the flag even though the target had not been hit. Now surely a world in which the flag is raised by mistake, but otherwise is identical with ours with respect to the fact that in neither is the vital enemy installation destroyed, is much more similar to ours than the world in which the flag is raised in consequence of the success of inflicting an enormous damage upon the enemy. And here of course we are comparing the worlds with respect to their states before the time $t(A)$. Consequently, according to Davis, S_3 should be false. It appears, however, that the relevant factor in determining the truth value of S_3 is the consideration that it is much more probable for the flag to be raised when the target has been hit than by mistake. The comparative resemblance between the worlds we mentioned is left out of consideration altogether. It will be obvious to the reader that here too we constructed our counter-example on the basis of our prior knowledge of what is wrong with Davis' analysis and our realization of what are the genuinely relevant factors in determining the truth values of counterfactuals.

To make sure it is entirely clear *why* the possible world analysis is completely off target, let us consider for a moment the predictive conditional counterpart of S_3, namely

S_3' =   If the flag is going to be raised at 12.05 then the enemy's C.-in-C. will resign approximately at 1.00

which has been asserted a considerable time before twelve o'clock. Let us assume that the mission was quite likely to succeed, but in case it should fail the chances of the flag being nevertheless raised by mistake were less than one in ten thousand. It seems obvious that under those conditions everybody would agree that S_3' was a true statement. Clearly what would influence our judgement is the high probability of the mission's success and the very small probability of the flag's being raised by mistake rather than as a true signal of the success of the bombardment. The factors determining the truth of the predictive conditional S_3' ought to be exactly the factors determining the truth of the parallel counterfactual S_3. All philosophers, including Lewis and Stalnaker, would unquestionably agree that the fact that the world would be vastly different at the crucial time 12.05 if the vital enemy installation lay in ruins is not of the slightest relevance to the truth value of S_3'. It is of no relevance to the truth value of S_3 either.

The last example I would like us to look at briefly is not merely a counter-example to the possible world analysis but it tends also to support the thesis I should like to maintain, namely that contrary-to-fact conditionals and straightforward predictive conditionals are intimately related. Suppose that when a group of identical cells of type c are irradiated briefly by δ-rays, some of them are destroyed while others remain intact, and that this is wholly a matter of chance. Given, for example, 100 c-cells, then it is equally probable that any number between 1 and 100 is going to be destroyed when the group is subjected to radiation. We shall now consider a laboratory where a series of demonstrations of this interesting, indeterministic phenomenon is given. The first demonstration takes place at 8.00 in the morning, when a batch of 100 c-cells are exposed to a burst of radiation by δ-rays and it is observed that 17 of them have disintegrated. At 8.05 the second demonstration takes place under identical conditions; however, this time 84 cells are destroyed. Consider now the following counterfactual:

If the first demonstration had been held at 7.55 the number of cells destroyed would still have been 17.

I do not believe many people would want to maintain that under the circumstances stipulated there would be any good grounds for regarding this counterfactual as true. Since we are dealing here with what scientists have firmly established as a perfectly indeterministic phenomenon, surely there is just no basis on which we could establish the number of cells that would have been destroyed if the first experiment had been conducted five minutes earlier. In fact, on the basis of universally shared scientific knowledge, the probability that the number of cells disintegrating would have been exactly 17 is no more than 1:100.

Obviously, however, the possible world which is different from ours in that the first experiment is conducted five minutes earlier but otherwise maximally similar to ours is unquestionably the world in which exactly 17 cells are destroyed in the first demonstration. Apparently, however, this is of no relevance. What does matter is that there is no law to determine the number of cells destroyed under such conditions. The absence of such a law, just as it renders it impossible to make a correct prediction of what number is going to be destroyed at a given time to come, also renders it impossible to assert a correct counterfactual concerning the number that would have been destroyed at a given time in the past.

Counterfactuals and metaphysics

This seems to be the right moment to introduce an important aspect of counterfactuals, one that appears to have been completely neglected. The first point I shall try to make is that the same counterfactual sentence may be used to express widely different propositions that have entirely different truth-conditions. This topic deserves a more extensive treatment than I am able to give it.

Let us suppose that in a show involving highly venomous snakes a performer executes a variety of stunning feats while all the time maintaining a distance between himself and the snakes. Consider:

S_4 =   If the entertainer had touched one of those snakes he would have died within two minutes.

Let me first list a number of facts we are to suppose as obtaining and that are relevant to our discussion. The performer is the kind of person who would under no circumstances expose himself to any kind of danger. He has no skill in calming vicious animals. The circumstances are such that if one of the snakes were to be replaced by a plastic replica this would not be likely to be noticed by the spectators in the hall. The entertainer is not so honest that he would be unwilling to practise a little deception in order to startle the spectators. In other words, the conditions are such as to render the probability that if the performer touched one of the snakes he would do so under safe conditions as almost one (i.e., he would make sure that he touches a plastic snake). Consider now the cases of three different speakers who assert S_4.

The first speaker is not interested in the performer's personality or behaviour. He wishes to say nothing about his skill, courage, honesty and so forth. The speaker is in fact an expert ophiologist who wants to impress upon us how exceedingly ferocious and poisonous this particular species of snakes is. Reason dictates our accepting his assertion as representing established scientific truth. In the present context it turns out to be entirely irrelevant that a prudent man like our performer would almost certainly not deliberately provoke a deadly reptile. Our speaker does not wish to query this; all he wants is to convey to us important information about the effects that the slightest interference with these beasts is likely to produce. His statement is to be regarded as true.

In the course of our conversation it has become evident that a second speaker dislikes the performer. It is obvious that he wants us to know that the performer has no skill in pacifying aggressive animals and also is not averse to engaging in a little deception. He denies S_4 in order to convey to us that we may be quite sure, given the performer's character, that if he touched one of these snakes, which he might well want to do in order to impress the spectators, he would do so only under safe conditions. So he would have introduced a plastic snake and, by touching that rather than a genuine snake, would make sure not to expose himself to any danger. There is every reason to regard this speaker's denial of S_4 as representing the truth.

It is most important that we note that the circumstances surrounding the two cases are identical. In particular, it is entirely correct to assume in both cases that the performer would touch one of these agitated serpentine objects only if he first ensured his safety. This is quite irrelevant in the first case, where the speaker is focusing on the causal relationship between a slight provocation and the swift retribution that follows from the species of reptiles he is talking about. For him, if *per impossibile* the performer should so much as touch one of these vicious creatures, this would indeed inevitably result in his death, which would be sufficient for his proposition to be true. The second speaker has no intention of denying the existence of the causal link affirmed by the last speaker but tells us something quite different, something that concerns the personality of the performer.

In brief: speaker 1, who affirms S_4, and speaker 2, who denies it under identical conditions, may both be right because they are not contradicting one another. They are using S_4 to express entirely different, logically independent propositions.

The third speaker is the fond keeper and trainer of the performing snakes, who is completely familiar with their behaviour down to the minutest characteristic wriggle of each one of them. He wishes to assure us that he recognizes each animal by its unmistakable pattern of movements and that it is out of the question that there might be among them a mechanically-driven plastic snake. He asserts S_4 and, as he is an honest and reliable expert of his trade, he is to be believed.

It is to be noted that speaker 2 would not disagree with the last speaker since the latter's observation is of no real concern to him. Assuming speaker 3 to be telling the truth, it follows that if the performer had touched one of those wriggling things then of necessity the circumstances would have had to be different from what they are now. Under the existing circumstances all the snakes on the stage are genuine; the performer would definitely not touch any of them under these circumstances.

Once more speaker 2 who denies S_4 and speaker 3 who affirms it do not contradict one another.

To summarize the important points made let us assume the existence of a causal law requiring that iff P & Q becomes true, then facts are generated bringing about the truth of R. It follows that

$$P \ \& \ Q \rightarrow R. \ . \ . \ (i)$$

as well as

$$P \ \& \sim R \rightarrow \sim Q. \ . \ . \ (ii)$$

Also assume that currently $\sim P$, Q, and $\sim R$. Consider the case in which the speaker asserts $P > R$.

The crucial point to be realized is that he may be intending to convey one of a variety of quite different propositions, for example:

(1) He may wish to affirm the existence of the causal link between the events referred to by P & Q and by R. In this case, it is entirely irrelevant whether the person who has the power to determine whether P should hold is anxious to prevent R becoming true. By asserting $P > R$, the

speaker in no way implies that P would be permitted to become true under circumstances that would also bring about the truth of R.

The condition required to ensure the truth of P > R is that there should indeed be a law of nature linking the relevant events causally.

(2) He may wish to convey that we may be assured that R would be true as soon as P becomes true since the necessary condition, i.e. Q, does prevail. Here he is focusing on the desire to affirm the truth of Q.

(3) The speaker wants to assure us that R would be true if P were true since the person who determines which of the relevant facts obtains is not bent upon preventing R from becoming true.

It may be added as a suggestion that if the speaker should assert P > ~ Q when (i) and (ii) are given, then we take him to be denying what he would be asserting in the third proposition P > R.

It is hardly necessary to point out that in (1), (2) and (3) the factual conditions that need to obtain in order to render the same counterfactual true are very different. Also, under certain circumstances we may know from the context whether we are faced with (1), (2) or (3), but under others we may not. Thus we may not be able to determine the truth value of the counterfactual even though we have perfect knowledge of every relevant fact surrounding P, Q and R.

The first simple but important conclusion that follows is that in general all the standard approaches assuming that a specific counterfactual and thus the particular possible world analysis has a unique truth-value must be radically mistaken. We can see this as soon as we remember that in the context of S_4 an A-world is one where the counterpart of the performer actually touches one of those wriggling snaky things on the stage.

Let both W_1 and W_2 be A-worlds. In W_1 the snake that is touched is a mere imitation and the performer is not harmed. In W_2 the snake that is touched is genuine and the performer perishes. We now ask: which of these two is closer to the actual world?

It is of no interest to find out what features of the situation Lewis would treat as more significant than others, for whatever approach he may take one thing is certain: *either* W_1 *or* W_2 is the closest A-world. But if W_1 is the closest A-world we have no explanation why speaker 1 and speaker 3 are both regarded as telling the truth, and if W_2 is the closest A-world we cannot understand why speaker 2 is telling the truth. In other words, what is wrong with Lewis' approach, and for that matter with virtually all other known approaches, is that it takes it for granted that every particular counterfactual has one specific set of truth conditions. In reality, however, since one and the same counterfactual can be used to express diverse propositions, there are as many sets of truth conditions for each counterfactual as there are propositions that may legitimately be expressed through its use.

However, the point that is of greater significance for our purposes is this. The widely adopted attitude, as we have seen, is to regard counterfactuals as referring to unrealized possibilities, to potential situations that may obtain in some other world but not in the actual world. In contrast to the case of most other statements, it is therefore believed that it is impossible to determine their truth-values simply by directly observing some actual facts they might be mirroring. We may, however, have access to some clues, to certain conditions prevailing in the actual world, that may serve as indirect indications of whether they are true or not. For example, it is through examining the actual world where A is false that we figure out the nature of the A-world that must be closest to our world.

According to the view I am advocating, counterfactuals are sentences that are used in one way or another to refer *directly* to *actual* facts that obtain here and now. In case (1) what is asserted is that a particular causal law actually obtains in *this* world. In case (2) the speaker is understood to assure us that Q is *actually* true, while in case (3) he is understood to be affirming that the person who can bring it about that P is *actually* not anxious to prevent R from becoming true.

Thus I maintain that the answer to the much debated question of what are the truth-conditions of counterfactuals is simply: precisely the same as those of all sentences. The required conditions are that their assertion that certain facts obtain should correspond to reality, and that those facts should actually obtain. On a sober consideration counterfactuals do not appear to have any features that would require that they be classified as metaphysical statements.

The indexical theory and the mystery of existence

So much for the subject of counterfactuals. Now we shall take a closer look at the fascinating metaphysical claim that reality is immensely larger than we would have suspected, this whole universe of ours amounting to no more than an infinitesimal fraction of the total. Our universe, according to this view, is just one of infinitely many equally real worlds. I shall discuss David Lewis' version of realism, the boldest and most straightforward version. He holds that the expression 'the actual world' means only 'this world', that is, the world we ourselves are in. If I am a non-solipsist I shall admit that while from my point of view there is an asymmetry between you and me, in fact you are no less real than I and therefore from your point of view – which in an objective sense is as good as mine – the asymmetry is reversed. According to Lewis' theory of actuality – the indexical theory – the same is correct in the context of different worlds; while every universe is privileged from its own point of view, no universe is more real than any other from an absolute point of view, that is, from a point of view outside all universes.

Lewis' view, which has also been called the extreme realist view, has numerous implications some of which differ greatly from the positions to which other logicians who hold other views on the status of possible worlds are committed. He is naturally aware of this and does not find it disturbing; on the contrary, he claims that the remarkable nature of some of the implications of his theory constitutes a positive advantage. There are, however, some quite far-reaching implications, which I shall soon touch upon and which have not previously come to anyone's attention. The well-known consequences of his theory have been debated in detail by logicians and described in other works. I should nevertheless like to refer to one of them briefly in order to qualify what has been said in the previous section.

We have looked in some detail at the view according to which a counterfactual 'If Oswald had not shot Kennedy . . .' is analysed in terms of possible worlds. This enterprise presupposes, of course, that a person like Oswald exists in many different worlds, in some of which he shoots Kennedy and in others of which he does not. According to the non-realist view this presupposition does not strike us as obviously incoherent, but on the realist view it does. There is only one actual world. The uniqueness of this world consists solely in the fact that it is the one world which is inhabited by me; it is the world which is mine. It is therefore a contradiction to claim that I may exist in other worlds as well. Thus there does not exist a single world in which Oswald exists but does not shoot Kennedy, since there does not exist a single world other than ours that contains an individual who is identical with our Oswald, just as there is no world, besides the actual world, that contains any individual identical with me.

Lewis however, not only accepts quite calmly the conclusion that there can be no 'transworld' individuals, he even welcomes it. After all, it has been claimed that the notion of a transworld individual involves great difficulties. Let me mention one briefly. Even if Oswald existed in just one world other than ours, w, this would amount to a violation of the Leibnitzian principle of the indiscernibility of identicals: in w, Oswald has some property other than those he has in the actual world, for example, he fails to shoot Kennedy. Consequently, Oswald could be claimed to inhabit *w* as well as our world only if all his properties were identical in both. But this would give rise to at least two decisive objections. First, Oswald in *w* who is identical with our Oswald loses all his usefulness, for he can be of no help in the analysis of the relevant counterfactuals. By definition, any counterfactual involving Oswald refers to facts other than those obtaining about our own Oswald, and none of these facts obtain about Oswald in *w* either. Secondly, so long as *w* contains even a single feature F that is absent from the actual world, Oswald in *w* has a relational property with respect to F that he cannot have in the actual world. In order to avoid this, it must be stipulated that *w* does not have any such feature. But then by the converse of the Leibnitzian principle of the identity of indiscernibles, *w* is none other than our own world.

It is not that this objection could not be met, but Lewis is able to avoid it altogether by refusing to admit the notion of a transworld individual and proclaiming 'Nothing is in two worlds.' Consequently the analysis of 'If Oswald had not shot . . .' involves individuals in other worlds who are sufficiently similar to our Oswald to qualify as his counterparts, some of whom do and some of whom do not shoot an individual who is the counterpart of Kennedy, the President of the counterpart of the United States.

How unfamiliar we still are with this vast new metaphysical territory so recently opened up for exploration may be illustrated by the fact that this elementary implication of Lewis' extreme realism has not yet generally been recognized. William Lycan very helpfully provides a summary of the various theses held by Lewis:

(i) There are nonactual possibles and possible worlds, and 'there are' here needs no scare quotes; nonactual possibles and possible worlds exist in exactly the same sense as that in which our world and its denizens exist.

(ii) Nonactual objects and worlds are of just the same respective *kinds* as are actual objects and the actual world. Nonactual tables are physical objects with physical uses; nonactual humans are made of flesh and blood, just as you and I are.

(iii) Nonactual objects and worlds are not *reducible* to items of less controversial sorts; worlds distinct from ours are not sets of sentences, or mental constructs of any sort, but blooming, buzzing worlds.

(iv) All individuals, actual or merely possible, are world-bound; there is no genuine identity across worlds. You and I are not world-lines, but merely have *counterparts* in other worlds who resemble us for certain purposes but are distinct individuals in their own right.

As Robert Stalnaker points out, it is crucial to see that most of the foregoing claims are independent of one another and the discriminating theorist might well accept some of them but disagree with Lewis over others. (iv) and (v) are perhaps the most obviously expendable. [13]

But of course (iv) is quite obviously not expendable since, as we have seen, given (i), (ii) and (iii) the actual world is in no way more real than any other possible world and its uniqueness therefore can consist in nothing else, as Lewis clearly explains, but in its being my world. It is a plain contradiction therefore to maintain that I may exist in other worlds too. (iv) is therefore logically implied by what came before.

The obvious question to ask is: are there any good arguments why we should subscribe to extreme realism? Lewis, who usually prefers conducting complex formal arguments to engaging in metaphysical flights of fancy, does at one point permit himself to soar into the speculative stratosphere when he cites his strongest reason for adopting what he calls the indexical analysis of actuality. He says:

> The strongest evidence for the indexical analysis of actuality is that it explains why skepticism about our own actuality is absurd. How do we know that we are not the unactualized possible inhabitants of some unactualized possible world? . . . The indexical analysis of actuality explains how we know it: in the same way I know that I am me, that *this* time is the present, or that I am here. All such sentences as 'This is the actual world,' 'I am actual, 'I actually exist,' and the like are true on any possible occasion of utterance in any possible world. That is why skepticism about our own actuality is absurd. [14]

I find this most puzzling. That is, while his reply to the sceptic sounds very good, I am at a loss to understand what the sceptic may have been worrying about. It is generally agreed, for instance, that it makes no sense to suggest to someone complaining of excruciating toothache that he is imagining it and in reality has no pain at all. One reason is that if one does not claim that there is some difference between the 'feel' of a real toothache and that of an imagined one, it makes no sense to maintain that there are two such distinct types of acute discomforts. Now Lewis' sceptic, who thinks we may be inhabiting some unactualized possible world, is sharply to be distinguished from the better-known sceptic we shall be meeting in the last chapter, who doubts the reality of the external world. Lewis' sceptic doubts the reality of everything including his own mental world. So obviously we should want to ask him whether, in consequence of this world's unreality, his toothache is somewhat less unpleasant.

One could, however, say something more down-to-earth in defence of extreme realism. One could claim that it provides a completely satisfactory answer to a question that has puzzled many people, a question a number of philosophers would probably agree was legitimate. It has been often asserted that explanations of physical phenomena can go only so far and that beyond a certain point matters must be left unexplained and accepted as unexplainable. We may be able to explain a certain phenomenon by showing it to be required by a given law of nature L_1 and then in turn explain L_1 by deriving it from some more basic law L_2. Eventually, however, we shall reach a basic law L_n that is not implied by any other true statement and is hence in principle unexplainable in the normal sense of that word. We are thus required to resign ourselves to the fact of the ultimate mystery of the universe; we shall never know why things are the way they are and why we have these basic laws and not others. Some philosophers would, of course, try to comfort us by saying that actually there is no occasion for regret since it is not the case that there is some precious piece of knowledge that is to remain for ever beyond our reach. The 'knowledge' we are after does not exist at all; hence not having it does not amount to being deprived of anything. To know the explanation of L_i means exactly having the ability to state the laws implying it. But since there is no law that implies any one of the basic laws of the universe there is nothing we actually fail to know. No sensible person feels frustrated because he does not know what is the highest integer. Even an omniscient person would not know this. He might also be supposed to lack the knowledge of the explanation of basic laws.

Most people, however, have not been happy with this kind of answer. No one will deny that if it is indeed the case that there is no empirical law from which L_i may be derived, then L_i cannot be explained in the sense that we may find the higher order generalization from which it can be shown to follow. But that need not stop us searching for an explanation in some other sense. The urge to solve the mystery of existence has been acute enough to give rise to attempts to show that the basic laws of nature are derivable from the laws of logic, or at least from the laws of thought or from such a fundamental principle as the principle of sufficient reason. Some have tried their hands at teleological explanations: they have assumed the existence of some 'obvious' goals to be attained and then attempted to argue that the existing laws of nature are the most suitable means of achieving these goals. However often such attempts may have failed in the past, our quest for an answer continues.

It could be claimed as a great merit of the extreme realist position that it provides a fully effective answer for those who crave for an explanation why the world is exactly as it is and not one of infinitely many other things it could have been. The answer is a radical one: the question why reality has this or that peculiar feature, while lacking others, cannot actually be raised. Reality embraces every conceivable state of affairs. The so-called basic laws of nature are not really unique since there are infinitely many other fully fledged worlds exemplifying all possible sets of laws.

What one may perhaps still feel inclined to ask is this: given all these worlds, with the widely different set of laws governing them, why am I in this particular world and not in some other? It is plausible to suggest that this question is meaningless. With few exceptions, philosophers agree that it makes no sense to wonder whether I could have been someone else. Neither does it make sense to ask whether some person P, characterized by what has been called his unique set of 'essential' properties, could have been anyone but P. It may well be claimed that when it comes to universes each one of their properties is essential, since a slight change in W_1 turns it into a distinct world W_2. This world must have the properties it has otherwise it would be another world. It makes no sense therefore to ask why I am in this world.

Objections to extreme realism

Now we have to ask the obvious converse of our previous question: are there any good arguments why we must not subscribe to extreme realism? The most immediate objection seems to be the immense extravagance involved in that thesis. Can a philosopher postulate at will any number whatsoever of universes? Lewis has seen this objection and proposed a way of dealing with it:

Realism about possible worlds might be thought implausible on grounds of parsimony, though this could not be a decisive argument against it. Distinguish two kinds of parsimony, however: qualitative and quantitative. A doctrine is qualitatively parsimonious if it keeps down the number of fundamentally different *kinds* of entity; if it posits sets alone rather than sets and unreduced numbers, or particles alone rather than particles and fields, or bodies alone or spirits alone rather than both bodies and spirits. A doctrine is quantitatively parsimonious if it keeps down the number of instances of the kinds it posits; if it posits 10^{29} electrons rather than 10^{37}, or spirits only for people rather than spirits for all animals. I subscribe to the general view that qualitative parsimony is good in a philosophical or empirical hypothesis; but I recognize no presumption whatever in favor of quantitative parsimony. My realism about possible worlds is merely quantitatively, not qualitatively, unparsimonious. You believe in our actual world already. I ask you to believe in more things of that kind, not in things of some new kind.[15]

This is strange reasoning indeed. If a scientist should propose an entirely new kind of elementary particle, one that travelled ten times faster than light, or that turned electrons that came into its vicinity into neutrons, or that had any other unheard-of properties, he would have to offer compelling arguments in support of his proposal before anyone would be willing to entertain it. But Lewis' vast assortment of universes contains infinitely many of the strangest types of particles. And yet are we to believe that to postulate the existence of all these universes does not amount to a qualitatively unparsimonious hypothesis? Furthermore, it is not at all clear what basis there is for Lewis to 'recognize no presumption whatever in favor of quantitative parsimony'. Suppose Neptune was observed to move in an orbit inexplicable in terms of the attraction of the known planets. Suppose also that one scientist postulates an additional planet which is too far away to be observed with present-day telescopes and is thus capable of fully accounting for Neptune's strange orbit. A second scientist achieves the same by postulating 17 different planets so situated as to partially cancel each others' effect. The two would differ in quantitative parsimony only, yet it seems that there would be a strong presumption in favour of the first scientist's hypothesis.

But perhaps what he could have said instead is that the principle of parsimony is essentially an injunction against the introduction of unwarranted entities. We are not supposed to postulate new entities before we have evidence for their existence. But then it might well be claimed that the principle does not apply to this special case. It is, after all, in the nature of things that within any world it is possible to interact only with whatever exists in that world; anything but the actual world is by definition absolutely inaccessible to us. It would therefore be senseless to legislate that we must not postulate other worlds before we have evidence for their existence. In addition, of course, Lewis could have also claimed that the principle of parsimony applies only to rival hypotheses that are of equal explanatory power. If the realist's claim that his hypothesis is of greater explanatory power than the non-realist's can be sustained then the principle does not necessarily apply to it.

Be that as it may, most philosophers who have objected to Lewis' view have done so on the general ground of its excessive wastefulness. They have found his position far too extreme and maintained that whatever its benefits they are outweighed by the disadvantage of having to commit ourselves to the existence of such immense stretches of reality. R. M. Adams has, however, raised some more specific objections. One of them is:

We normally believe that actuality as such is, absolutely considered, a special metaphysical status – that the actual is, absolutely considered, more real than the merely possible. We do not think that the difference in respect of actuality between Henry Kissinger and the Wizard of Oz is just a difference in their relations to us. [16]

However the realist need not be too disturbed by this objection. To begin with, he may reply that from my own subjective point of view there is good reason to treat Kissinger as someone more real than the Wizard of Oz, since the former inhabits the same world as I do; we can interact with each other and many of his policies may have had a direct impact on my life. Subjectively speaking, the Wizard of Oz – although very real in his own universe, and even from an absolute point of view as fully fledged a being as Kissinger – is as good as non-existent, since nothing he does can have the slightest effect on me, and vice versa. Different worlds are absolutely segregated causally from one another.

He might add to this that should it really follow from the realist position that the Wizard of Oz ought to be taken more seriously than he actually is, that should constitute no source of difficulty either. The purpose of philosophy is to find out by rigorous method what the truth is. Often its results clash with the common-sense view. In such cases it is reasonable to maintain that our relatively unexamined common-sense views should be abandoned to give way to the conclusions of rigorous philosophical analysis.

Adams has another objection, however, which is much stronger:

Our normal belief in the absoluteness of actuality is reflected in our value judgments too . . . I think that our very strong disapproval of the deliberate actualizing of evils similarly reflects a belief in the absolutely, and not just relatively, special status of the actual as such. Indeed, if we ask what is wrong with actualizing evils, since they will occur in some other possible world anyway if they don't occur in this one?', I doubt that the indexical theory can provide an answer which will be completely satisfying ethically. [17]

This is a stronger objection, because here we cannot reply that all we have is simply another situation in which logical analysis leads us to a conclusion that is incompatible with common sense and once more it is common sense that has to yield. I do not believe that Lewis or any other realist would advocate abolishing all ethical restraint, no matter how many logical arguments he had in favour of doing so.

Yet this objection, though interesting, is by no means conclusive. Lewis could defend his position against this attack; its success really depends on what meta-ethical view one subscribes to. According to one view, for instance, to be ethical is to act according to what is ultimately in one's own enlightened self-interest. By acting decently and compassionately I advance the cause of morality in the society in which I live, which in the end is bound to benefit me, since the higher the moral standards adhered to in a given society the better off its members are likely to be. Anyone then subscribing to this particular answer to the question 'Why should I be moral?' will have good enough reason not to actualize evils, but will have no reason to worry about what happens to creatures in other worlds with which we do not interact.

I would like now to consider another objection to the realist view, one which seems to be more decisive. Suppose we are about to launch a projectile and have determined on the basis of the simple laws of mechanics that it will hit the ground in spot L_1. Since these laws are thought to be firmly established we shall be confident in our prediction, even if something vital for our welfare depended on it, that L_1 is going to be the landing spot of our missile. Of course, there are infinitely many other spots in the universe besides L_1, and it is logically possible that any one of these will be hit by the missile; yet, given the vast amount of evidence supporting the universally accepted laws of mechanics, the missile's landing in any spot other than L_1 would violate a firmly established conclusion of inductive reasoning. Consequently we are convinced that no such unlawful event is going to take place. But that event, though empirically unlawful, is still logically possible, and we know that for any logically possible situation there corresponds a world in which that situation obtains. There is therefore an infinite number of worlds, W_1, W_2, . . . W_n, each perfectly identical to our world until now, so that the laws established inductively in each one imply that L_1 is going to be the terminal point of the projectile. Yet in all except one that projectile will of necessity fail to hit L_1. Since there is only one universe among infinitely many indistinguishable universes in which the missile does in fact arrive at L_1 as required by inductive reasoning, and in all the others the conclusions arrived at by standard empirical inference must turn out to be false, surely it ought to be rational to expect with virtual certainty that ours is also one of those worlds where induction is going to be violated in the present case. In a lottery in which there are a billion tickets, for instance, only one of which is going to win, if I hold only one ticket I am not if I am rational going to assert with confidence that I shall be the winner.

Let me hasten to add that I am not trying to discredit the inductive method in general. I am ready to go along with the suggestion that we are entitled to place our confidence in this unique method, to which we are all instinctively drawn even in the absence of any strong argument showing that our confidence is well placed. Undeniably, however, this could no longer be a tenable approach once it were found that it is positively contrary to logic to expect inductive reasoning to yield correct results. Now a non-realist at least seems to be able to maintain that there are no positive arguments against having any trust in induction. He is fully aware, of course, that inductive reasoning always leads to a prediction that the future is going to unfold in one particular way among infinitely many others. Yet he accepts the result of inductive reasoning, maintaining that although from a logical point of view L_2, L_3 and so on are as good landing spots as L_1, they are *not* by a long way equiprobably likely to be the actual landing spot in the real world. In fact, he maintains that the statement 'The event of the missile landing on L_1 is one that is going to occur in the actual world' is more likely to be true than the infinitely long statement, 'In the actual world the missile is going to land on L_2, or L_3 or . . . .'

I shall not inquire now into the question of what the basis might be for this kind of probability judgement and how confident we are supposed to be in its soundness. However, I should point out one important feature of our belief that all the other spots are more likely to be hit in non-actual worlds than in the actual world: it certainly does not violate the principle of insufficient reason. For suppose that someone accused the non-realist of violating elementary good sense since, when faced with infinitely many worlds that are objectively not in the least distinguishable from one another, he picks the one world which suits him subjectively – namely the one he inhabits – as precisely the one world in which induction is going to be complied with. The critic would claim that this is a most blatant violation of the principle of treating equal cases equally. The non-realist may well reject this charge by insisting that he is not assigning different probabilities to the occurrence of the same event in essentially similar situations. All the worlds under consideration are identical up to the time of the launching of the projectile, but there is one vast difference between our world and all the others: ours is the real world and the others do not exist at all.

Lewis, however, seems entirely defenceless against the same charge. He certainly could not make his position more tenable by claiming that he believes it to be a fundamental aspect of reality that events obey the laws we arrive at by using inductive reasoning. After all, each one of the infinitely many worlds under consideration is equally real, and we know that only in one of them is L_1 going to be the landing spot demanded by the inductively established laws. It is impossible to imagine a set of cases whose members qualify more for the status of being regarded equiprobable than our set here. By definition, all the worlds we are dealing with here are perfectly identical and become distinguishable from one another only after the landing of the missile. If we should insist that L_1 is more likely to be hit in our world, our counterparts will similarly insist that L_1 is more likely to be hit in their worlds. From an absolute point of view, each one of us has the same chance of having L_1 as the landing spot, which is practically zero. By the elementary principle of insufficient reason it seems absurd to maintain that a world arbitrarily chosen from among perfectly identical worlds has a diffrent chance from the others of turning out in a given way.

It seems therefore that according to the realist view of the status of possible worlds one cannot give a viable account of one's confidence in inductive reasoning. This in itself may constitute strong enough reason for rejecting that view.

It is important to take a careful look at what precisely our objection amounts to. It follows from logical consideration alone that there are infinitely many worlds W_1, W_2, . . . W_n which are perfectly identical up to time t. At time t each world differs from every other in that in one world the missile hits L_1, in another it hits L_2, and so on. Suppose we pick at random a world W_i and ask: will the missile land on L_1 in W_i, or rather on a spot other than L_1 in definite contravention of the inductively-established laws? Surely it must be regarded as virtually certain in the extreme realist view that it will land on a spot other than L_1. Let me stress once more that it is not now my intention to query the reliability of the inductive method in general. I am fully prepared to concede that for whatever reason, or even in the absence of any reason, we would not be unjustified in believing that all regularities that were taken in the past to represent laws of nature are going to continue into the future. The trouble is that from a realist position it is impossible to apply the principle of induction in a coherent manner. This is easily seen as soon as we look at matters objectively, that is, from a point of view which lies outside all the worlds.

Suppose we are determined to apply the principle of induction. Are we to say therefore that the missile is going to land on L_1 in all the worlds? Certainly not, for we have already stated that logic demands that there be infinitely many worlds in which the missile on this occasion behaved contrary to what is required by the laws firmly established by induction on past experience and came to rest in some spot other than L_1. Is there any rule that could help us to pick out the one exceptional world in which the missile continues to obey the laws established by standard empirical method, and thus in which it lands on L_1? It seems quite obvious that there exists no such defensible rule. As Lewis has clearly stated, there are no privileged worlds; objectively speaking, nothing distinguishes one world from any other. The probability of any specific spot being hit in any world must be the same.

But of course the attitude of all of us, including Lewis, is that the probability is exceedingly high that it is L_1 that is going to be hit in the actual world, and we are prepared to stake much that is precious to us on the proposition that this is so. In the non-realist view there is no difficulty in explaining coherently what we are doing. We may not be able to offer good justification for our belief in induction, but we have no difficulty in explaining how the principle applies. Admittedly, there are infinitely many worlds in which L_1 is not going to be hit. However, we apply the inductive principle to say that in the actual world L_1 is going to be the landing spot of the missile, assuming that induction applies to the privileged world, namely, a world that is the only world which really exists. This is also the way to look at matters from an absolute point of view since according to the non-realist, the viewpoint of the inhabitants of the actual world and the absolute point of view are identical.

It is hardly necessary to stress that the objection is entirely general. In every instance of inductive reasoning we conclude that some statement s_1, rather than any one of its contraries s_2, s_3 and so on, is going to be true. The difficulty for the realist is to state coherently the basis upon which he assumes that our world is the one world in which s_1, and not s_2 or s_3 and so on, is true. There are after all no more worlds in which s_1 is true than worlds in which s_2 is true, or in which s_3 is true, and so how can we have any great confidence in our prediction that s_1 is going to be true? The non-realist does not face this problem since he maintains that not all worlds are of equal status and, for whatever reason, s_1 is much more likely to be true in the unique real world than anywhere else.

The conclusion to be drawn is by no means entirely negative. The last argument, after all, does not show extreme realism to be logically defective. It shows only that even its most ardent advocates seem to have repudiated it in their everyday behaviour. The firm trust Lewis and his followers place in the reliability of predictions based on inductive reasoning is inconsistent with their affirmation of the fully fledged reality of all possible worlds. It is also to be noted that my argument does not undermine the effectiveness of realism in allaying any puzzlement over the question why the universe has the specific set of features it happens to exhibit and not one of the infinitely many other sets it could have exhibited.

Indeed, from a metaphysical perspective the most important point to emerge from our discussion of the status of possible worlds concerns the so-called mystery of existence, that is, why is the universe not other than it is? This question greatly exercised the minds of fourteenth-century philosophers but has also attracted the attention of some in the twentieth century, for example A. Eddington, who proposed that certain basic facts about the universe may be shown to follow from mathematical considerations alone. However, the majority of contemporary analytic philosophers do not regard a question such as why ultimately the universe is the way it is as a useful or even legitimate question. P. W. Bridgman, in his celebrated book *The Logic of Modern Physics*,[18] makes an impassioned plea that we desist from asking questions which, though they may on the surface appear penetrating and probing, are in fact devoid of meaning. He warns that the 'matter of meaningless questions is a very subtle thing which may poison our thoughts more than dealing with purely physical phenomena'. He then compiles a list of questions with which the reader may amuse himself by finding out whether they have meaning or not. Among the questions we find:

(11) Why does negative electricity attract positive?
(12) Why does nature obey laws?
(13) Is a universe possible in which the laws are different?[19]

The implication seems to be that all these questions are meaningless. Of course, not many philosophers subscribe any longer to Bridgman's extreme operationalistic standards of meaningfulness. Nevertheless, many will agree that questions (11), (12), (13) and their like are meaningless. The explanation why this is so may be said to be as follows:

1 If we assume that the attraction of positive and negative electric charges is a basic fact, it follows by definition that there is no true statement that refers to a more basic fact and implies the statement that opposite charges attract one another. Hence (11) cannot be explained in the standard way in which explanations are offered in science.

2 Assuming the illegitimacy of postulating any cosmic aims to be pursued, all teleological explanations are ruled out as illegitimate. There is no point in trying to show that certain states of affairs are best realized if the world has this or that basic property, since we must not postulate any desirable goals the universe is supposed to be striving for.

3 Empiricism bids us to maintain the complete separation of logic and experience. All knowledge about the world is a posteriori: an a posteriori statement is one that can be confirmed or disconfirmed only by experience and observation. Logic, mathematics and such 'necessary' principles as the principle of sufficient reason do not imply a single fact about the universe.

Now (1), (2) and (3) exhaust all the possibilities there might have been for explaining basic facts. We are thus forced to conclude that there can be no way of seeking an answer to the seemingly momentous question why the universe is as it is. In fact the question is devoid of meaning. We must not allow it to 'poison' our thoughts in the sense of our persisting in worrying about a question that can have no answer and can lead only to frustration and confusion.

My point is that this conclusion is unwarranted. I would like to emphasize that I do not now wish to question the soundness of (1), (2) or (3). What I do wish to question is the reasoning that, since certain kinds of answer to the ultimate question concerning the nature of the universe have been ruled out, no answer in principle is even possible. It is beyond our scope to decide that all possible avenues leading to a meaningful answer have already been explored, for we are not in a position at any given time to foresee the limits of new approaches that may be devised in the future. Our discussion of the doctrine of extreme realism provides a vivid illustration of this point. Though I have not the slightest wish to defend the doctrine nor any need to do so, it clearly provides an illustration that (1), (2) and (3) by no means exhaust all the possible ways in which the question of the ultimate nature of reality may be approached. Anyone to whom the doctrine appears plausible will maintain that the statement that negative electricity attracts positive does not follow from the laws of logic or mathematics; neither can it be shown that it has to be true in order that certain desirable states of affairs can be realized. However, puzzlement as to why reality has the peculiar feature the statement says that it has is quite unwarranted. Reality has no peculiar features. Reality embraces the fact that negative and positive charges repel one another as well as that they do not interact all, since worlds in which the former or the latter is the case are no less real than our own.

Thus the extreme realist allays our metaphysical worry in a most fundamental way. He removes altogether the basis for puzzlement over the question why reality has this or that special feature to the exclusion of others. Nothing is in fact excluded. Every logically possible state of affairs, every consistent set of laws, is instantiated by one of the infinitely many equally real universes.

6

The problem of universals and linguistic analysis

Universals: an elusive problem

The problem of universals, unlike the problems discussed in the previous two chapters, is a metaphysical problem which has a long history and which has excited the attention of most philosophers throughout the ages. However, progress has been rather slow in elucidating this issue because of the special difficulties involved in its handling. This should serve also as an explanation of why I have less to say about it than about nearly every other issue in this book. Part of the difficulty arises out of the fact that universals form a unique category which does not necessarily resemble any other category, and therefore any inference we might wish to make from characteristics of other items which all agree exist can always be defeated by claiming that we are trying to compare incomparables. Often, therefore, when a philosopher believes he has at last succeeded in gaining a grip on the problem, it slips out of his hands; the position he thought he had nailed down is easily qualified to render the attack made on it irrelevant. Universals are a rarefied species not easily captured in our conceptual net.

Let me illustrate. One of the well-known objections to the realist position has been that if, for instance, redness is something the roof of that cottage has, which is literally identical with the redness of a car parked many miles away, then it follows that the same thing is in two different places at the same time. But it is a well-known principle that the same thing cannot be in two different places at the same time. The realist, however, was able to repel this attack quite easily: the principle is known to apply to particulars, but there is no reason to assume that it is also binding upon universals.

This quick reply indicates clearly enough that indefinitely many other moves one might think of attempting will also fail. In general it will be useless to discover that F is an essential feature of all genuinely existing things and point out that universals lack this feature. The answer will be that F may be essential to all existing things that belong to categories basically different from the category of universals.

I should mention that other realists reacted differently to the above attack. They explained that as a matter of fact the universal redness is neither on the roof of the cottage nor on the surface of the car, since universals are not spatial entities at all. It is only the exemplification of redness that we find in different objects that are red. There is no reason why various exemplifications of the same universal should not occur at different locations. This reply makes it hard to devise useful arguments about this peculiar aspect of universals, arguments that are likely to advance us towards a resolution of our problem. There is certainly no hope that we shall be able to draw analogical inferences about the nature of the alleged relationship universals have to particulars since this relationship is, of course, sui generis, exhibited by no other pairs of entities.

It is not hard then, to see why the problem of universals is so elusive. A closer look at the realist's position reveals it to be much more guarded and qualified than it might appear at first sight. Those who insist that universals exist by no means intend to go so far as to claim that they exist in the same way that particulars do. It is a special kind of existence that realists wish to ascribe to universals – indeed, so special that their position may be compatible with the discovery of any number of properties of alleged universals, properties that everywhere else are inconsistent with existence.

It should be obvious that it is not much easier to attack nominalism. No matter how many features a realist may find, features characteristic of existing entities and which he succeeds in demonstrating to be possessed also by universals, he can never have enough. It is by definition impossible that universals should have all the features of particulars, and hence the nominalist can always refuse to grant universals the status which the realist claims for them. He may insist that one of the features which all admit is absent from universals must be possessed before something can be said to exist in any sense.

This brings us to the subject of linguistic analysis, the investigation of the properties of language with a view to using the results to establish some philosophical thesis. This method has been employed in all areas of philosophy, but because those wishing to investigate the issue of universals are considerably restricted with respect to the kinds of argument available to them, they may be forced to resort to this method more than others. I have used the term 'resort' to indicate that the method would not be everyone's first choice. This is because the use of linguistic analysis as a tool for establishing the nature of reality has a somewhat tenuous status.

I wish to touch upon the important meta-philosophical question whether the features of the English language may be assumed to provide evidence concerning the hard facts of the extra-linguistic world. Could it be relevant to the ontological status of anything how terms representing it are correctly used in everyday discourse? Philosophers of different persuasions differ widely about the right answer to this question. Some believe that careful linguistic analysis is the most fruitful method for investigating the ultimate nature of reality at the disposal of the philosopher. At the other extreme are those who think there is no reason to assume that the properties of the English language mirror the properties of facts that language is used to refer to.

I shall be brief on the subject of linguistic analysis because it has probably received more attention in the last few decades than any other method. I shall thus not attempt a comprehensive study of all aspects of the question of the relationship between language and philosophy in general, or even between language and ontology in particular. I do wish, however, to make what seems to me a very important point, albeit a fairly simple one, and yet one to which not much attention has been paid. Briefly, it is that linguistic analysis is an invaluable heuristic tool, which, on its own, however, may never be sufficient to establish any fact. When a certain feature of language is discovered that in itself is no guarantee that something parallel to it exists in reality and is reflected by the linguistic feature. I shall attempt to indicate what else needs to be done in any given instance to establish a correspondence between language and reality.

Realists and nominalists have often turned to language to discover how we talk about alleged universals and thus to infer their status. One famous realist argument is based on the fact that, while in 'Socrates was wise' the term 'wise' is merely a predicate, the sentence 'Wisdom was the most striking characteristic of Socrates' treats 'wisdom' as the subject, which seems to denote a thing that existed in Socrates. Nominalists have tried to defend themselves by arguing that all statements referring to universals can be translated into statements referring to particulars that are assigned a given property. In the next section I shall consider in detail this particular debate between realists and nominalists.

Translation into nominalistic language

Frank Jackson, in an interesting short note,[1] raises three objections to the nominalist's claim that it is never necessary to refer to a universal.

1 His first example alleged to create a difficulty is 'Red is a colour' which refers to 'red' and 'colour'. He considers the possibility of translating this into 'Necessarily, everything red is coloured', but he finds it unsatisfactory. The last sentence does not entail 'Red is a colour.' For if it did, then given that 'Necessarily, everything red is both shaped and extended' is true, it would follow that 'Red is a shape and an extension' was true as well, which is absurd.

2 His next example is:

(a)   Red resembles pink more than blue

which refers to three universals. He considers that a nominalist may want to claim (a) could be translated into

(b)   Necessarily anything red colour-resembles anything pink more than anything blue.

Jackson believes that this response is not satisfactory. He asks us to consider:

(a′)   The colour of ripe tomatoes resembles the colour associated with girl babies more than the colour associated with boy babies.

This is a true statement. Now if (b) were really equivalent to (a), as claimed by the nominalist, then clearly (a′) would have to be agreed to equal (b′):

(b′)   Necessarily anything with the colour of ripe tomatoes colour-resembles anything with the colour associated with girl babies more than anything with the colour associated with boy babies.

But Jackson maintains (b′) is certainly not equivalent to (a′) since (b′) is false. It is not necessarily true that tomatoes are red and the colour associated with different babies could certainly have been different.

3 Finally he asks us to consider:

(c)   The most conspicuous property of ripe tomatoes is a colour.

Jackson argues that (c) cannot be translated into:

(c′)   Everything with the most conspicuous property of ripe tomatoes is coloured.

Even if we ignore the term 'property' and agree to look upon (c′) as not causing any difficulties to the nominalists, the problem remains that (c′) is not an adequate translation of (c). The most conspicuous property of ripe tomatoes could possibly have been their smell, in which case (c) would be false, whereas (c′) could be true if it happened to be the case that everything that smells like tomatoes is coloured.

Thus Jackson claims to have produced three sentences that treat universals as entities and that cannot be translated adequately into a nominalistic language. This, he concludes, considerably strengthens the realist's position.

No doubt there will be readers who will point out that Jackson was far too hasty in arriving at his conclusion. Consider, for example, 'Red is a colour.' Why not suggest 'To be red is to be coloured'? Then again consider:

(a′)   The colour of ripe tomatoes resembles the colour associated with girl babies more than the colour associated with boy babies

which he has shown cannot be correctly translated into (b′). But why not translate it into:

(b*)   Anything coloured as ripe tomatoes *happen* to be coloured *necessarily* colour-resembles anything coloured in a way that baby girls *happen* to be associated with . . . ?

And finally we could consider that:

(c)   The most conspicuous property of ripe tomatoes is a colour

is to be translated as

(c*)   What is most conspicuous about ripe tomatoes is how they are coloured.

However, it may not be such an important question whether Jackson's examples do effectively illustrate his point since it seems there is indefinite scope for finding some example which it will not be possible to translate into a nominalistic language. These of course need not involve colour predicates but any of thousands of other predicates. Let us consider one example:

(d)   Politeness is a greater virtue than punctuality.

There does not seem an obvious way to translate (d) into a nominalistic language. It would certainly not be adequate to suggest:

(d′)   Anyone who is polite is more virtuous than anyone who is punctual.

since (d′) is obviously false. Suppose A is a worthless person of whom nothing good can be said except that he happens to be polite. On the other hand, B embodies all the desirable human qualities except that he is not very polite. On the other hand B is always meticulously punctual. We would not say that A was more virtuous than B. We might try:

(d″)   For any x and for any y, if x and y are equal in all their characteristics with the only exception that x is polite but not punctual when y is punctual and not polite, then x is more virtuous than y.

It indeed seems that (d) entails (d″); however, (d″) does not entail (d). According to (d) politeness is always a higher virtue than punctuality, and not only in the special case where x and y are identical in every other regard. That is, even in the extreme case of A and B the addition of politeness to the rest of A's properties reduces the degree of his unvirtuousness more than the addition of punctuality raises the virtuousness of B.

Another suggestion that may have initial plausibility would be to translate (d) into:

(d‴)   Any person who has been neither polite nor punctual becomes more virtuous by becoming polite than by becoming punctual.

But this is not adequate either. For one thing (d‴) does not imply that politeness is always a greater virtue than punctuality even in the context of persons who have been polite or punctual or both all their lives.

Let me consider one more attempt to translate (d) which may seem the most promising. I shall then explain why, in my opinion, this whole enterprise is not very useful. Consider:

(d⁗)   For anybody to be polite is more virtuous than for him to be punctual.

If this were an adequate translation, then obviously

(e)   Truthfulness is a greater virtue than x.

is correctly translated into

(e′)   For anybody to be truthful is to be more virtuous than for him to be x.

But there are many ways of objecting to this. One way is to consider two thoroughly wicked people X and Y, who differ mainly in one respect: X is quite candid about his ambition to obtain power over as many people as possible without the slightest regard to their interests or feelings, whereas Y, who has the same kind of ambition, is embarrassed to a certain degree and wants to hide it. There will be some who would argue that Y's lack of truthfulness is a sign of residual decency. Thus, even though Y may behave quite atrociously, he is somewhat ashamed of his own wickedness and thus claims to be acting ultimately for a good cause in order to fool not only others but even himself. X, however, has hit a moral bottom and no longer knows or cares at all about the difference between good and evil. Furthermore, it may be said that Y's reticence is bound to restrain him to some extent and make him avoid too conspicuous criminal acts.

Those who hold this view may argue that admittedly truthfulness is intrinsically nobler than x (where x is one of the less important virtues). Nevertheless, in the case of special people like X and Y, who are comparable as moral monsters, it we add truthfulness to X but not to Y, X is bound to be degraded even further by acquiring this quality, which considered on its own is a valuable virtue. Consequently (e) is true because truthfulness is indeed a greater virtue than politeness. Yet (e') is false, since it is not the case that for anybody to be truthful is for them to be more virtuous than to be x. Similarly, for example, it is true that gold is far more precious than aluminium and that a large chest of gold is greatly to be preferred to the same chest filled with aluminium. Nevertheless, my expensive motor boat may not rise more in value if we put a chest of gold in it than if it is loaded with a chest of aluminium; or it is not necessarily preferable for the boat to contain the former rather than the latter. A chest of gold is much heavier than a chest of aluminium, and under the weight of the former, but not the latter, the boat may sink to the bottom of the ocean and be irretrievably lost.

I realize that there may be people who would oppose the moral judgement just described and argue that an honest crook is preferable both morally and practically to a devious one. I shall not consider this matter any further since it is of hardly any importance to us. First of all, if (d) and (e) are not adequate counter-examples to the principle of the translatability of all sentences into a nominalistic language, that would show very little. Since there are indefinitely many predicates it would take an exceedingly long time before we could examine a sufficient number of putative counter-examples and come to a reasonably well-founded conclusion concerning the status of this principle. But what is really important to realize is that the discussion we have had so far is of little relevance. The crucial point that must be understood is that the whole question of the translatability of sentences into a nominalistic language is devoid of genuine philosophical interest. I shall try to show that even if the principle is false, and even if there are many sentences that make essential and ineliminable reference to universals, the case of the nominalist is not thereby weakened.

Linguistic phenomena and the nature of reality

Let us begin by considering an argument by A. Prior that also concerns the question of what kinds of thing exist. Prior holds the view that propositions do not exist. In the course of discussing his thesis he considers:

(f)   The proposition that the sun is hot was true before anyone asserted it.

(f) makes references to propositions and hence Prior thinks it suggests that propositions do exist. This, however, is not so, he claims, because (f) can be translated into:

(g)   The sun was hot before anyone said so.

Given that (f) and (g) are logically equivalent, and seeing that (g) makes no reference to propositions, we can continue to maintain that it is not necessary ever to use a sentence referring to propositions, as well as that propositions do not exist.

We should now consider for a moment what we would say to someone who objected to Prior by asking us to assume that the following definitions have been generally accepted:

tomeating   = eating tomatoes
tomcooking   = cooking tomatoes
tombuying   = buying tomatoes etc.

Under such circumstances it would never be necessary to mention the word 'tomato', though we could fully describe all facts that involved tomatoes. The objector would thus ask: would Prior agree to the absurd suggestion that under these circumstances we should be committed to the view that tomatoes do not exist either? Surely not, but then there is no reason to hold that the possibility of translating (f) into (g) supports the view of those who deny the existence of propositions.

I believe few would agree that this is a sound objection. However, to state correctly what precisely is wrong with the objection will require some thought. For example, the obvious point that the word 'tomeating' is not an integral part of the English language does not invalidate the objection. The English language as it happens to be at the moment is surely not of any special significance. First of all, the objector could argue that as there are more than 2000 living languages in the world today as well as some obscure languages no longer spoken by anyone, if a philologist came along and made a strange claim about an esoteric language we know nothing of, then many of us would not have a criterion by which to measure the likelihood of his being truthful. In particular, if he told us that in the language in question it is actually the case that the word 'tomato' is never used because of the availability of terms like 'tomeating', I would certainly not feel any confidence in opposing him, not being able to cite any good reason why no language could have such a property. But are we then to say that speakers of English may not – while speakers of some other languages may – arrive at certain ontological conclusions? Surely the nature of reality does not vary with different languages.

Secondly, the English language changes all the time. Scientists, lawyers, journalists and others who feel the need for new words to refer to new concepts that emerge in the area of their expertise introduce such words without apology. Why then should a philosopher whose ontology has no room for certain entities not be permitted to introduce new words to suit his needs?

But what is wrong with this objection is that whether it is possible or not to eliminate a certain word cannot as such be relevant to the question whether a certain feature of reality exists. Let me explain. If we look at a person A, who has been described as 'tomeating', and a person B, of whom it has been said that he is eating chocolate, we cannot help observing that although the two descriptions seem to assign different activities to A and B their behaviour in fact has many identical features, namely, those characteristic of ingesting food. At the same time there are aspects of their activity which differ to the extent that tomatoes differ from chocolate. A's activity therefore naturally splits into two parts: the first one he shares with everyone who consumes food and the second is specific to the kind of food he is partaking of. Using a single term to describe A's behaviour does not disguise the fact that what A and B are doing is identical in that they are both eating, and different in what they are eating. It is quite correct to insist therefore that the reason why 'A is tomeating' is true is because it corresponds to the objective facts that A is engaged in the intake of food and that the particular food he is eating is tomatoes.

The situation is radically different in Prior's case. The possibility of expressing by (g) exactly what has been said by (f) is of substantial significance. The fact that the word 'proposition' can be dispensed with, and more particularly the way in which it can be dispensed with, reflects a unique feature of the concept of a proposition not shared by anything else. The reason I can avoid making a reference to 'proposition' is that whenever I affirm that something is the case, I of necessity affirm the proposition that something is the case. It follows from the very nature of a proposition that I can simply assert that the sun is hot, and thereby actually give voice to the proposition that the sun is hot, without having to mention that this is what I am doing. The eliminability of the term 'proposition' from (f) by translating it into (g) is a genuine reflection of an intrinsic feature of propositions themselves, namely, that when I am asserting that p what I am actually doing is asserting the proposition that p is true.

Now it is possible to see what is so fundamentally wrong with the well-known realist's argument discussed by Jackson. Let us assume that he is right and that, using the vocabulary now available in the English language, it is indeed impossible to construct a nominalistic sentence that would be the exact equivalent of 'Red is a colour.' Surely this is of no significance so long as it is not construed as a genuine reflection of some describable feature of the notions of 'red' or 'colour' themselves. But no such feature seems to suggest itself. Therefore, as long as we find no obstacles to defining a new term with whose aid we can construct the desired sentences, our present inability to do so is to be ascribed to a mere accidental feature of the language. And of course there are no obstacles to doing so; in fact there are many ways in which the task may be accomplished.

Earlier I mentioned that Jackson considered translating the sentence in question into 'Necessarily everything red is coloured', but rejected this as inadequate since it is also true that 'Necessarily everything red is both shaped and extended' and hence we would be committed to the absurd 'Red is a shape and an extension.' To overcome this difficulty, we need only to have two concepts of necessity, Nec_A and Nec_B, where it is made clear that Nec_A (x) $(Fx \supset Gx)$ says something about the nature of F – it asserts that F-ness essentially amounts to G-ness; while Nec_B (x) $(Fx \supset Gx)$ says something about the nature of particulars that have F – it asserts that they are the kind of thing that must also have G. Clearly, then, it is correct to say that 'Nec_A everything red is coloured' which is equivalent to 'Red is a colour.' On the other hand, we are entitled to say only 'Nec_B everything red is shaped and extended' which of course is not equivalent to 'Red is a shape and an extension.'

Assuming that we are permitted to use words that do not happen to be currently a part of the English language, nothing should be untranslatable into a nominalistic language. Consider again

(e)   Truthfulness is a greater virtue than x.

We have considered the suggestion that it may be translated as

(e′)   For anybody to be truthful is more virtuous than for him to be x

but found it objectionable. The objection is, however, easily overcome by introducing two concepts to correspond to 'more virtuous$_A$' and 'more virtuous$_B$'. When we say that 'X is more virtuous$_A$ than Y' we shall mean that X itself is superior in virtue to Y. However, when we say that 'X is more virtuous$_B$ than Y' we shall mean that X possesses a virtue Y lacks that is intrinsically a superior quality; however, X himself, because of a special condition that may prevail, does not have his moral character enhanced by possessing this virtue. It should then be clear that, if in (e′) we use 'more virtuous$_B$', the objection we have raised before no longer applies.

The basic difference we have found between the two issues reviewed suggests a simple but quite important conclusion. A philosopher should certainly pay close attention to the characteristics of the English language. The discovery of some interesting linguistic phenomenon should alert him to the possibility that it may be a symptom of a parallel feature of reality. The importance of a linguistic peculiarity thus lies in the fact that it often serves as a clue to some extra-linguistic, metaphysical fact. Thus one must not stop as soon as one has discovered something noteworthy about the way we speak. One must continue by asking: are we confronted here with a property of language that truly mirrors something in reality? Can we trace the extra-linguistic facts that have apparently imposed upon our language the peculiar feature we have discovered?

In other words, the properties of language, even the most general and fundamental ones, are of no interest in themselves to the metaphysician. They are significant to him only in so far as they may lead to the discovery of some independently characterizable fact, one whose reality is not solely confined to a given property of the language.

As I have already indicated, it is not my intention to give a full account of all aspects of linguistic analysis in its role as an aid to discovering the furniture of the universe; however, I shall attempt to make at least one more point. It would seem reasonable to expect that a feature of the English language that is not found in all other languages is, from a metaphysician's point of view, an accidental feature. On the other hand, one that characterizes all languages may confidently be expected to reflect some genuine aspect of reality. This is indeed often the case, but not always, as we shall see. In some instances where we are clearly confronted with a linguistic phenomenon that is peculiar to a few languages only, it is possible to explain why, even though the phenomenon in question has its counterpart in the extra-linguistic world, many languages in fact fail to register it. Then again, in some cases a universally shared linguistic property may be shown not to have been imposed on all languages by external reality. This constitutes one of the factors that complicates the task of conducting metaphysical inquiry via linguistic analysis. It is not sufficient to discover some phenomenon exhibited by the English language, nor is it sufficient to establish that this is or is not a universal linguistic phenomenon. We have to probe deeper before we know whether a given linguistic phenomenon is indicative of some genuine ontological truth.

The limitations of linguistic analysis

1 Since ancient times philosophers have held that there is a basic ontological difference between individuals such as oranges, bricks or houses on the one hand, and stuff or matter such as water, metal or wood on the other. Much of the argument over this distinction has been based on linguistic analysis. There is, for example, a well-defined distinction in English between terms and phrases that have the grammatical features of count nouns, which are nouns that are coupled with 'many' and 'few' (in contradistinction to the noun 'water', for example, which is used with 'much' and 'little'), and phrases that are mass nouns (which among other things lack the contrast between plural and singular).

Although I have not found it asked anywhere in that part of the vast literature on the subject that I have read, a most obvious question seems to be: do these grammatical distinctions exist in all languages? The answer is 'Definitely not'. To name but two languages, in Hebrew and Hungarian there are several expressions denoting 'great quantity', but the distinction marked by the English words 'many' and 'much' is not reflected. In Hungarian, for example, the most frequent word for 'great quantity' is *sok*, and it may be applied to water and metal just as well as to tables and chairs. The same holds true for words that stand for 'small quantity'.

Earlier, however, I claimed that the most elementary point about theoretical attempts to arrive at ontological conclusions from a study of language is that before we do anything else we must make sure that we are not confronted merely with an accidental feature of language. It would seem that a linguistic phenomenon exhibited by some languages but not by others cannot be claimed to have been imposed by reality upon the language that does exhibit it, for why then is it absent from others?

The answer must be that it is one of the complicating factors in the study of reality via language, as I have indicated before, that there is no such simple rule that no linguistic phenomenon not shared by all languages can have ontological significance. In our particular case, the proponents of the view that there is a fundamental difference between particulars and matter will claim that this difference is echoed by English but not by some other languages that are plainly not sensitive enough to have registered this feature. It may be pointed out that after all no language is rich enough to represent all the distinctions that exist in nature. There are many languages that have considerably fewer colour-words than English, even though it is undoubtedly true that the various distinctions made in English stand for real distinctions that exist among colours. Or there are many more species of animals as well as plants than are acknowledged in any language, which again shows that no language is rich enough to reflect the lushness of nature.

When it comes to 'much' and 'many', it may be claimed that those languages that do not have counterparts for these words simply lack the refinement to give expression to a real and quite important distinction between different categories of things. How is this claim justified? One quick way seems to be to point out that an English speaker who, for instance, has never before heard any reference to a large quantity of oil or to a large quantity of teacups will quite unerringly say 'much oil' and 'many teacups'. This is not so, for example, with someone proficient in German, who is not likely to know whether *die*, *der* or *das* should precede a word he has not heard used before. It is quite reasonable to explain this by saying that 'many' and 'much' mark real differences that exist in nature, which once understood make it obvious that oil belongs to one category and teacups to another.

2   As we know, the issue of universals arose from the fact that all sentences are of the subject – predicate form, which led to the desire to distinguish between the entities that these two represent. The subject term usually stands for a particular, while the predicate, it was assumed, stands for something else – also a thing, but a more abstract thing, a universal, which is exemplified by the particular in question. Bertrand Russell has advanced the suggestion that the issue would never have arisen in a language in which there were no predicates at all. He is not concerned whether there exist any such natural languages, and the likelihood that all natural languages distinguish between subjects and predicates does not intimidate him. He finds it sufficient if we are merely able to conceive of an artificial language in which the distinction

is absent. Thus Russell suggests that 'white' could be treated as the proper name of a particular, various parts of which may be found in different places. Instead of saying 'This wall is white', which refers to the wall and ascribes to it the property of being white, we would use 'White and wall are there', which is not assigning whiteness to the wall any more than wallness to the white, but points only to two particulars located side by side.

Russell's example surely shows his approach to be radically different from that of those who believe that the possibility or impossibility of eliminating references to universals is of serious metaphysical significance. He is clearly of the opinion that even one of the most fundamental features of language, namely the division of sentences into subject term and predicate term, need not be taken as a reflection of a genuine ontological difference. Neither is he concerned by the fact that possibly all languages possess this feature. It suffices that we should be able to suggest an artificial language in which this distinction does not exist for us to conclude that the feature in question was not imposed upon the spoken language by reality. As long as we can lay down generally applicable rules of translation we are dealing with a legitimate language.

3   This is a somewhat less important point but may still be worth stating. In order to demonstrate that a given linguistic feature does not reflect an aspect of reality itself it is not invariably necessary to find or construct a language free of that feature. Let us consider briefly a point made by D. Greenslee that it is a part of the definition of universals that they are 'things *common* to other things'.[2] He then raises the objection that many things we regard as particulars are common to a variety of things; for example, a man can be a member of different clubs and thus be common to many clubs, a fence can be common to bordering properties and so on. His answer is that universals are common to things in an 'appropriate sense'. The appropriate sense is just the sense in which a universal is said to be common to the different things it qualifies.

Some may find this objectionable. It may seem that what Greenslee is saying makes no more sense than if we said that '*a* is red' and '*b* is red' *assign different* properties to *a* and *b*, since the sense in which *a* is red is unique to *a*'s being red while *b* is red exactly in the sense in which *b* is red. This would not be quite fair. What Greenslee is saying is that, if we stop focusing on the words alone and do not allow ourselves to be misled by the fact that the same term 'common' is used in different contexts but instead pay attention to the sense of that expression, we are bound to realize that a man's relation to the different clubs he belongs to is basically different to the relation of 'whiteness' to the different surfaces it belongs to.

Thus what Greenslee is trying to say, I believe, is that it can be seen without the aid of any other languages that the use of the word 'common' in different contexts is incapable of masking the actual difference in the relations themselves. It can be seen as soon as we go beyond the word and look at the relations it represents.

4   Finally, we shall look at an important example which suggests that the scope of inferences to be drawn from the properties of languages about the nature of reality is even more severely limited. The second example above was taken to show that even when we find a feature shared by all natural languages, we cannot be certain that we are confronted with a genuine reflection of a feature of reality so long as we are able to invent a language not possessing this feature. Still we would be strongly inclined to say that not just any language will do: it has to be rich enough for us to convey through it everything we can convey in natural languages. Now we shall find that even this may not be required under all circumstances.

As we have seen in chapter 4, one of the great ontological issues is the question whether there exists a moving NOW, and whether it is correct to maintain that events and moments undergo real changes, for example when they first have the temporal property of futurity and shed it to acquire the property of presentness. Without attempting now to support one or other side of this debate, I should like to refer to the universally acknowledged fact that English, in common with most languages, contains not one, not a few, but indefinitely many expressions that clearly assign movement to time. 'The day of judgement is *coming* (*approaching*)', 'The laser age has *arrived*' and 'World War II is *receding* further and further into the past' are common examples, as is 'I have *become* middle-aged and time seems to have *speeded up.*' We should be justified in saying therefore that if any linguistic phenomenon is ever to be taken as evidence for some feature of reality, then the movement of time relative to the NOW must surely be such a feature since it is hard to think of any other metaphysical hypothesis for which language provides so much evidence. Nevertheless, many philosophers, including self-confessed practitioners of ordinary language philosophy, have permitted themselves to ignore the seemingly overwhelming evidence provided by language.

We must, of course, remind ourselves that, beginning with Russell, philosophers have suggested ways in which some expressions that seem to point towards a transient nature of time can be translated into sentences that imply only static temporal properties. For example, as we saw, Reichenbach suggested that a sentence like 'E is occurring now', which apparently refers to a momentary property of E, a property E did not have a while ago when it had futurity and which it is about to lose in the next instant, can be translated as 'E's occurrence is simultaneous with this utterance', where the word 'this' points at the utterance just being made. Of course, Reichenbach's sentence assigns no transient properties to E, since if it is ever true that E is simultaneous with a particular utterance made at a specific time, then it is for ever true. Nevertheless, Reichenbach's sentence is not part of ordinary English, nor most probably of any other language either. But there is a much more serious difficulty: there are sentences which cannot be translated into this kind of language even by adopting Reichenbach's ingenious but artificial device. For instance, Reichenbach might suggest that 'World War II is receding further and further into the past' could be translated perhaps into 'World War II is earlier than this utterance and even earlier than any utterance considerably later than this utterance.' But obviously this is not a full translation, since the sentence 'The number 3 is earlier than the number 7 and much earlier than the number 27' is true and carries no suggestion that anything is receding or advancing.

Reichenbach will admit this; his sentence indeed does not carry the connotation that something is moving, but this is just as well since nothing is in fact moving. Thus his translation of the sentence about World War II is a partial translation only. It expresses that which can be expressed and omits that which makes no sense.

Thus we have here a seemingly extraordinary situation. Language is full of expressions clearly implying that time moves. Nevertheless, Russellians refuse to regard this as a crucial factor in determining whether there are transient temporal properties. They construct an artificial language from which all reference to such properties is eliminated. The question that arises at once is: since this new way of phrasing certain sets of sentences, apart from being artificial – in the sense that no one, not even the followers of Russell, ever uses it – has also the critical disadvantage of failing to facilitate the expression of a number of things we are able to say in a natural language such as English, is it not evident that time's motion is a genuine feature of the universe that is successfully mirrored in natural languages? Does this not show that Russellians expurgate certain vital phrases from our language which do express some fundamental aspects of temporal reality?

In reply Russellians will concede that the linguistic features in question do indeed carry extra-linguistic implications. However, what we can take as being implied is not necessarily some real property of time itself but some deeply entrenched property of our own mind. It is undeniably the case that we think of time as moving, and this is reflected in our temporal discourse. Russellians claim however to have constructed a way of talking that fully reflects the nature of time itself without also reflecting anything extraneous imposed upon time by our minds.

We have thus seen some of the ways in which we are restricted in making inferences about the nature of reality from our discovery of various features of language. As to the problem of universals, the issue remains elusive; progress will continue to be slow, as it is difficult to determine which aspect of reality might contain the clues to the resolution of the problem.

7

Other minds and explanations

Other minds: a unique problem

The metaphysical belief that others have minds differs from other deeply entrenched metaphysical beliefs, such as in the existence of an external world or that the universe did not spring into being five minutes ago or in the uniformity of nature. Nowadays, the average person untutored in philosophy is willing to concede that there may be some basis for doubting that everybody is minded. The construction of increasingly more sophisticated computers capable of simulating human behaviour more and more precisely has vividly brought home to many people that the kind of behaviour that tends to be unquestioningly taken as manifesting the capacity to have sensations, to experience pain and pleasure and to possess consciousness and awareness is not necessarily really connected to any such capacity. We now have actual cases of physical systems that exhibit such behaviour to different degrees, and yet most of us would not ascribe mental properties to them. This is not to say that the development of the computer has affected the objective status of the doubt about the existence of other minds, only that it has facilitated a more effective way of explaining it.

As for the alleviation of this doubt, I believe it is fair to say that with the decline in the popularity of the Wittgensteinian Criterial Argument more philosophers subscribe nowadays to the view that this is best achieved by the good old inductive argument. In this chapter I shall discuss various problems connected with the different methods of applying induction to our problem. Finally I shall advance a somewhat novel suggestion about how the use of induction may help lend adequate credibility to the belief in other minds.

Allegedly non-inductive arguments

I shall begin by making a point which deserves at least a brief mention: not only are there a considerable number of philosophers who maintain that the right solution to the problem of other minds is based on an inductive argument, but several philosophers who claim to be subscribing to some different solution can also be shown to be actually relying on a disguised form of an inductive argument. One fairly well-known approach of this kind attempts to equate the status of the hypothesis that others have a mind with that of the scientific hypothesis postulating the existence of theoretical entities. It will be quite easy to show, however, that the attempt fails and that the argument employed reduces to no more than an inductive argument.

The suggestion that we might postulate the existence of other minds just as a physicist postulates the existence of theoretical entities is based on the idea that when grappling with philosophical problems it is helpful to look for the key to the solution among the results of modern science. As I have said before, the idea that we should try and employ in philosophy some of what we have learned from the practices of scientists is a sound idea as such, but it must not be assumed that it will always work. Metaphysical hypotheses are, after all, related to experience in a way fundamentally different to that of scientific hypotheses.

Let us look at the specific suggestion of C. S. Chihara and J. A. Fodor on the way the existence of other minds might be postulated to account for people's overt behaviour.[1] These two authors share with Wittgenstein the view that the inductive argument for the existence of other minds is faulty, and they scrutinize Wittgenstein's own alternative argument. According to Wittgenstein, people's manifest behaviour constitutes no mere evidence but indeed the very criterion that they have inner experiences. One reason for saying this is that our way of forming such a concept as pain is through the pain behaviour exhibited by people who are supposed to be in pain. Thus, when a person exhibits pain behaviour in a manner in which simulation must be ruled out, it is simply conceptually true that he is experiencing pain. Chihara and Fodor raise a number of objections to this view, objections which sound quite reasonable, and then advance their own theory. In their opinion, behaviour is not a criterion for mental properties; it is correct to look upon behaviour as evidence for mental properties but not in the inductive sense, rather in the sense in which various observations in physics are taken as evidence for the existence of theoretical entities postulated in order to explain these observations. Chihara and Fodor use the example of the Wilson cloud-chamber. Just as Wilson regarded the formation of tiny, thin bands of fog on the glass surface of his instrument as indicative of the passage of charged particles through the chamber, so pain behaviour should be regarded as indicative of the existence of experienced pain. Chihara and Fodor say:

On this view, our success in accounting for the behavior on the basis of which mental predicates are applied might properly be thought of as supplying *evidence* for the existence of the mental processes we postulate. It does so by attesting to the adequacy of the conceptual system in terms of which the processes are understood. The behavior would be, in that sense, analogous to the cloud-chamber track on the basis of which we detect the presence and motion of charged particles. Correspondingly, the conceptual system is analogous to the physical *theory* in which the properties of these particles are formulated.[2]

It seems that Chihara and Fodor have seriously misunderstood scientific methodology and the way in which theoretical entities are introduced into science. The postulation of entities additional to those already observed is never regarded as justified unless it brings about a reduction in the number of assumptions which would otherwise have to be made. If, for example, we do not postulate the existence of charged particles, then the appearance of thin bands of fog on the glass surface of the Wilson cloud-chamber under his experimental conditions would have to be accepted as an independent law of nature, supported by nothing else but this experiment along with a number of other phenomena p_1, p_2, . . . which would each have to be separately established by experiment. But as soon as we postulate the existence of charged particles and assign a few elementary properties to them, the formation of fog tracks on the walls of the Wilson cloud-chamber under specified conditions as well as p_1, p_2, . . . can be inferred. Hence by introducing the charged particles we gain in that we reduce the number of logically independent laws of nature.

Consider another somewhat more elementary example, the kinetic theory of gases. The following are three of the laws which are derivable within that theory:

1   The law connecting the volume, pressure and temperature of a gas.
2   The law describing the relationship between the coefficient of viscosity and the density of a gas.
3   The law describing the coefficient of viscosity and the specific heat of a gas.

Without the kinetic theory these cannot be derived one from another, for the three laws are independent of one another and have to be established separately, each one through the experiment relevant to it. But if we postulate that a gas is not a continuous substance but consists of discrete particles with certain properties familiar from mechanics, we no longer need three separate sets of experiments to establish (1), (2) and (3). These laws follow from the nature of the ultimate constituents of the gas we postulate.

However, the postulation of mental properties cannot be similarly justified since it does not achieve any economy. Consider three laws in the science of human behaviour:

1   Stimulus S_1 gives rise to R_1.
2   S_2 evokes R_2.
3   S_3 evokes R_3.

If it is not assumed that a given body B is a mind-possessor, the three laws have to be established independently of one another, either by observing that whenever B is subjected to stimuli S_1, S_2 and S_3 it responds by R_1, R_2 and R_3 respectively, or by assuming that B obeys the same set of stimulus – response laws as some other body for which we have already established that laws (1), (2) and (3) apply. Now suppose we assume that B has a mind. From this alone it surely does not follow that (1), (2) and (3) apply. Indeed, we shall not know that these laws govern B's behaviour unless we experiment with B to establish that they govern the behaviour of some other body. Of course, the other body may be our own, but if we already know that we ourselves obey (1), (2) and (3) we may infer that B also obeys these laws without having to assume that B is a mind-possessor like ourselves but merely by assuming that he is subject to the same stimulus – response laws as we are.

It might be claimed that in our own case we do not necessarily need three separate sets of experiments to establish that (1), (2) and (3) apply to us. Having a mind renders us capable of establishing by introspection some psychological laws which apply to us. Simply by imagining how it would feel if we were subjected to S_1 we may become convinced that our response would be R_1. This of course may be true. But it does not change the fact that the inference that B also obeys (1), (2) and (3) is made in exactly the same way irrespective of whether B is assumed to have a mind or not. Even if B is not supposed to have a mind he is supposed to obey the same laws of stimulus and response as I do. Mental properties are therefore quite redundant as far as accounting for B's behaviour is concerned. We might still be inclined to assign these properties to him on the basis of the argument that since all the stimulus – response laws that apply to me apply also to him, why should we not assume that B also resembles me in having a mind? But in this case we would be using inductive reasoning. It is obvious that if Chihara and Fodor do not wish to rely on the force of plain inductive reasoning alone they have no basis at all upon which to establish their belief in other minds.

We may look for a moment at an example provided by Paul Ziff. He also believes that the defence he advances is quite different from plain induction. He says 'What is in force and active here then is not a silly single hypothesis that there are other minds, this naively supposed to be somehow based on an unexplored analogy.'[3] His defence claims to be based on the superior simplicity and reasonableness of the conceptual scheme that assigns minds to others and contrasts with the strangeness and inexplicability of the scheme that denies others minds:

The question again then is: could the other one and I relevantly differ only in this: I do and he does not have a mind? Suppose we opt for yes. Then how do we account for the fantastic state of affairs? Why do I have a mind? Why doesn't he have a mind? Do minds just come and go in the universe? Did one just happen to alight in my head? Is there no bait for this bird?[4]

Inductive reasoning, we should remind ourselves, consists in the argument that if everything so far observed which had the property A also had the property B, then we should assume that everything in existence which has A also has B. It is based on the claim that it is more reasonable to assume this kind of uniformity than to assume that some things which have A have B and others which have A do not have B. When we can produce a reason for regarding the observed As as having a special feature that explains why they should also have B, while some other As without this feature may not have B, then we are entitled to say that although all the observed As had B there may yet be As that do not have B. Otherwise rationality requires that we assume the unobserved As are like the observed ones. In other words, inductive reasoning is based exactly on those sentiments expressed by Ziff in the quoted passages. His defence is in no way different from the inductive defence.

Anyone who rejects this argument and feels that there is nothing inexplicable about some As being Bs and other As not being Bs and that the unobserved may be different from the observed – in other words, anyone who rejects the validity of inductive reasoning – has no further argument to fall back upon to explain why it is better to assume that others have a mind than that they do not. Strangely enough, Ziff thinks otherwise. He thinks, for example, that the efficacy of aspirin, mescaline and opium is somehow indicative of the existence of other minds. But the efficacy of these and thousands of other drugs is not in the least indicative of anything to someone who denies the validity of induction in establishing the existence of other minds. Various drugs induce in me a great variety of inner experiences; they also affect in all sorts of ways my physical behaviour. In the case of others I make no assumptions about the ways in which their minds are affected. I assume only that their behaviour is affected in the same way as mine is.

Plantinga's objection to the inductive argument

In *God and Other Minds* A. Plantinga produces an unusual and even surprising argument to show that the form of inductive reasoning leading to the conclusion that other minds exist is such that it violates a basic principle and is therefore illegitimate. Remarkably enough, even though the rules of induction have been subject to much study in the past 30 or 40 years, Plantinga's elementary principle has never been heard of before. Yet he argues that there is a decisive reason why we must accept it. Subsequently his far-reaching conclusion is that in view of the fact that the only solution to the problem of other minds we can hope for is that involving induction, we are now left without any prospects for solving the problem. Thus the existence of other minds is to be accepted without any justification.

It is to be noted that Plantinga's claim to have demolished the inductive reasoning designed to establish the existence of other minds has not impressed many philosophers. As we shall soon see, his claim has no foundation whatever. Yet it is useful to look at it in some detail, for it provides an excellent illustration of the hazards associated with the method of counter-examples as discussed in chapter 5. Here we shall see a vivid example of a principle constructed without any inquiry at all into its whys and wherefores and with the sole purpose of formally accommodating a counter-example. It should be obvious that there is no good reason for accepting the principle.

Plantinga formulates the inductive argument for other minds in the following way:

Every case of pain-behaviour such that I have determined by observation whether or not it was accompanied by pain in the body displaying it, *was* accompanied by pain in that body.

Hence

probably every case of pain-behaviour is accompanied by pain in the body displaying it.[5]

We shall denote this as argument (O). The premiss of (O) obviously refers to the pain-behaviour of my own body, since it is only thus that I can actually determine whether or not it was accompanied by pain. For a moment it might seem that the premiss of (O) is not necessarily true, since there might have been occasions on which I have merely simulated pain-behaviour. This, however, is easily taken care of. Pain-behaviour is supposed to include microscopic changes in my blood and nervous system and these may safely be taken to be absent – no matter how good an actor I am – in cases of pretended pain.

Plantinga, however, claims to have found a fundamental objection to argument (O), namely that it violates what he calls Principle (A).

(A) = A simple inductive argument is acceptable only if it is logically possible that its sample class contain a counter-instance to its conclusion.

Before we examine the reason that allegedly compels us to adopt Principle (A) we may ask how Plantinga's version of the argument for the existence of other minds violates it. Plantinga reminds us that it is logically possible for others to feel pain in my body. Thus there could never be counter-evidence to the claim that all pain-behaviour of my body is accompanied by pain in my body. For suppose that my body manifested pain-behaviour but I definitely did not feel any pain. I would not have any evidence that this was a case of pain-behaviour in my body not accompanied by pain in my body because I could never have evidence that concurrently no one else in the world experienced pain in my body.

Now to the reason why Principle (A) must be adopted. Plantinga argues that if we were allowed to violate it then the following argument (R) would have to be accepted:

(R) = Every physical object of which it has been determined whether or not it has ever been conceived (i.e. perceived or thought of) has been conceived. Therefore: probably every physical object *has* been conceived.

But argument (R) is obviously absurd. In order to avoid it some such principle as (A), which it violates, must be adopted.

A. Hyslop and F. C. Jackson have attempted to meet this difficulty by reformulating (O) in such a manner that it does not violate principle (A):

Every case of pain-behaviour such that I have determined by observation whether or not it was accompanied by a pain in the body displaying it *which belonged to the person whose body displayed the pain-behaviour*, was so accompanied which leads to:

> Probably every case of pain-behaviour is accompanied by a pain which is in the body displaying it and which belongs to the person whose body is displaying it. [6]

This, they claim, constitutes a simple inductive argument which does not violate (A) because it is possible to determine by observation that my body does not contain pain which belongs to the person whose body it is, that is, that it does not contain a pain of mine.

But the reformulation does not really help. It is logically possible that the same body belonged to the same extent to two different minds. A counter-instance to the conclusion would not be possible because even if I did not feel pain when my body displayed pain-behaviour it would still be possible that the mind sharing my body felt it. I have no evidence that such a mind does not exist.

But the way out of this difficulty would seem to be to resort to the well-known device of formulating a principle (α) which is less restrictive than (A) so that (α) does not rule out argument (O), while (α) is still stringent enough to rule out argument (R), and adopt (α) instead of principle (A). We note, for example, that there is a difference between its being logically impossible that there exists a counter-instance to the conclusion, and its being logically impossible that there is evidence that a given instance is a counter-instance. When it comes to argument (O) it is obvious that it is not logically impossible that there should exist a counter-instance to the conclusion, since it is logically possible that there be pain-behaviour in my body which is not accompanied by pain felt either by me or by anybody else – except that I could never know this to be so. With respect to argument (R), however, it is logically impossible that there could be a counter-instance to the conclusion in the sample class, since it is contradictory to say of an object that it has been determined whether or not it has been conceived, and yet it has not been conceived. Thus we could adopt a weaker principle which demanded that in order for an inductive argument to be valid it must be the case that it is logically possible that its sample class contains what *might* be a counter-instance to its conclusion rather than that it contains what is also *known* to be a counter-instance to its conclusion. This weaker principle would still rule out argument (R) but not argument (0).

Another way of constructing an adequate principle is by pointing out first that, with respect to the hypothesis that all Xs are Ys, there are three types of X observable:

1 Xs which provide supporting evidence for the hypothesis, that is, Xs which are found to be Ys.
2 Xs which provide counter-evidence for the hypothesis, that is, Xs which are found to be not Ys.
3 Xs which are neutral with respect to the hypothesis, that is, Xs of which it cannot be determined whether or not they are also Ys.

Now in the case of argument (R) it is clear that not only (2) but also (3) is impossible. Every physical object which has been examined is a positive instance of having been conceived, and thus not only counter-instances but also neutral instances are excluded from the sample class. Consequently the need to invalidate argument (R) provides support only for a weaker principle (A*).

(A*) = A simple inductive argument is acceptable only if it is not logically necessary that its sample class contain supporting instances only.

According to this principle, an inductive argument based on observations which could have contained at least neutral instances is valid. Hence the inductive argument whose premiss describes the supporting instances of the hypothesis that all pain-behaviour by a body is accompanied by pain felt in that body, does not violate principle (A*). It is logically possible that the sample class contains neutral instances, the sample class being described as 'pain-behaviour such as I have examined with a view to determining whether it was accompanied by pain' – which is equivalent to saying 'pain-behaviour of my body'. Note that it is necessary to reword argument (O). If the argument were left standing as it was then it would be impossible even for a neutral instance to be a member of the sample class, which is defined as 'All pain-behaviour of which it has been determined whether or not it was accompanied by pain.' It is logically impossible to fail to determine whether or not something so described was accompanied by pain. If, however, the sample class is described as 'all pain-behaviour of my body' then of course a neutral instance could be a member of it, namely an instance of pain-behaviour of my body which was definitely not accompanied by pain felt by me, and thus of which it has not been determined whether or not it has been accompanied by pain felt by some person.

Now we come to the major point of this section, which, as I have indicated before, is of great general significance to philosophical methodology. What we have seen here is a typical example of an approach all too popular among contemporary analytic philosophers.

Plantinga has described argument (R), which no one would want to admit to be a valid argument, and subsequently constructed principle (A) for the specific purpose of disqualifying (R). In formulating (A) he seems to have been concentrating exclusively on his determination to invalidate (R), without any concern for the question whether there is anything in the nature of induction which would provide good reason for maintaining (A). In our reply to Plantinga we have done no better. We have tailored principle (A*) precisely in such a manner that it will rule out (R), but not the argument for other minds, without paying attention to the questions what (A*) actually amounts to and why it should be adopted.

The correct approach to the construction of a restrictive principle is to ask what restraints seem warranted on an understanding of the nature of induction. The answer that becomes evident in a quite elementary investigation is that a restriction similar to what is implied by Plantinga's principle, but which does not disqualify argument (0), naturally applies to inductive reasoning. Suppose we are trying to confirm the generalization (x) $(Px \supset Qx)$ and all the members of the sample class have a feature $\emptyset$ and we know of a good reason why any individual having $\emptyset$ should not have $\sim Q$. Also suppose that outside the sample class there are many individuals with the property P but without the feature $\emptyset$. Clearly there is compelling reason in this case why we ought not to argue inductively to the desired conclusion on the basis of our sample class. Everyone is bound to agree that there would be no justification for assuming, just because we could find no Ps that had $\emptyset$ that also possessed $\sim Q$, that the case must also be true for Ps that lack $\emptyset$.

Now in the case of argument (R), all the members of the sample class may be said to have $\emptyset$. This is the feature of having been observed, which provides the strongest possible reason, a logical reason, why no member of the sample class could not have been conceived. Material objects outside the sample class do not of course have this feature. Clearly, therefore, (R) is invalid. In the case of (O), however, the feature $\emptyset$ which ensures that we cannot know that pain is absent in the body in question exists no less in all instances that are outside the sample class; it is true with respect to every body that it is never possible to be certain that there is no pain felt in that body. There is no basis for invalidating argument (O).

Elementary consideration shows therefore that instead of (A) the following restrictive principle (A´) applies to inductive reasoning:

(A´) = In all those cases where it is logically possible that some particular provides a counter-instance to the conclusion, a simple inductive argument is acceptable only if it is possible that its sample class contains such a counter-instance.

Plantinga's objection is without any foundation.

Arguments based on a single case

But there is another, very famous objection to the claim that the existence of other minds can be established by inductive reasoning. The objection is that such reasoning would be based on the known mindedness of one body, that is, on the evidence of a single instance, and this is generally regarded as insufficient.

It may seem that the objection can itself be questioned. Is it not a fact that in science inductive arguments are quite often based on a single instance? The way in which scientists have arrived at the generalization 'All lead melts at 327 °C' seems a good case in point. Virtually after the first experiment showing a sample of lead melting at 327 °C it was taken as confirmed that all lead melts at the same temperature. If further experiments were performed to determine the melting point of other samples of lead, their purpose was not to strengthen the credibility of the hypothesis that all lead melts at the same temperature. These additional experiments had only one aim: to approximate more exactly to the value of lead's melting point by refining experimental techniques and eliminating possible sources of error. Scientists never stopped to ask themselves if perhaps the particular sample of lead experimented upon, but not all others, melted at 327 °C. They started with the assumption that whatever temperature represented the melting point of one particular sample was the melting point of all lead. The source of this attitude is to be found in the fact that previous experience taught them that different samples of lead share all sorts of properties: specific weight, coefficient of thermal expansion, hardness and so on. Consequently, all samples of lead are believed to belong to the same natural kind. Members of the same natural kind are expected to have the same melting point; experiment is required only to determine what this melting point is.

Now, one might wish to argue that the case of lead is similar to that of human bodies. Human bodies share with one another innumerably many biological, physiological and behavioural–psychological properties. Human bodies may be regarded, therefore, as members of a natural kind. Hence it should be sufficient that a mind has been found to be associated with one of these bodies in order to conclude that minds are associated with all of them.

However, this argument will not do. It is not enough to know that a collection of particulars belong to a given natural kind; it is also required that we know with respect to what properties they belong to a natural kind. After all, it is a fact that there are many properties that members of natural kinds do not share. While different samples of lead share properties such as specific weight, specific heat, coefficient of thermal expansion, thermal and electrical conductivity, latent heat, elasticity and hardness, they may differ in temperature, electric charge and potential, as well as in weight, momentum, shape and size. How do we distinguish between properties which we assume are shared by all members of a natural kind and properties in which they are allowed to differ? This is done on the basis of a further assumption: that the natural kind of lead is itself a member of a higher-order natural kind, namely the natural kind of metals. Members of other species of metal have been found to share uniform properties such as melting point and others mentioned above. It is assumed, therefore, that members of the species lead do likewise. (Incidentally, the assumption that our sample of lead observed to melt at 327 °C on a single occasion has a constant melting point is also based on what we know to be the case with respect to other metals.)

Now, different human bodies share many properties and differ in many others. There is nothing that would indicate to us whether the property of having a mind belongs to the first or the second group of properties. For the essential thing we are lacking here is a higher-order kind – which contains all human bodies as a member kind and also other natural kinds – from which we could determine whether the possession of a mind is the sort of property shared by all members of various natural kinds such as human bodies. We are not entitled here to generalize from a single instance.

It may seem that a case could be made for claiming that our argument is based on many instances. All of us have acquaintances whom we know to be reliable and trustworthy. A number of these have consistently told the truth in the past – whatever they asserted to be a fact invariably turned out to be a fact. It would, therefore, be only reasonable to argue that because so far every statement these acquaintances have made was true, the next statement they make is bound to be true. So we ask them whether they possess a mind and they all answer 'Yes'. It is rational to believe that what they say is true. But this in itself will not establish that everybody has a mind. To do that I shall still have to use the classical argument based on the resemblance of human bodies. But it will no longer be based on a single instance, namely, that of me, but rather on the case of me and all my trustworthy acquaintances.

I do not think one can defeat this argument by saying: these acquaintances are not lying but do not know what they are affirming; for if they have no minds then they simply lack the whole concept of mind. My past experience may also include instances of my having asked questions that involve concepts my acquaintances lacked, and in these cases they always readily admitted they did not understand the question. Furthermore, to have a grasp of a concept amounts to always employing it correctly in one's discourse, and these acquaintances have always used the notion of a mind in the accepted manner.

One way of countering this argument, however, is by pointing out that the sample class contains statements whose truth could be checked by me, whereas the conclusion is about a statement which is basically different; its truth cannot, in principle, be verified by me. There is good reason to hold that one cannot make an inference from what is the case with one type of statement to what is the case with a fundamentally different statement. It is easy to explain why people tend to utter nothing but the truth whenever there is a possibility that they might be found out if they did otherwise. The same explanation does not hold when it comes to the crucial utterance in which they assert that they have a mind; the latter cannot, in principle, be verified by me.

But something else that seems to be wrong with this attempt to establish the existence of minds among my trustworthy acquaintances is that it compares statements made about different sorts of facts. It compares statements whose nature we cannot foretell to the statement about possessing a mind, a statement which could have been predicted on the basis of the solipsistic hypothesis. After all, the solipsistic hypothesis consists in the assumption that while others do not possess minds their behaviour is entirely indistinguishable from mine who has a mind. When asked whether I have a mind, I will, if truthful, answer 'Yes', and so by the solipsistic hypothesis it follows that they, too, will give the same answer. Their answer cannot be taken, therefore, as evidence that they have minds.

The argument from myself

Probably the best-known attempt to reply to the objection that the inductive argument of establishing the existence of other minds is too weak, as it purports to establish its conclusion on a single case, is that of Ayer. He has contended that the objection vanishes once we realize that what is being done is not arguing from a single case of one body being correlated with a mind, but rather arguing from a large number of correlations between an indeterminate number of instances of behaviour and as many different mental events: namely, those which are associated with my own body. There have been some philosophers who found this argument attractive. For example:

> we do not need to proceed from a single case of one mind correlated with one body, . . . we can proceed instead from an enormous number of correlations between instances of behavior and experiences. The experiences and the instances of behavior all belong to the same person, but this does not preclude there being an enormous number of correlations between the two sorts of event.[7]

This argument is likely to seem rather strange to some of us. After all, we should certainly be reluctant to accept the generalization 'All ravens are black' if we had never seen more than a single black raven. And it seems to me that we would not be greatly impressed if someone pointed out that although all we have encountered so far was a solitary raven, our generalization is supported by more than just a single case: we have found a large number of correlations between instances of ravenness and blackness since our raven was black in the morning as well as in the evening; in the winter and in the summer; in flight as well as when perched on a branch, and so on.

It seems, however, that Ayer could defend his position against this particular objection. He could claim that in the context of the generalization about ravens, given our background knowledge, the so-called different cases that support it are not really independent of one another. It has, after all, been well established that hardly any bird changes its colour between the morning and the evening. Hence as soon as a particular raven has been observed to be black in the morning we are fairly certain that it will remain black at the end of the day. Consequently, on observing our raven to be still black in the evening we cannot be regarded as having learned something new that we did not know from our first observation; similarly with winter and summer and so on. However, in the context of the generalization that behaviour is accompanied by mental events, there is no background knowledge on the basis of which I could have anticipated that if (1) my perspiring is accompanied by the sensation of feeling hot then (2) my scratching my ear is likely to be accompanied by feeling my ear itch, or indeed by any other inner experience. Hence (1) and (2) may justifiably be looked upon as two genuinely independent and hence separate pieces of information.

But Ayer's position seems untenable all the same. Suppose we have observed no more than one raven and found it was completely black. This means that we have seen that each one of its hundreds of feathers was black. It will be agreed that in this case we are not in the possession of any background knowledge indicating that if feather a is black then feather b is likely to be too so long as a and b belong to the same bird. After all, we have often found in the past that one and the same bird may have variously coloured feathers. Nevertheless, we are not prepared to argue that we have observed hundreds of different raven-feathers and found them all black and therefore it is reasonable to conclude that all raven-feathers are black. The reason, apparently, is that the feathers we have observed belong to a very limited class by virtue of their all belonging to a single raven. Similarly, then, even if I know that hundreds of different instances of my behaviour were accompanied by mental events, we are not allowed to generalize from it since the different instances were limited to a single person.

At the end of this chapter I shall suggest a way of overcoming this difficulty. I shall also be in a position to resolve another problem which may not appear at once to be obviously related to it. The second problem, which I shall now describe, has been discussed by a number of philosophers and has sometimes been referred to as the problem of the 'inverted spectrum'. The problem is: how can I know that I do not have systematically delusive colour-perception so that when confronted with a given surface that looks red to me everyone else has the experience that is identical with mine when I see a blue surface, and vice versa?

There are famous discussions on this problem by C. I. Lewis, M. Black and J. J. C. Smart and, more recently, by William Lycan[8] and J. Harvey.[9] I shall not go into the various arguments they devised, but I should like to draw attention to the fact that the different writers are mainly concerned with this issue: is the inquiry whether different people have the same experience when viewing various coloured surfaces at all meaningful? The general concern is that, since it is hard to conceive a way in which any observation may be relevant to deciding whether different people have different experiences when subject to the same visual stimulus, the inquiry may be devoid of cognitive significance. The various attempts to deal with this question have consisted in the ingenious construction of situations in which some facts could be claimed to be relevant to the question and in consequence of which the problem of the inverted spectrum is in principle resolvable with the aid of possible experience.

Now with regard to the question of other minds, in general what philosophers have been after is a way in which the belief could be established as credible. As we have already said, many philosophers have been satisfied that it can be done by arguing inductively from one's own case. The obvious question arises: why has it not occurred to anyone to employ the same kind of inductive argument in the problem of the inverted spectrum? Why should my own case not provide the basis for actually verifying the claim that all people have the same colour experience, in consequence of which verifiability in principle does not even arise? It should follow from elementary inductive reasoning that just as I have a certain experience whenever I look at a surface I call red, so does everyone else.

Searching through the writings of philosophers of mind I could not find any explanation why the two questions (1) do others have a mind? and (2) do others have the same visual experience as I do? should not be dealt with in an exactly similar fashion, at least so far as the applicability of induction is concerned. To the extent to which inductive reasoning is effective in producing an affirmative answer to (1), it should also be effective in producing an affirmative answer to (2); and whatever reservations we may have about applying it to (2), we ought to have the same reservations about applying it to (1). At the end of this chapter I shall advance a reason why these two problems are to be treated differently.

Explanation as redescription

In order to be able to advance convincingly my suggestion as to how these two problems may be solved, I shall attempt to clarify a few basic aspects of explanation in general. In the past 20 years there have been hundreds of papers on the nature of explanation, containing various attempts to describe the necessary and sufficient conditions a set of statements must fulfil in order to qualify as an admissible explanation of a given phenomenon. On the other hand, very little has been said about the comparative power of different explanations. It seems obvious that a phenomenon is not simply either explained or unexplained; it can be explained to different degrees, some explanations being better, more illuminating, than others. I believe virtually all agree that explanations admit of degrees, and so it is unnecessary for me to defend this claim at great length. Let me mention only the famous saying that the hypothesis which best explains our observations is the one which is confirmed by those observations. 'Best' implies degree.

I think it would be generally agreed that Hempel's account of scientific explanations is the best-known and most frequently discussed account. As we saw in chapter 5, he says that if we have an explanandum E (which asserts that a certain event has taken place) then, if T is a theory and C is a true singular sentence, T & C explains E provided T & C entails E while C on its own does not entail E. It seems clear that no provisions have been made for comparing the explanatory powers of different Ts and Cs, for there is nothing in Hempel's conditions which admit degrees as, for example, T & C cannot entail E to a lesser or greater degree.*

There is however an important view that is far less well known and that focuses on a much neglected characteristic which is possessed by different explanations to indefinitely many degrees. One of the few philosophers to allude to this most fundamental feature of explanations is J. J. C. Smart, who pointed out that when, for instance, a scientist explains why iron rusts by stating that this is caused by the fact that iron oxidizes then

(1) The scientist changes the meaning of 'rusting' from its commonsense one of 'reddening of iron when it is left out in damp' to 'oxidation'. . .
According to (1) the nerve of the explanation lies in the shift of meaning of the word 'rust', or in other words to the *redescription* of reddening when exposed to moisture as rusting.[10]

According to this, when we ask for an explanation why a key which was left out in the damp has turned red, we may be given different answers with different explanatory powers. For example:

1 The key is made of iron and all iron reddens when left out in the damp.
2 The key has undergone a process of oxidation (and we may be given the details of this process).

There is little doubt that the second explanation is better than the first. Admittedly the first explanation fulfils the conditions necessary to qualify as a legitimate explanation. From the universal generalization 'All iron reddens when left out in the damp' conjoined with the description of the initial conditions, namely that the key is made of iron and was left out in the damp, we can derive the explanandum. However, (1) is a minimal kind of explanation. It offers very little redescription of the phenomenon to be explained. Not that it offers none; after all (1) informs us that the event we have witnessed

---
* We are here ignoring probabilistic explanations.

exemplifies a physical law. In addition, while earlier we might have described the explanandum as the event of our object reddening by virtue of its shape or weight or whatever, now we know that we are confronted with a case of an object reddening by virtue of its being made of iron. Yet (2) obviously offers more information about what is actually going on by telling us that what we have observed was the result of the molecules of the key uniting with the air molecules to produce a new compound.

Clearly the 'redescription' thesis is compatible with a number of different accounts of explanation, and in particular with Hempel's account. It draws attention to a vital ingredient all admissible explanations have to a greater or lesser degree. I do not believe anyone would wish to deny the existence of this aspect of explanations. We may formulate the following principle which embodies Smart's thesis:

(∅) = Σ is a superior explanation of E to Σ ' if both explain why E but in doing so Σ provides more information about E than Σ '.

Principle (∅) expresses the common-sense observation that the more we know about what happened, the more we know why it happened.

It is important to note that when the 'redescription' aspect of explanation is brought to our attention we begin to understand how scientific explanation is related to explanations in other spheres. On Hempel's account alone it is not at all clear how, when someone does not see what is funny about a given joke and it is then explained to him, this activity is related to what scientists do when explaining why a given event took place. Some will not mind if it turns out that the two activities have nothing in common. Yet it seems that the view according to which the two activities described by the same term share something in common is preferable. We can indeed see that the two activities are related. A person may fail to understand a joke because it is an ethnic joke and he does not know about the ethnic characteristic that is being ridiculed; because he does not realize that a given word has another meaning; because he has not heard the latest political news that is being alluded to; and so on. He will understand the joke as soon as the missing information is supplied and he has a more complete knowledge of what the joke actually says.

The most obvious illustration of the centrality of the provision of information about what the explanandum is would be provided by the case in which a difficult text or one written in a foreign language is being explained to us. We may know how to describe the sentences in terms of the letters they contain but not in terms of their content. On receiving the appropriate explanation we have significantly increased the number of true descriptive statements we know about the text in question.

Of course, we must not forget that in science the demand for explanation is usually made in the form 'Why did this happen?', whereas in the last example what is customarily asked is 'What does this sentence say?', rather than 'Why is this sentence included in the text?' Yet it is essential to realize that scientific explanations also contain an element whose function is to increase our information about what is going on.

Grades of explanation

I shall not attempt to develop an accurate method for measuring the amount of information conveyed by different sets of explanatory statements. In quite a number of cases the disparity in the amount of information provided by the different sets is sufficient to be immediately recognizable without any rigorous criterion. For our purposes it will be sufficient to consider only these straightforward cases.

Let us consider the story of a patient who goes to see his doctor and asks for an explanation why he feels so tired lately when he has done less work than usual. After a thorough examination and various tests, the doctor's answer to the question is:

1 Your condition is caused by a virus.
2 The virus is lodged in your lungs.
3 The virus interacts with the fluids of the lungs to produce a toxic substance.
4 The virus was discovered only five years ago.
5 There is a new Swiss drug which is effective in such cases.

I submit that each additional statement increases the amount of explanation the patient receives in reply to his question. It is unlikely, for instance, that the latter will complain: 'But doctor, I was asking why I am tired all the time, so why are you changing the subject and telling me (4) and (5)?' No, he will find those statements relevant to his question even though, for instance, neither (4) nor (5) gives extra causes of his illness or describes any laws of nature relevant to his case. However, both (4) and (5) furnish him with information about what is going on. The patient was puzzled by his tiredness when he had done hardly any work. Now he is informed that he is exhausted because of the depletion of his body's resources, which have been used up in the struggle against the invaders in his lungs. His fatigue is further described and hence explained by the information that it is caused by the fierce battle his body is waging against a virus which produces a toxic substance, a virus which was discovered only five years ago and which is controllable with a Swiss drug.

Vacuous explanations

If we accept (ø) we are virtually committed to the following principle:

(ψ) =   When Σ provides no additional information at all about the fact described by E, then no matter what conditions Σ may fulfil, it is not an admissible explanation.

Principle (ψ) is of great importance, but I shall discuss it only briefly since it is not an essential factor in the solution of our problem.

In chapter 5 I offered an argument why Kepler's laws, K, cannot legitimately be explained by the conjunction of K and B (Boyle's law) even though K & B → K. The essence of the argument was that ∼K & B bears a logical relationship to ∼K that is exactly parallel to K & B's relationship to K, and hence the tendency of ∼K & B to explain ∼K cancels the tendency of K & B to explain K. Now we can see even more clearly why K & B must be ruled out as acceptable explanans for K. Surely the conjunction of K & B does not provide additional information about the facts described by the explanandum K, since the first conjunct is merely the explanandum and the second conjunct B has nothing to do with it. After all, it is entirely immaterial from the point of view of this explanation schema what the explanandum is; it matters not if it is K or ∼K or indeed if it is X, where X is any possible generalization. The relationship of X & B to X is not a function of B. Conjoining B to K cannot therefore contribute any specific information concerning the subject matter of K, for otherwise the conjoining of B to any X would contribute specific information concerning the subject matter of X.

In other words, we adopt the simple and compelling principle that a statement purporting to make an assertion about everything makes no assertion about anything specific. But, if we were to assume that when B is added to K this results in the making of some assertion concerning the subject matter of K not made by K alone, then it would have to be admitted that when B is added to X, where X stands for any statement, this always results in the making of some assertion concerning the subject matter of X not made by X alone. This, however, would contradict the principle just enunciated, and hence the assumption is false, that is, K & B says no more about the facts described by K than K itself. Thus K & B cannot constitute a redescription of the facts described by K and therefore lacks the essential feature of admissible explanations.

The principle that a statement purporting to make an assertion about everything makes no assertion about anything requires no great deal of buttressing but I shall briefly refer to Goodman's treatment of the notion of 'about'.[11] One of his central points is that although the statement 'Florida is Democratic'' entails 'Maine or Florida is Democratic', the first statement cannot be regarded as a statement about Maine. The reason is that the first statement entails every statement of the form 'x or Florida is Democratic' where x may stand for anything at all. He says 'that S yield logically a statement mentioning Maine is not a sufficient condition for S to be absolutely about Maine; S must, roughly speaking, yield such a statement without yielding a parallel statement for everything else.'[12] Goodman, of course, is dealing with the question when is a given statement about a certain particular, whereas we are concerned with the question when is a given statement about a certain fact. Still, his point is that a statement cannot be about some specific thing by virtue of the fact that it entails a statement mentioning that thing, if at the same time it entails parallel statements for everything else as well.

Other minds and the inverted spectrum

Now we may return to where we began to consider the issue of the use of induction to establish the existence of other minds. The idea was that my own case should serve as the basis upon which to establish the credibility of the hypothesis that others have a mind too. In saying this we are offering an explanation for other people's behaviour. The conclusion of the inductive argument is that any person who exhibits behaviour B does so because of an inner experience I, since everyone who undergoes experience I exhibits behaviour B. Thus we may have:

E = Person P is scratching his nose.
T = Experiencing an itch on the nose prompts a person to scratch it.
C = P's nose itches.

T & C is a legitimate explanans with the aid of which we can explain E. One might assume unthinkingly that all we have here is the routine kind of explanation exemplified by the way we explain why a given raven is black. In that case we have no more than a minimal explanation, since all we add to what is already asserted by the explanandum is that the blackness of individual i is an instance of a universal generalization according to which all ravens are black. Similarly, it may be thought that all we have here is what we have shown, that E is an instance of T, for from T universally instantiated and C, we may infer E.

But in fact we have much more. Upon assuming that C is true we infer that E, not merely because of the generalization T. We can also infer that E is true because we are directly acquainted with the unpleasant experience of having an itching nose. We know by virtue of ourselves having had such an experience that it is something that strongly calls out for scratching, which brings prompt and positively pleasant relief. Thus we are in a position substantially to redescribe E. We can say that P is stimulating the itching region of his body so as to obtain the pleasant feeling of being relieved from an irritating tickle.

We may look once more at the question: can the credibility of a generalization be established by observing a single instance? It is important that we answer this question while bearing in mind that generalizations may differ radically from one another, and what may be true of one kind may not be true of another. Some generalizations provide very little illumination of their instances while others provide a great deal more. We must remember that we may not have good enough evidence for saying that in all cases a single instance cannot establish a generalization: though we find this to be so in some cases, in those cases the resulting explanation is very weak.

Suppose we have so far observed only one black raven. Then, as we have already stated, the general hypothesis that we can construct on the basis of this observation is of minimal explanatory power. It is not unreasonable, therefore, to maintain that from the fact that we would not be allowed to establish that all ravens are black on the basis of a single observation we cannot infer that the same must apply to the generalization concerning the mindedness of all human beings. This latter generalization may well be adopted more readily, for it is a superior generalization, one that results in a much more powerful explanation of its instances. I cannot think of a generalization that results in a comparably powerful explanation where it is known that a single instance is regarded as insufficient.

The solution to our second problem should now be obvious. In the case of the inverted spectrum, we saw that no one has suggested that we should argue that since my experience when seeing a red surface is of a specific kind everybody else's must be the same. But of course, to derive such a conclusion would amount to arriving at a conclusion by an argument based on a single instance only, in which case the resulting explanation is an inferior one. Unlike the case of mental experiences, whose typical behavioural reaction – such as the sensation of itching producing the act of scratching – is an act we fully understand as being called for by that particular experience, we do not in the least 'understand' or 'see' why electromagnetic radiation of a given wavelength should produce the particular experience of seeing red. I do not, of course, wish to maintain that philosophers actually had this in mind, but the distinction does provide a justification for distinguishing the belief that others have mental experiences from the question whether their colour perception is the same as ours.

8

Induction, infinite regresses, the uniformity of nature and the intelligibility of nature

Strawson on induction

It is only natural to begin this chapter with the basic question: should a discussion of induction be included in this book at all? Is the belief in the reliability of conclusions arrived at by inductive reasoning a metaphysical belief? In fact there are philosophers who would deny that induction has anything to do with metaphysics. One of these is the well-known philosopher Strawson, who has claimed that our commitment to the inductive method reflects no metaphysical beliefs on our part since it does not imply an affirmation that the universe has this or that particular feature. To subscribe to the rules of inductive reasoning amounts to no more than accepting a certain linguistic convention without adopting any given view of the nature of reality. The question whether there are good reasons for believing in conclusions arrived at inductively simply does not arise, for by the very rules of our language 'having good reasons to believe that *p*' simply means '*p* is the conclusion of inductive reasoning'.[1] At most one can inquire whether, by the rules of ordinary language, if it has been established by induction that a certain event is going to occur, then would expecting that event to happen be called 'having a rational attitude'; and the answer is 'Yes'.

There is an important point here that has not always been appreciated. Some opponents of Strawson have been tempted to argue impatiently that the rules of ordinary language are of little value in helping us to discover the nature of reality and cannot create facts. Whether a certain event E is going to happen or not is a factual question which cannot be decided by linguistic legislation. But Strawson explains that the linguistic rule according to which, if it can be shown by inductive reasoning that E is going to happen, then it is reasonable to believe that E is going to happen, is entirely safe from empirical refutation. For if it turns out that E after all does not happen it can still be maintained that it was reasonable to expect it to,[2] even that, in the context of the circumstances prevailing at the time, it was correct to maintain this. Strawson ridicules the question 'Is the universe such that inductive procedures are rational?', since the nature of the universe has nothing to do with the question what beliefs it is rational to hold. It is purely a matter of convention, which may be upheld in the face of any future experience, that it is rational to assert that I have good reasons now to believe E is going to happen if this belief is a conclusion of inductive reasoning.

While some philosophers have been antagonistic to Strawson's view that the problem of induction is a pseudo-problem, many others have endorsed it. Indeed, the measure of his influence may be gauged from the fact that nowadays, when someone is said to be engaged in investigating the problem of induction, he is quite often automatically assumed to be engaged not in trying to justify induction but in trying to describe in detail its rules. It should be mentioned here that at one point Strawson becomes inconsistent and suddenly attempts to argue that beliefs about the unobserved not based on induction are irrational not simply because it has been agreed to call them irrational; he is determined to say something stronger in their disfavour. He considers a person who, wishing to surmise what the future is going to be, closes his eyes, asks himself the relevant question, and accepts the first answer that comes into his head. Suppose we were to ask him whether he usually obtains the right answer by this method. Strawson says 'He might answer: "You've mentioned one of its drawbacks; I never do get the right answer; but it's an extremely easy method." One might then be inclined to think that it was not a method of finding things out at all.'[3] This remark is either irrelevant or unwarranted. When Strawson says that this person's method 'was not a method of finding things out', he must have meant either that in the past it was found not to be or that in the future it will be found not to be such a method. In the former case we must ask: not assuming now that induction is the only valid method of predicting the future — for surely such an assumption would amount to begging the question — why should it be thought relevant that the method was unsuccessful in the past? What has past failure to do with future failure? In the latter case we may ask: what is the justification for this attitude? Since we are not now assuming the validity of induction, what makes us inclined to think that the method may not be successful in the future? There does not seem to be any way in which Strawson's remark can be presented as both relevant and justified.

Now we shall have a closer look at Strawson's main thesis and shall see that a number of difficulties arise. He points out that it makes good sense to ask about a particular belief concerning the future whether its adoption is warranted, for then we are asking whether, by the accepted standards of induction, it follows that the belief should be adopted. However, it makes no sense to go on and ask whether the application of those very standards is well-grounded. The situation, according to him, is similar to that which obtains in the case of questions concerning the legality of certain practices. One may sensibly inquire whether a given action is legal, to which the answer will be provided by an appeal to the existing legal system which sanctions or prohibits that particular action. However, Strawson says 'it makes no sense to inquire in general whether the law of the land, the legal system as a whole, is or is not legal. For to what legal standards are we appealing?'[4] Strawson's comparison is a very useful one and I shall use it in my effort to get a better picture of what his position amounts to.

1 Strawson is surely correct in saying that a person may well ask, for instance, 'Is it legal to bring into the country merchandise from abroad valued at $1,000?' However, upon being told that it is not, he is not to ask 'Is the law that prohibits such an act legal?' Suppose, however, that we were told that in every country in the world it was the law that the limit for bringing in undeclared goods acquired in a foreign country was exactly $300. Also suppose that we were told that this limit has been fixed by the appropriate authorities in each country without any prior consultation with foreign authorities and even without any knowledge of the law anywhere else. Surely we would regard this as quite incredible. How can it be that, without any collusion, all the authorities arrived at exactly $300 as the limit to the value of what may legally be imported from abroad? Surely there is no distinct feature of the universe which makes $300 the natural sum for that purpose.

Similarly, in the case of induction, what constitutes a valid form of inductive reasoning happens to be agreed upon to the last detail in all the languages in the world. How is it that all peoples without exception arrived at precisely the same convention when there is nothing in the objective nature of reality that would call for such a convention? It is, for example, a convention in the English language that 'green' stands for the colour green, and we may leave it at that. However, if in every language in the world the colour green was denoted by 'green', then surely we would regard this as most remarkable and investigate the reasons for it.

Against this objection, however, Strawson may perhaps defend himself by saying that he wished to claim only that we cannot give logical reasons for adopting inductive practices, but by this he did not mean to imply that the rules that govern these practices are entirely arbitrary; we can and should give an explanation why there is a convention of employing these particular rules in empirical inquiries. The explanation will be psychological. That is, while Strawson will deny that inductive reasoning is objectively superior to any other form of reasoning from the observed to the unobserved, it does have features that are psychologically attractive. The explanation why all people everywhere in the world subscribe to the same rules of induction is that it is a universally shared human urge to anticipate that the unobserved will turn out in the way it is predicted to turn out on the basis of these rules.

2 While good sense precludes us from asking whether the law prohibiting the import of an unlimited amount of foreign goods is legal, it is perfectly in order to ask why such a law has been enacted in the first place. And such a question would not be left unanswered; the economic factors which necessitate the law could be stated in detail in defending it. The same applies to every law: we do not ask, of course, that they be legally justified but we do ask that they be justified in a satisfactory manner, that is, that they be shown to fulfil some legitimate purpose. It may safely be stated that if the citizens of a country were to reach the conclusion that a particular law did not serve any useful purpose, that it merely caused inconvenience and that its origin could not be explained by anything but that it fulfilled a psychological need of the legislators, then they would fight for the abolition of that law.

When it comes to linguistic conventions, in some cases we are justified in being quite indifferent to the fact that there is no objective basis for their adoption. For instance, we are not worried about why the colour green is denoted by the word 'green' and not 'red'; but then it makes no practical difference what word denotes green. We should, however, not be indifferent to the question what linguistic convention determines the circumstances under which we say of event E that it is reasonable to expect it to happen. This convention may have a large number of practical implications. Suppose E is a highly undesirable event which we very much want to avert but that according to the rules of induction action of considerable complexity and strenuousness is required to prevent E. In such a situation we should want a good explanation why these rules, which impose upon us the need for such burdensome activities, have to be adopted. As in the case of a law about which we were told that the sole reason for its enactment was to satisfy some psychological quirk on the part of the authorities, here too we ought to feel that the linguistic legislation in question is an unwarranted imposition upon us. But in fact we never question the adequacy of the rules of inductive reasoning. Thus Strawson's claim that they are rules adopted merely by convention, and his comparison between these rules and the legal rules which govern our behaviour, seem implausible.

3 In the case of the law against importing foreign goods above a certain value, we can easily imagine that if the law was abolished we would not give another thought about what we brought back with us from our visits abroad. Would Strawson maintain that if by the general consent of writers, journalists and others who shape linguistic practices the convention concerning what is to be called a well-grounded belief was altered then all of us would cheerfully go along with this change? It would seem that we would not, but it might be contended that the reason is something we have already mentioned: inductive reasoning has strong psychological appeal. But if the convention were changed we would be left with no rational grounds upon which to defend the beliefs we arrived at by the old rules of reasoning. Yet I am sure there are many people who feel, like me, that even if all the philosophers who had the highest regard for universally proclaimed conventions tried their hardest they could not talk me into accepting any new rules to determine the meaning of 'a well-established hypothesis'.

4 The most serious objection to Strawson's view is also the simplest. It is quite clear that our commitment to the use of induction, contrary to what Strawson has claimed, is related to the nature of the universe. Strawson, as we have seen, has maintained that if a prediction based on inductive reasoning turned out to be false it would make no difference, for it could still be contended that it was reasonable to expect that it was going to be proved true. He is of course quite right, but only so long as this is the case once or twice, or at any rate not too frequently. What he fails to consider is what we would say if inductive arguments persistently failed to yield correct results. It seems obvious that there is no basis for claiming that even this would make no difference. On the contrary, it is quite clear that under those circumstances we would not say that it is rational to expect the conclusion of an inductive argument to turn out to be true.

Popper on induction

One other, even more extreme view postulates that there is no such problem in metaphysics as whether reality corresponds to the conclusions of inductive arguments, since such arguments simply do not exist; what have traditionally been construed as instances of inductive reasoning are actually instances of a different kind of reasoning. This view was advanced by K. R. Popper in 1934, and while it has not been adopted by many people there are a few philosophers even today who are willing to defend it enthusiastically. For example, a highly spirited defence was provided by David Miller, who declared that 'scientific knowledge is everything that a classical epistemologist says it ought not to be: it is unjustified, untrue, unbelief.' [5]

One of the first things that is likely to puzzle the reader is the everyday behaviour of Popperians. It is hard to understand why, if they take a view of the status of scientific hypotheses so radically different to classical epistemologists, they, no less than anyone else, readily trust their very lives to any hypothesis that scientists assure them has been well confirmed. When on the basis of standard inductive methods some highly unpleasant event is said to loom ahead, why is it that they seem to place confidence in the truth of such predictions, just like the so-called 'justificationists'? And why is the incidence of concern, fear and even panic among Popperians as frequent as among ordinary folk? Miller does not touch upon this. He concentrates on stressing the fundamental difference between followers of Popper who are falsificationists and those philosophers who 'would commit themselves to the absurdities of inductive logic and the search for justification.' [6] According to falsificationists, scientists do not assume that the future is likely to be like the past; in fact they do not postulate any specific hypothesis about how the future is going to be. What they do is to admit provisionally all hypotheses into the realm of scientific knowledge provided that they are falsifiable in principle by experience. Subsequently tests are performed, and any hypothesis that fails any of these tests because it is falsified by them is expelled. In the end we uphold all the hypotheses that have not been falsified and have been left unexpelled.

These views have been subjected to a great deal of criticism. For one reason or another, the critics have not been as effective as they could have been, and Miller seems to be able to defend Popper against them. I shall not cite here all the many inadequate objections that have been raised. However, Mary B. Hesse, who has developed an important approach of her own to confirmation theory, has this to say:

Objections can be made to Popper's view on the ground that it is impossible even to state it without making some inductive assumptions. For example, it is not clear that the notion of a 'severe test' is free of such assumptions. Does this mean 'tests of the same kind that have toppled many generalizations in the past', which are therefore likely to find out the weak spots of this generalization in the future? Or does it mean 'tests which one should expect on the basis of past experience to refute this particular generalization'? In either case there is certainly an appeal to induction. Again, one past falsification of a generalization does not imply that the generalization is false in *future* instances. To assume that it will be falsified in similar circumstances is to make an inductive assumption, and without this assumption there is no reason why we should not continue to rely upon falsified generalizations.[7]

The second of these two objections can at once be seen to be in error. While according to Popper scientists are not seeking hypotheses anyone is capable of knowing to be true, they decidedly will not entertain any hypothesis they know for sure to be false. When an event that a given hypothesis clearly implies will not occur has been observed to occur, then the falsity of the hypothesis has conclusively been demonstrated and it must be rejected for this reason.

As to the first objection, Popperians could reply that in order to determine what constitutes a 'severe test' they do not have to appeal to induction, as it can be done on purely logical grounds. On the basis of our understanding of the contents of a given hypothesis we are able to evaluate how improbable various events would be if the hypothesis were true. The type of event we judge the most improbable will be identified as the event that most seriously threatens the hypothesis. We should therefore endeavour to produce the circumstances that will enable us to observe whether such an event does or does not occur. The production of those circumstances amounts to putting the hypothesis in question to its most severe test. But of course the question that remains is: how do we know how to produce the appropriate circumstances? How do we know, for instance, what to do in order to find out whether water boils at 100 °C? This is a very good question, which, however, is not specifically connected with the notion of a 'severe test', since it is a completely general question. How do Popperians, for example, know where to go when they want to have a meal? If one is to believe them, then apparently not for a moment do they assume that they are more likely to satisfy their hunger in a restaurant than in a hardware shop. However, they go to a restaurant because of the implications of the hypothesis they have been instructed to act upon on the basis of their falsificationist methodology.

It is sufficient to confront Popperians with the following. Let us consider for a moment two hypotheses:

h_1 =   All unsupported bodies fall to the ground.
h_2 =   All unsupported bodies fell to the ground until this moment but all the rest will remain suspended in the air.

Nobody is prepared to entertain h_2. Even if we offer a Popperian a vast amount of money to take just one step beyond the edge of the roof, pointing out to him that on the basis of h_2 no harm will come to him, he will resolutely reject our offer. We may go on to point out to him that according to:

h_3 =   All unsupported bodies fell to the ground until this moment but all the rest will descend slowly with a gentle impact,

there is nothing to be concerned about either. The same goes for indefinitely many other hypotheses we may construct. He will refuse to consider, even for this single occasion, adopting any one of these hypotheses. But surely each one is as admissible as h_1 by the criterion that a scientific hypothesis must be falsifiable. The next instance of an unsupported body will just as readily falsify h_2, if it turns out to behave according to h_1 as it will falsify h_1 if it turns out to obey h_2! And of course in the past not a single observation has been in conflict with h_2, h_3 and so on. These hypotheses remain just as unfalsified in practice as h_1 is.

One might perhaps attempt to evade the required conclusion by contending that the actual reason we adhere to h_1 is not because we subscribe to the principle that the unobserved will be like the observed but because we subscribe to the principle of simplicity. One needs no elaborate explication of the notion of simplicity to see at once that of all the hypotheses h_1, h_2, h_3 and so on, h_1 is the simplest. The principle of simplicity thus instructs us to reject all the other hypotheses.

This move is, however, quite useless. First of all, it is worth noting that Popper indeed incorporates the principle of simplicity into his methodology, but the reason he has given is that it follows from the basic methodological rule of selecting the most falsifiable hypothesis. He has said 'Simple statements, if knowledge is an object, are to be prized higher than less simple ones because they tell us more; because their empirical content is greater and because they are better testable.'[8] Such is the influence of Popper that a number of philosophers have been prepared to take his word about the validity of such a substantial claim without much investigation of its factual basis. For example W. Kneale has stated 'the policy of assuming always the simplest hypothesis which accords with the known facts is that which will enable us to get rid of false hypotheses most quickly.'[9] Similarly, F. S. Barker maintains that it is an important feature of reality that the simpler hypothesis always runs the greater risk of being contradicted by the evidence and that it therefore 'says more'.[10]

Now Popper seems to believe that it is sufficient in order to establish his thesis to cite a few examples where there is some correlation between degrees of simplicity and falsifiability. He ignores the fact that in infinitely many other cases there is no such correlation. In particular, in the case of h_1 and its infinitely many rivals h_2, h_3 and so on there is no difference in falsifiability and consequently the principle of simplicity cannot be invoked in order to defend our choice of h_1.

A more damaging objection is to point out that even if Popper felt entitled to use the principle of simplicity in contexts similar to the present one, he could not do so unless he subscribed to the important generalization that in all cases where a hypothesis postulates that the unobserved will be like the observed, and its infinitely many rivals postulate that the unobserved is going to differ in some way from the observed, the first hypothesis must be regarded as the simplest. But, if so, his insistence that he has revolutionized the philosophy of science and overthrown classical epistemology becomes empty of substance. His principle of simplicity, without which he cannot adjudicate between competing hypotheses in a single case, is just another name for the standard inductive principle.

What follows is based then on the clear understanding that all of us subscribe to the important metaphysical belief in the uniformity of nature. This means that we believe nature obeys a set of unchanging laws which can be inferred with considerable probability from our past observations. When described in the required fashion these observations yield statements about regularities that are assumed to hold in general. The question we shall concentrate on is: what is the objective basis for this belief?

Different types of regress

I would like to advance a suggestion for the justification of induction based on an infinite regress argument. I want to present a discussion of this important argument form, one of the most versatile weapons in the armoury of the metaphysician. This principle of reasoning has been used throughout the history of philosophy up to the present day and yet it has hardly ever been subjected to thorough analysis. To my knowledge there has been no serious inquiry to determine the number of different kinds of infinite regress and to establish the exact structure and scope of each kind. I am aware of the existence of one small book by John Passmore, *Philosophical Reasoning*,[11] in which he examines a number of methodological principles philosophers employ and in which he devotes one chapter to a discussion of the infinite regress argument. The book has of course the distinction of being a pioneering work; otherwise, however, it is of only limited use. For example, he treats all the different kinds of regress as if they were of a single type when in fact there are many types, some of which are basically dissimilar to the rest. In this section I shall attempt to describe the outlines of four of the better-known varieties of this argument. Passmore has noted the distinction between vicious and benign regresses, but this distinction is one that applies *within* some types of regress, that is, the very same type may have a destructive or a constructive effect on a given philosophical claim. I shall now discuss four kinds of regress argument.

(R$_1$) This is a simple and entirely harmless variety. For example, given that proposition p_1 is true then of necessity it follows that

$$p_2 = p_1 \text{ is true}$$

as well as

$$p_3 = p_2 \text{ is true}$$

and so on ad infinitum. Everyone seems to agree that this causes no worry. Admittedly , for any i, no matter how large, it is the case that there is a p_{i+1} such that

$$p_{i+1} = p_i \text{ is true}$$

but this creates no difficulty. There is nothing wrong with the notion of an infinite chain of something as such. No problem arises unless it is shown that to admit such a chain creates some specifiable trouble.

(R$_2$) As we have seen in chapter 4, after a painstakingly thorough examination of the nature of time Broad argued against the transient theory of time – that is, against the idea that time passes and that there is a particular called the NOW that is relentlessly moving into the future – for that would require that there be infinitely many separate time systems. As will be remembered, I argued that one extra time system is sufficient and, furthermore, that even this system need not actually exist; the mere possibility of its existence suffices to render the notion of a time flow coherent. However, let us assume that Broad is right. What logical difficulty arises from the postulation of infinitely many time systems?

Broad does not offer an explanation; he neglects to make explicit the point of his objection. The most reasonable interpretation seems to be that his objection is not a logical one, that is, Broad does not wish to claim that there is a fallacy involved in trying to lend meaning to the movement of the NOW by resorting to higher and higher order time series. What he is likely to have had in mind is that it is far too extravagant to have all these time series. After all, there exists an alternative account of time, one that does not admit a moving NOW, and whatever advantages the transient view may offer it can be had only at an exorbitant price. Sound ontology requires us therefore to abandon that view.

A second example of (R_2) is provided by the famous argument against the realist position, according to which universals as well as particulars exist. G. Ryle has argued[12] that a proposition like 'The grass is green' is taken by the realist as saying 'The grass exemplifies the universal greenness', which means that the particular grass and the universal greenness are related to one another by the relation of 'exemplification'. Of course, the relation of 'exemplification', like every other dyadic property [i.e. a property that amounts to relationship between two particulars] is itself a universal and is itself exemplified by the exemplification of greenness by the grass, and so on ad infinitum.

A. Donagan called this regress vicious without offering any explanation, and it is hard to see what he had in mind.[13] Landeman, on the other hand, conceded that the regress is not vicious logically but violates Occam's razor.[14] He argues that what Ryle wanted was to show how much better off nominalists were in that they did not have to admit such vast numbers of entities. Thus an appeal is made once more to the prohibitive extravagance involved in postulating an infinite chain of entities.

It is, however, not the case that philosophers will avoid regresses of this kind under all circumstances. Consider, for example, the famous dictum 'Every event has a cause.' It clearly implies an infinite chain of events the end of which can never be reached. Yet no one has suggested that the principle of causality ought to be rejected on the ground that it violates the injunction that one should economize with postulated entities. But of course the case of causality is very different to, for example, the case Broad was arguing about. In the latter case, in order to be able to sustain the notion of a moving NOW we were going to postulate an infinite number of time systems when there isn't the slightest evidence that there exists even one such system. In addition none of these systems is of any use apart from permitting us to assign movement to the NOW. In the case of the principle of causality, on the other hand, we know already of the existence of long causal chains consisting of indefinitely many events and hence there is inductive evidence for the claim that the chain continues for ever. Furthermore, the principle of causality is of immense value; it is a central principle providing much of the motivation for scientific progress.

Thus (R$_2$) may be described as a regress that generates an infinite chain of physical entities. The regress is set in motion by some philosophical thesis. The rule to be adopted is to reject the thesis so as to avoid the ontological extravagance involved in admitting the chain of entities, for whose existence there is no independent evidence and which serves no useful purpose other than sustaining the thesis in question.

(R$_3$) Gilbert Ryle has claimed that there are philosophers who subscribe to what he describes as the 'intellectualist legend'. Their position, he shows, is involved in an infinite vicious regress:

The crucial objection to the intellectualist legend is this. The consideration of propositions is itself an operation the execution of which can be more or less intelligent, less or more stupid. But if, for any operation to be intelligently executed, a prior theoretical operation had first to be performed and performed intelligently, it would be a logical impossibility for anyone ever to break into the circle.[15]

The infinite regress here (which Ryle refers to as a 'circle') is (R$_1$), which consists of a series of sentences and, unlike the next kind of regress, which consists of a series of arguments, of a series of acts which are to precede one another. This regress represents a straightforward state of affairs and requires no lengthy discussion. If indeed there are philosophers who hold precisely the view Ryle attributes to them then he has conclusively refuted their argument. Since not one of the acts in the series can be performed unless some other act has preceded it, it is not possible to execute any act.

(R$_4$) Now we come to the most frequently encountered type of regress, and also the most controversial one. There is no agreement among philosophers in any given instance whether any specific regress of this kind is to be taken as supporting or refuting what it is relevant to, nor about the general question: what are the crucial features of this type of regress that determine the way it is to be treated?

(R$_4$) may be roughly characterized in the following way. The first step to be taken is to raise a certain problem; the second step consists in providing a solution to that problem. However, it is immediately shown that the type of problem raised at the first step may be raised once more. This is the third step. The fourth step leads to the solution of this problem along the lines provided by the second step, and so on ad infinitum. The point of dispute in general is what to make of (R$_4$): are we to say that, since essentially the same problem keeps arising no matter how far we progress along the regress, we are faced with an ineradicable problem, or that, since every time we raise a problem we can at once come up with a solution, we are left with no difficulty?

I shall discuss here one particular view of how to handle (R_4) properly. This view may have been tacitly assumed by a number of philosophers but I have only once found it clearly stated. It has been described in a discussion of a regress generated in the context of the hypothesis – defended by K. Lehrer – that nobody knows anything.[16] The reason he offers for his sceptical position is the alleged possibility that our brains are manipulated by super-beings he calls Googols, who mislead us into seeing non-existent sights, hearing non-existent sounds and so on. He then goes on to claim that these Googols themselves may also lack knowledge since their own brains may in turn be manipulated by higher order Googols. The thesis Lehrer is concerned to establish is that no being whatever in the whole universe knows anything, for the knowledge of these higher order Googols is once more subverted by yet higher order Googols, and so on, thus generating an infinite regress which, he assumes without any argument, supports the contention that no one knows anything. Oliver A. Johnson, who examined Lehrer's thesis, expresses the opinion that some sort of an argument is required before we are able to decide whether the regress that has been generated supports the position of the sceptic or the position of one who believes in the possibility of knowledge.[17]

Before going any further I should perhaps acknowledge that many readers may find the whole issue somewhat strange. To begin with, even though it has become a tradition since Descartes to present the sceptical hypothesis by postulating some extraordinary being such as an evil demon because of the pedagogical value of such a practice, from a logical point of view there does not seem to be any need for it. The sceptic may well wonder whether our brains, without any outside assistance, perhaps generate the perceptions that deceive us. This is a point I shall touch upon in the next chapter. What is even harder to understand is why, even if we do have to introduce these strange beings, it should be of any interest to us whether they do or do not know anything. The question of human knowledge is obviously of considerable concern to all of us, but I cannot imagine anyone being very curious to find out whether Googols know anything.

But I am discussing this specific issue only because what Johnson has to say about it is of general relevance to the nature of (R_4). It seems obvious that Lehrer's regress is an instance of (R_4). He advances the thesis that possibly no one knows anything, whereupon the objection is raised that we make many observations on the basis of which we ought to be entitled to assert that we do know a large number of facts. Lehrer's reply is that we cannot rely on our observations with sufficient confidence because of the possible existence of higher order beings who manipulate our minds. The immediate objection to this is: if such beings exist, then they possess knowledge. However, the answer given is 'No, their knowledge might be subverted by yet higher order beings', and so on ad infinitum. And these are Johnson's comments:

These two kinds of infinite regresses can be distinguished from each other, as far as the question of knowledge is concerned, in the following way: If, to establish the truth of any proposition, A, one must establish, as a necessary condition, the truth of an infinite number of propositions $B_1. . .B_n$, the regress is vicious, because one is, as a consequence, logically incapable of ever establishing the truth of A. If this consequence is not entailed, the regress that can be generated, although infinite, is nevertheless benign. Now the proposition whose truth the skeptical hypothesis is designed to establish is that no being knows anything. And the argument offered is that all beings at any given level are deceived by beings at the next higher level. That the regress thus generated is infinite we have already seen; that it is vicious, as well, is apparent, since, should we bring it to a halt at any level, we contradict the original proposition that no being knows anything, because we are left with a being that is not deceived hence knows something. To establish the truth of the original proposition, we *must* generate an infinite ascending series of deceivers. But – and this is the crux – it is now obvious that it is *not* the truth of the thesis of cognitivism but rather the truth of the thesis of skepticism which, in order to be established, logically requires a never-ending argument. Ironically, the vicious regress that Lehrer generates by his skeptical hypothesis fails altogether in damaging cognitivism but succeeds brilliantly in destroying skepticism.[18]

Thus Johnson raises the problem we have mentioned before, and it is a problem that always arises in connection with (R_4). One way of looking at the situation is to say that there is knowledge in the world because knowledge is provided for us by our observations. Should anyone question this by introducing Lehrer's Googols then we shall claim still that *some* beings possess knowledge, namely, these Googols. Should anyone try to destroy the knowledge claim of these by introducing super-Googols, then we shall reply that those at least have knowledge. In general, as soon as the sceptic invalidates the knowledge claims of beings of order n by introducing beings of order $n + 1$ we are provided with a new type of being who, we shall claim, possess knowledge. Thus we are capable of frustrating each attempt to establish scepticism.

However, to look at matters in an alternative, pessimistic way, one can say that there is solid basis for doubting whether there is any knowledge in the universe. We humans certainly cannot claim to have confidence in any of our beliefs in view of the possible existence of Googols. The cognitivist may want to suggest that after all these Googols would then possess knowledge. The immediate reply of the sceptic is that the knowledge claims of Googols are in turn subverted by other beings who stand to them in the way that they stand to us. It should be clear therefore that as soon as the cognitivist makes an attempt to attribute knowledge to some beings of order n the sceptic introduces beings of order $n + 1$ to subvert their knowledge. Thus the sceptic is capable of frustrating each attempt to alleviate scepticism.

Johnson's solution to this dilemma is to claim that in the context of this type of regress the crucial question is: what is the philosophical thesis we are required to establish? In the case before us, the universally held view has been that it is perfectly reasonable to rely on our senses to provide us with reliable information about the external world. It is the sceptic who proposes to introduce the novel hypothesis concerning the existence of mind manipulators and thus tries to shake our faith in all cognitive statements. The burden of proof is therefore upon him, and he must demonstrate the soundness of his hypothesis. He should not impose it on us until he can advance it in a manner such that it is not at once subject to an obvious rebuttal by the cognitivist. Johnson seems to base his solution on the principle that (R_4), which is essentially a two-edged weapon, always works against the side that attempts to introduce a novel thesis and that therefore needs to show that it is well founded.

Johnson might claim that his approach can help us to understand the way (R_4) applies in other cases as well. Let us, for example, look once more at J. L. Mackie's attack on the theists' attempt to solve the problem of evil, which we discussed in chapter 3. The theist suggests that suffering is to be condoned because it is an indispensable prerequisite for the possible existence of a number of noble and highly desirable human acts, for it is logically impossible, for example, to have any manifestations of human compassion in a world completely devoid of suffering. We have seen that Mackie accepted the theists' suggested solution: the assertion that the existence of first order evil, consisting in a variety of human misery, is justified because it creates the conditions necessary for higher order good, specifically second order good, which consists of acts associated with efforts to eliminate instances of first order evil. But then Mackie points out that the world undeniably also contains second order evil, which is the counterpart of second order good and consists of wicked acts associated with the effort to perpetuate first order evil. The need to have second order goods may explain the existence of first order but not of second order evil.

Mackie considers the possibility that the theist would try to defend his position by saying that the existence of second order evil could be justified as constituting a necessary prerequisite for a yet higher order good, that is, third order good, which comprises acts designed to combat second order evil, that is, acts aimed at curbing those who are trying to perpetuate first order evil. The theist would claim that third order good has all the merits of second order good as well as an extra merit which clearly elevates it above the latter. Those who fight the wicked contribute to the lessening of first order evil and enhance their moral status as well as enriching the moral content of the world, and in addition tend to decrease the amount of second order evil. The existence of third order good could perhaps be claimed to be precious enough to justify the existence of second order evil. Mackie rejects this defence by arguing that it at once gives rise to the question why there is also third order evil, which will presumably be explained by the need for fourth order good – and so on leading to an infinite regress.

In spite of the fact that the regress he has generated is central to his main argument, Mackie has not attempted to offer any explanation why it must be looked upon as doing damage to the theist. His regress, after all, is of type (R_4), which, on the surface, does not seem to be pointing in one direction more than in the other. Admittedly we can look at the regress pessimistically, as we have pointed out in chapter 3, that is, in a way that suggests we cannot escape our difficulties since as soon as we have justified the existence of evil of level n by explaining that it provides the necessary conditions for good of level $n + 1$, the atheist objects that we are left with unjustified evil of level $n + 1$. Thus every attempt to solve our problem is defeated by the existence of evil of the same level as the good we were so eager to bring into existence. But there is also an obvious way of looking at matters optimistically, asserting that when the question is raised why a certain type of evil is permitted, we can at once come up with a solution. So why is it obvious that the regress works against the theist?

It seems, however, that Mackie, if he accepted Johnson's solution, could well explain why his regress (assuming it is an infinite regress – but as we have explained in chapter 3, it is by no means clear that it is) affects the theistic position adversely. It is reasonable to claim that it is the philosophical thesis that defenders of theism have specifically constructed to save their seemingly vulnerable position that needs to be placed on a solid foundation, for in the absence of some positive, novel argument proving otherwise, the difficulties with the belief that there exists an omnipotent and omnibenevolent being are all too evident. The truth of the claim that there is misery in the world has been clear to everyone from the beginning of human existence. Furthermore, the conviction that to cause and condone unnecessary suffering is incompatible with goodness has always been taken for granted in almost all human societies. The novel and controversial thesis we are confronted with is the suggestion that even though the world is full of suffering it does not follow that unnecessary evil exists, because suffering is logically necessary for the possibility of certain noble acts. It is the defenders of this suggestion who are required to demonstrate the soundness of their claim and formulate it in a manner that does not expose it to rebuttal. But we have seen that at any point along Mackie's regress at which the theist argues that the existence of evil of level n may be justified, on the grounds that it is a precondition for the possibility of manifestations of goodness of level $n + 1$, the atheist can immediately raise the question why there is also evil of level $n + 1$. There seems good reason therefore for maintaining that the problem of evil remains unsolved.

Another example is provided by the famous regress employed by McTaggart in his argument for the unreality of time. This is a subject that has perplexed many, but fortunately we need not go into the intricacies of the argument; a superficial look will suffice for our limited purposes.

According to the most widely accepted interpretation, McTaggart begins by pointing out that the statements 'E is in the future', 'E is in the present' and 'E is in the past' are incompatible statements as they stand and yet all are true of E. To remove the contradiction it should be pointed out that these statements, which are indeed incompatible, may all be truly asserted only if asserted at different times. 'E is in the future' may be true if asserted at M_1, 'E is in the present' is true if asserted at a later time M_2, and 'E is in the past' is true if asserted at a yet later time M_3. This neatly removes the problem of the incompatible statements that are true of E. But what about statements we may assert about M_1, for example? It seems that three incompatible statements, similar to the statements made about E, can be formulated, that is, 'M_1 is in the future' etc. The answer, of course, is that these difficulties too can be eliminated in the way in which we eliminated the difficulties concerning E; the incompatible statements are true only if asserted at different times, that is, 'M_1 is in the future' is true when asserted at M_4, and so on. But as soon as we remove the difficulty concerning M_1 we raise difficulties about M_4, and so on ad infinitum. No matter how many difficulties we solve, new ones can always be generated. This involves us in an infinite regress, as a result of which we must abandon the view that properties such as being in the future, in the present or in the past are real properties of events or moments. But if such basic temporal properties do not really exist, then it would seem to McTaggart that time is altogether unreal.

The above argument sounds pretty unconvincing and there have been countless replies. For our purposes the most instructive objection has been raised by A. Prior. He disagrees with the claim that there is any difficulty to begin with and hence denies that we need to take even the first step along the regress. He says further:

Even if we are somehow compelled to move forward in this way (i.e. taking further and further steps along the regress) we only get contradictions half of the time and it is not obvious why we should regard these, rather than their running mates, as the correct stopping points. [19]

Prior is unique among the many commentators in explicitly pointing out that McTaggart's regress is essentially involved in an ambiguity. On the one hand, we may be inclined to conclude that we are facing an inescapable difficulty, for no matter how many contradictions we eliminate among statements assigning temporal properties to moments, new contradictions may be generated among statements involving other moments. On the other hand, it is possible to conclude that there is no real problem here, since no matter how many contradictions are pointed out we are sure of being able to eliminate them. On the assumption that Johnson's thesis is correct, Prior's objection seems to refute McTaggart's argument. The novel thesis that has been introduced, and which needs to be argued for, is McTaggart's thesis that certain temporal predicates harbour a contradiction. On Johnson's principle the regress works against that thesis, which meets with rebuttal every time it is advanced.

In my book *Aspects of Time* [20] I explained that McTaggart would agree that his claim that certain temporal properties are incompatible stands only if we stop at any odd step of the regress (i.e. the first, third, fifth stops etc.). Hence he would also agree that in the absence of any further argument the conclusion that time is unreal does not follow. However, he has another argument, one that has gone unnoticed by most commentators, as to why it is impossible to stop at any even step along the regress.

Induction and an infinite regress argument

Now we shall look at the suggestion that an infinite regress argument could be constructed to defend our belief in the efficacy of induction. In the past, several attempts have been made to justify inductive reasoning through what was called 'self-justification'. Briefly the argument runs as follows. We know that

$$(\emptyset) = A_1 \text{ has been successful in the past}$$

is true, where A_1 is the rule of induction that is applied to a premiss like 'All as in the past have been found to be bs' to derive the conclusion 'All as are likely to be bs.' Next we may apply the parallel, second-order rule A_2 to $(\emptyset)$, which we now treat as a premiss and derive the conclusion that A_1 is likely to be successful in the future as well.

Max Black, one of the philosophers who has advocated this approach, has insisted that, contrary to what many have maintained, the foregoing argument is not circular. A truly circular argument employs premisses that state what is asserted by the conclusion. However premiss $(\emptyset)$ is definitely not based on the truth of the conclusion to be arrived at; it is based on an immense number of observations.

A number of philosophers found Black's approach hard to accept and raised objections to it. In essence, what they did was to construct some clearly absurd arguments and claim that if Black's defence was valid then we would be forced to admit the soundness of these unacceptable arguments as well. Black has made vigorous attempts to show that this is not so. Let us assume that he has been successful. There still remains a simple objection that has not been mentioned and seems damaging. Black's argument supporting the reliability of A_1 employs the rule of inference A_2. Is there any reason to believe that we are entitled to use A_2, that is, that we may regard A_2 as a valid rule of inference? A_2 is a rule of induction and is therefore admissible if and only if inductive reasoning is valid. But if inductive reasoning is valid then we do not need A_2 since then A_1 can automatically be treated as valid. Obviously we do not take the validity of the rule of induction as given and hence we are not entitled to use A_2.

However, while it is clear that Black's argument as it stands is unsound, it may be treated as the first part of a more elaborate argument which one might wish to defend. Suppose we are inclined to believe that all as are bs since this result has been established by scientists applying rule A_1 to the premiss 'All observed as have been found to be bs.' But we are told by Hume that even though there is a very strong presumption in favour of A_1, in fact our premiss and our conclusion are logically independent and indeed the premiss is not incompatible with the statement 'In the future not a single a will be observed to be a b.' Consequently A_1 is incapable of lending any logical support to the conclusion we wanted to arrive at.

In order to meet this objection, however, we might point out that it is possible to cite a reason why A_1 deserves our trust: it is a well-established fact that A_1 has worked in the past, and hence by applying the rule of inference A_2 it is credible to conclude that A_1 is likely to work in the future as well. The Humean, of course, will now question our use of A_2 and point out that it seems to have no logical force. To this we shall immediately reply that it is a well-established fact that A_2 has worked in the past, and hence we treat the statement which asserts this as our premiss to which we apply A_3 – the obvious parallel of A_2 – and arrive at the conclusion that A_2 is likely to work in the future as well, and so on.

I believe it is clear enough that what we are confronted with here is a regress of type (R_4), for as we move along it we keep oscillating between wanting to assert that there is evidence for the reliability of A_1 and that there is not. As soon as the question is raised as to what the basis is for our confidence in inference rule A_n, which we used in trying to establish the soundness of A_{n-1}, leading ultimately to the support of A_1 itself, it is pointed out that A_n has been successful in the past and hence by A_{n+1} we are entitled to conclude that A_n is likely to be successful in the future as well. If we accept Johnson's approach to this kind of regress it seems that the conclusion to arrive at is that the regress works against the sceptical position of Hume. The method Hume is questioning is one that has always appeared to be the obvious method to use; it was adopted by prehistoric man and has served as our guide ever since in all our empirical inquiries. Nothing could be said to be more entrenched in the human mind than the belief in the efficacy of induction. Hence, if anyone should wish to query it, it is he who must formulate his objection clearly and in a manner that does not lend itself to refutation. However, as soon as the sceptic formulates his objection to A_n we introduce A_{n+1} to justify our confidence in A_n and hence remove his objection.

This proposal to justify induction by using (R_4) suffers, however, from the weakness that it is not very clear how to determine when something should be described as 'the thesis that needs to be established'. If it is claimed that the thesis that needs to be established is decided essentially by reference to the history of the relevant ideas, then we might well sustain the assertion that it is Hume's sceptical position that requires a sound argument to support it. A minimal knowledge of history shows clearly enough that the soundness of induction has always been taken for granted and that it is Hume who is trying to introduce and argue for a novel thesis. But Johnson's view would then be rather hard to defend, for it seems that purely formal considerations ought to be relevant in determining the nature of regress arguments. However, if we focus solely on the logical features of the situation it matters little that it has never before occurred to anyone to doubt the validity of induction. Hume may be said to have demonstrated that no one has any prima facie logical basis for assuming the reliability of induction in the first place. Consequently, until someone advances a clearly formulated argument, one not open to rebuttal, as to why conclusions reached by inductive reasoning are reliable, the original situation remains: A₁ has no logical foundations.

There is, of course, scope for further discussion of the question which thesis is in need of support in any given situation as well as of views other than Johnson's on the proper way to treat regresses of type (R₄). However, at the moment we seem to have no good reason to claim that induction can be defended by a regress argument.

A new approach to induction

Now I should like to advance an argument justifying induction that does not begin by trying in the traditional way to show that scientific method consists of rules which will lead, or at least probably lead, to true hypotheses. I propose to arrive at the methodological rules to be adopted by elimination: that is, I shall try to show that the set of rules we should adopt is the one we are left with after having eliminated everything else as unsuitable.

When it comes to justifying why a given candidate is *not* to be adopted as one of our methodological rules, then clearly we need not do this by demonstrating that the rule in question would lead to an unreliable hypothesis. Later I shall give many more examples of hypothesis selection rules that are to be rejected because their very form reveals at once their uselessness, but at this stage we may look for a moment at the rule 'Adopt the hypothesis which begins with the word 'the'.' It may be seen at a glance that it is out of the question for us to accept this as our hypothesis selection rule – not because it is likely to lead to a false hypothesis, but because it cannot possibly lead to any unique hypothesis. Any assertion may be expressed through a sentence beginning with the word 'the'; thus the rule could not possibly guide us in deciding which of conflicting hypotheses to adopt.

I shall begin with the assumption that even if there is no hope of justifying any set of rules as guaranteed to select hypotheses that are probably true, we still want to have rules for the selection of hypotheses. For no matter how unknowable everything might be we must act in one way or another, and a specific hypothesis that helps to resolve the question of how to act is preferable to no hypothesis at all. But once we begin to examine the problem of what we should adopt as our hypothesis selection rules, we see that there is a vast number of rules that do not come into consideration because they could not help us in selecting any hypothesis in particular. What I am about to argue is that our inductive method basically consists of a set of rules that are at least capable of selecting hypotheses uniquely, while any rule replacing a member of this set would be entirely useless in the sense that it would lead to no hypothesis uniquely. Everyone must agree that a minimal aim of science, an aim which precedes that of producing true hypotheses, is to produce some hypotheses upon which we can act in anticipation of allegedly impending events. The set of rules constituting current scientific methodology is arrived at by having eliminated all alternative rules as useless.

Let me explain the significance of what I have called 'the minimal aim of science'. If I were genuinely worried that perhaps all empirical hypotheses were unreliable and unsuitable for acting upon I should find myself in an impossible situation. I could neither sit nor stand, neither stay put nor go anywhere. After all, if I stay in this room it is because among other things I am tacitly making all sorts of assumptions, for instance, those concerning the laws governing the strength of materials which lead me to believe that the roof will not collapse on me; again, I remain seated, tacitly holding the hypothesis that the chair under me is not suddenly going to rise in temperature. Nor could I either eat anything or venture on fasting if I refuse to postulate any hypothesis: I could not presuppose that any food was not poisonous or that it was safe to abstain from all food. Thus in order to function at all I need a set of hypotheses which I accept and which will guide me in my everyday activities. Current scientific methodology uniquely provides such a set.

The following is a more detailed outline of how our scientific methodology is to be constructed. First of all, when we are about to select a hypothesis for adoption, our selection can certainly not be made from among those that have been falsified, that is, from among hypotheses h_1, h_2, h_3 etc. for which $p(b/h_1) = p(b/h_2) = p(b/h_3) = 0$ (where b states the observational data to be accounted for and $p(b/h_1)$ stands for the probability of b if h_1 were true). Since according to h_1, h_2, h_3 etc. b, which is known to be true, has a probability of zero, these hypotheses have been conclusively refuted. Though we may not be in any way able to ensure that any of our hypotheses is likely to produce correct predictions, it is clearly legitimate to insist that each should account for past observations as well as possible ones. We naturally want the hypothesis we adopt to be selected from among those that are furthest from having been refuted, that is, that account maximally for past observations. In other words, we want them to be selected from among hypotheses k_1, k_2, k_3 etc., where $p(b/k_1)$, $p(b/k_2)$, $p(b/k_3)$ and so on are of maximum value, if possible 1.

Next we want to adopt hypothesis selection rules that are generally applicable; that is, no matter what particular phenomenon is under investigation, the same rule should be capable of being applied to the selection of the hypothesis from among the maximally confirmed hypotheses. Suppose (R_1), (R_2), (R_3) etc., which are pairwise contraries, represent such rules. Let us assume that we find that R_i alone is a rule such that adopting it will lead us to the selection of a specific hypothesis, whereas all the other rules lead us not to a single determinate hypothesis, but at best to a whole group of hypotheses without giving us any clue as to which particular member of the group we ought to adopt. We shall thus reject all the hypothesis selection rules except R_i as being of no use to us; and by elimination we shall be left with R_i alone as the only *adequate* hypothesis selection rule in the sense that it is alone capable of yielding a particular hypothesis. The hypothesis we shall adopt on every occasion will be the one selected with the aid of the adequate rule R_i, which is the sole satisfactory hypothesis selection rule capable of handling appropriately the task of a hypothesis selection rule.

The situation is in reality somewhat more complicated, however. We shall find that not only R_i, but also R_j, R_k etc. are adequate, and that their adoption could lead to the selection of a particular, though different, hypothesis on each occasion.

We thus face a multiplicity of suitable choices and we must find a sufficient reason for selecting a particular adequate hypothesis selection rule. It seems reasonable that if R_i is the only one among the adequate Rs that is unique, in the sense that R_i is the only one of its kind, whereas all the other Rs have duplicates, we should choose R_i as the rule we should employ for selecting hypotheses. It is intuitively preferable to choose R_i, if it has no counterparts, than any rule which is just one among others of its kind. If this justification were to be articulated it would have to be by employing the Principle of Insufficient Reason: if someone were to suggest that we adopt R_k then we might well ask why we should adopt R_k rather than R_k' or R_k'' when these are all rules of the same kind. But if we decide to choose a rule of the kind to which R_i belongs we face no dilemma over which one to choose, as no other rule is of this kind.

According to the view I am advancing here, the system of propositions that constitutes science is essentially a set of hypotheses which account for past observations and which have been chosen with the aid of adequate hypothesis selection rules which are unique of their kind. Our determination to use 'adequate' selection rules in the sense here defined needs no elaborate defence since inadequate rules are simply not usable. It is also obvious that both the principle of considering only adequate

rules and the principle of adopting among these the one which is alone
of its kind are principles which help to prevent us from becoming
paralysed through having to face a superfluity of hypotheses, all of
which account equally well for our observations, and a superfluity of
hypothesis selection rules, all of which are equally adequate.

It is obvious that the principle of selecting the rule which is the sole
representative of its kind will not always lead to the choice of a particular
rule unless we are fortunate enough to find that, whenever we are faced
with a choice, there is one and not more than one relevant rule which is
unique of its kind. It is a remarkable feature of reality that, so far as I
can see, we are indeed fortunate enough not to be faced with
irresolvable dilemmas and are capable of arriving at a unique set of rules
which in turn leads to a unique set of hypotheses.

Inadequacy and elimination

We shall now look at how the central principle – of adopting from
among the equally confirmed hypotheses the one chosen with the aid of
the adequate hypothesis selection rule – works in practice. Suppose it
has been established that $y = f(x)$ represents the relationship between
two physical parameters x and y for all hitherto observed values of the
two variables. When I say 'represents', all I mean is that for all instances
so far observed the values of the parameters involved have satisfied the
equation $y = f(x)$. Then we are faced with the possibility of applying
straight induction or what has been described as 'counter-induction'. In
other words, we might apply the hypothesis selection rule.

(R_1) =   Assume that the regularity which has been obeyed by the
            instances we have checked is also obeyed by hitherto
            unknown instances (for brevity's sake these classes of
            instances will hereafter be distinguished as 'past' and
            'future')

or the contrary rule

(R_2) =   Assume that a different regularity from that which has
            been obeyed hitherto will be obeyed by future instances.

Both (R_1) and (R_2) are entirely independent of the nature of x, y and f,
that is, they are generally applicable irrespective of the particular
phenomena under investigation. The question is, is either of them
adequate?

It would seem that if we adopt (R_1), then the hypothesis we shall accept is that $y = f(x)$ will continue to represent the relationship between the parameters in the future. This amounts to the adoption of a concrete hypothesis, because for any value of x we can predict what the corresponding value of y will be. But if we were to use (R_2) we would be in no such position. All we would know then would be that $y = f(x)$ no longer represents the relationship between x and y. This allows the possibility that infinitely many equations will turn out to represent the way in which x and y actually covary in various instances. Thus knowing that $y = f(x)$ does *not* represent the relationship between x and y does not provide us with a specific hypothesis on the basis of which we can derive any value of y corresponding to any value of x. In the past, various arguments have been put forward by philosophers in support of the thesis that straight induction is preferable to counter-induction. Here, however, we have quickly disposed of counter-induction by showing that it is an inadequate hypothesis selection rule which can be of no use in helping us to choose a particular hypothesis for adoption.

Let us assume for the moment that (R_1) is adequate. Even then it seems that we have not completely vindicated the use of (R_1). Admittedly (R_2) is inadequate and has to be dropped, but there are hypothesis selection rules besides (R_1) which are adequate. It is possible, for example, to appoint a certain person, A_1, whose task it would be to name any particular law he wishes; the rule then is that in every case the law which will govern future phenomena is the law named by A_1. The suggestion may sound frivolous, but if all that we can say in favour of induction is that it produces unique hypotheses, then it does not seem that the rule to follow A_1's instructions can legitimately be denigrated as inferior to it. Alternatively we could devise a method M_1, whereby we list all the possible hypotheses in a given order, number them and then pick a number either by a randomizing device D_1, or by a particular way I_1 of interpreting sacrificial entrails, or by a particular manner F_1 of reading the flight of birds. Our rule then should be to adopt the hypothesis selected by D_1 or I_1 or F_1. Thus we have adequate hypothesis selection rules such as

$(R_3) =$ Assume that the law that will hold in the future is the one designated by A_1

$(R_4) =$ Assume that the law that will hold in the future is the one selected by D_1 from a list compiled by method M_1

and so on.

In the previous section I have already explained that in a case like this, where we are faced with a number of adequate hypothesis selection rules, we have to see which is unique of its kind. (R_3) and (R_4) are not.

First of all, we can see this by substituting A_2 for A_1 in (R_3), and D_2 for D_1 in (R_4), to obtain duplicate rules:

(R'_3) =   Assume that the law which will hold in the future is the one designated by A_2

(R'_4) =   Assume that the law which will hold in the future is the one selected by D_2 from a list compiled by method M_1

and so on. These rules are just as adequate as (R_3) and (R_4).

Another important way of demonstrating the uniqueness of (R_1) is by noting that it is the only adequate rule that does not use empirical facts extraneous to the facts our hypothesis accounts for. A hypothesis of the form $y = f(x)$ accounts for the way a parameter represented by y varies with the parameter represented by x. The fact that A_1 has chosen such and such a hypothesis, or that D_1, I_1 or F_1 has picked such and such a number, is extraneous to the facts to be accounted for. The only adequate rule that does not include such facts seems to be (R_1).

But there are other arguments, apart from those that follow from the Principle of Insufficient Reason, for preferring (R_1) to all other adequate rules. In order to be able to suggest a hypothesis postulating that $y = f(x)$ represents the covariation of y and x, we cannot avoid availing ourselves of information about the various values of x and y that have obtained so far. Information concerning the choice of A_1 or D_1 or the state of sacrificial entrails or the flight of certain birds is not being referred to by our hypothesis. We are capable of constructing a hypothesis to account for what has so far been observed without having to use such information. It stands to reason that we should prefer to be able to choose a hypothesis which also describes observations yet to be made again without using such information.

Matters are, however, not as simple as this. R_1 as it stands is not adequate. Elementary analysis shows that the plain assumption that whatever law governed a phenomenon in the past is going to continue to govern it in the future is not sufficient to lead to any specific hypothesis. Some 50 years ago H. Jeffreys of Cambridge showed that, given any finite number of observations, there are always infinitely many ways to account for them, each description resulting in a claim that a different law has been in operation and consequently leading to a different hypothesis concerning the course of future events. We may illustrate this with the aid of the example observed above, where the two parameters x and y have in the past been governed by the relationship that may be represented by $y = f(x)$. It is then of necessity the case that these parameters could equally well be said to have been observed as being governed by a relationship represented by $y = f(x) + g_1(z)$, where

$g_1(z) = 0$ for all the observations made in the past. The two equations are, of course, equivalent with respect to all past observations, and that is why these observations cannot be used to adjudicate between them. But they are not necessarily equivalent with respect to any future observations, and that is why it is a genuine problem which one to adopt. It can be shown that there are indefinitely many functions $g_2(z)$, $g_3(z)$ and so on, all of which are like $g_1(z)$ in this significant respect; they all equal zero for all the observations made in the past. Assuming then that in the future the same law will be observed as in the past, which law are we supposing to hold in the future – $y = f(x)$, $y = f(x)$ + $g_1(z)$, or some other?

The commonly accepted answer is that we should assume that the most parsimonious hypothesis, namely the one postulating that $y = f(x)$, will hold in the future. I should like to emphasize that the problem of the relative simplicity of hypotheses is a difficult one, and no attempt is made here to provide a general solution. It is only in the case where we have found that hitherto values of x and y satisfy $y = f(x)$, an equation from which we can automatically generate the parasitic equations $y = f(x) + g_1(z)$ and so on, that there is a simple solution: reject all the parasitic equations and adopt the equation which has no extra term at all representing a third variable. The important point, however, is that the rule 'Assume that the future will resemble the past in accordance with the most parsimonious description of the latter' has never been justified. Jeffreys stated that the most parsimonious equation is most likely to represent the truth, but makes no attempt to justify his claim.[21]

It is easily seen, however, that this last rule is also fully explained by what I have said is the principle underlying all scientific method, namely that we reject hypothesis selection rules which are incapable of leading us to any determinate hypotheses. Suppose for a moment that we adopted some alternative rule, for example 'Select the hypothesis with the maximum number of terms.' It does not take much to see that this would be an utterly useless rule. Its uselessness has nothing to do with the likelihood that it would not lead to the correct hypotheses, but with the certainty that it would not lead to any hypothesis at all; given a hypothesis with a vast number of g_1-like terms (that is, terms which equal zero for all past observations), one can always produce another with more terms. Thus there is simply no such thing as the equation with the maximum number of terms. But a rule instructing us to adopt the hypothesis that postulates, say, exactly five terms on the right hand side of the equation supposedly representing the law we are after would also be useless. There are indeterminately many equations in which $f(x)$

is followed by four g_1-like terms. Let us lastly suppose the following rule to be suggested: 'Select the second most parsimonious hypothesis.' We shall be able to convince ourselves quite quickly that this is not adequate either, but is in fact a useless rule. This is not necessarily because we should not be able to come to a general agreement about which *is* the second most parsimonious hypothesis; I am prepared to grant that it might universally be agreed that, of all the g-functions, $g_1(z)$ is the simplest, from which it may be said to follow that $y = f(x) + g_1(z)$ is the second most parsimonious equation. The trouble is that z may stand for indefinitely many different physical parameters, and the rule provides no guidance at all about which one we should take z to represent. Hence the rule would lead us to an indefinitely large group of equations and not to a specific equation. It is only the rule of adopting the most parsimonious equation leading to $y = f(x)$ that provides us with the specific guidance we require.

Thus (R_1) becomes adequate if we adopt it together with

(Q) =   Assume that the most parsimonious equation describes the regularity hitherto observed.

We note that (Q) is also a rule that employs no information about facts extraneous to those accounted for by our hypothesis. Which is the most parsimonious of the various equations that logically imply our observations is determined by looking at these equations and at nothing else.

We may deal in a similar fashion with what has become known as Goodman's problem. Some 20 years after Jeffreys, Nelson Goodman raised essentially the same problem, namely, that past observations lend themselves to different descriptions. Goodman called this the 'new problem of induction' and ever since philosophers have been referring to the problem of which admissible description of the regularities of the past we should adopt in order to project it into the future as 'Goodman's problem'. Goodman presented roughly as follows. Suppose we define 'grue' thus:

Grue =   observed before the year 2000 AD and found green, or observed after the year 2000 AD and found blue. [22]

It is obvious that all our past observations concerning the colour of emeralds permit us to say that all emeralds have been grue no less than that all emeralds have been green. If, however, we describe our experiences as having established that all emeralds were grue and assume this to be true in the future as well, then we shall not expect emerals to look the same after 2000 AD as we shall if we subscribe to 'All emeralds are green.'

A large number of solutions have been suggested. I shall consider some of them. I should like to emphasize first that I do not wish to defend any of these solutions and it makes no difference if the reader regards them all as unsound. My point is that each of these solutions advances a special hypothesis selection rule designed to disqualify predicates like grue; all are rules which, in spite of whatever defects we may discover afflicting them, have *prima facie* some intuitive appeal. These examples illustrate therefore the fact that hypothesis selection rules that seem intuitively satisfactory conform to the fundamental principle underlying methodology: to make use of adequate rules which are unique of their kind.

We may begin by considering W. C. Salmon's suggestion.[23] His proposed solution amounts to advocating that we should employ the following rule:

(P) =   Use purely ostensive predicates only in your projections where 'ostensive predicates' means predicates which can be defined ostensively and are such that the similarity between their instances lies open to direct inspection.

Salmon confines himself to stating as a fact that everybody regards it as natural to use ostensive predicates only; he makes no attempt to defend this principle. I should like to point out, however, that if indeed the question should arise whether we should use (1) only ostensive predicates or (2) non-ostensive predicates as well, or instead, in our projections, then by just once more applying the principle I have claimed to underlie our scientific methodology, we arrive at the conclusion that (1) must be adopted. For if we accept (1), then in a situation where we have made a large number of observations concerning the colour of emeralds, the only ostensive predicate we find applicable to our past experience is 'green', and we are therefore led to the choice of the specific hypothesis 'All emeralds are green.' If, however, we adopt (2), then we would not end up with the choice of any specific hypothesis. There are, after all, infinitely many non-ostensive predicates such as grue$_1$ – which is defined like grue except that '2001 AD' replaces '2000 AD' – and grue$_2$, and so on. In addition, we have gred, grite and so on where red and white respectively stand in for blue. (2) provides us with no instruction whether we should select 'All emeralds are grue$_1$' or 'All emeralds are grue$_2$' or 'All emeralds are gred' or any other.

Another solution is due to S. F. Barker and P. Achinstein.[24] They advance the rule:

(P′) =   Use non-positional predicates only in your projections.

Briefly, the difference between positional and non-positional predicates is this: for all instances of application of a non-positional predicate a single picture or representation can be given. On the other hand, at least two different representations are needed to cover all instances of application of a positional predicate. For example, a single patch of green paint in the present can represent the colour of all green things irrespective of their dates; but two present patches will be needed to represent all grue things: a green one for cases up to 2000 AD and a blue one for cases thereafter.

It can be seen at once that in the context of the example in which Goodman's problem has been raised (P′) is certainly adequate: it disqualifies all such predicates as grue, grue$_2$, gred, and grite and permits the use of green only, since green objects are such that they may be represented at present by a single colour alone.

Finally I shall mention Carnap's solution. It may be noted that Carnap is reported to have withdrawn his solution. However, this does not matter; his was a suggestion which occurred to him on first reflection and which seemed intuitively satisfactory, as indeed it should seem to everyone. He advanced the rule:

(P″) =   In your projections use only predicates that are time-independent.

'Time-independent' predicates are predicates which may be defined without reference to a certain point in time. Grue$_1$, grue$_2$, gred, grite are time-dependent and are thus disqualified. It is clear that (P″) is adequate for the same reason as are (P) and (P′).

It is also clear at once that all the three proposed rules are unique in the required sense. It is not necessary to obtain any information beyond what our hypothesis accounts for in order to be able to apply any one of these rules. We need not go further than noting the colour of emeralds, to which we referred in our generalization, in order to realize that 'green' is a predicate which is ostensive and non-positional and which can be defined without reference to time.

Thus the basic tenets of our methodology so far considered are: some version of (P); in addition (Q), concerning maximum parsimony; and (R$_1$) which bids us assume that the unobserved will be like the observed. These tenets have seemed to philosophers to constitute a disparate set of tenets. Each tenet needed its own justification or, if unjustifiable, had to be postulated independently of the others. But now we have clearly seen that these are not disconnected rules. (P), (Q) and (R$_1$) derive from one basic principle. The validity of this principle stems from the fact that, when all we are given is that the hypotheses we should include in our system of knowledge are to account for what has been observed so far, we are left entirely helpless in the face of an infinite number of candidates. The principle of using adequate hypothesis selection rules that are unique of their kind is not only a very reasonable principle but fortunately releases us from our state of paralysis by leading us to the choice of particular hypothesis selection rules which in turn instruct us in the selection of which particular hypotheses to adopt.

In conclusion, let me say that I do not claim to have dealt here with all the basic problems of empirical reasoning. There may be further problems whose solution may require the postulation of additional hypothesis selection rules or even the replacement of one of the rules presented above. What seems to me true almost beyond question is that the basic principle that guides us in the choice of the fundamental set of rules for the selection of hypotheses is the principle I have just described. Whatever rules will ultimately be decided as belonging to this set will, I feel, conform to this principle.

Vindication and justification

Anyone anxious to resist the suggestion that the inductive method is one we arrive at by the process of elimination just outlined might perhaps attempt to query my argument for the inadequacy of hypothesis selection rules such as (R$_3$) and (R$_4$). He might contend that my claim that the Principle of Insufficient Reason will always help us to decide which rules should be rejected has not been established rigorously enough in the context of this kind of alternative rule. It might be thought that my assumption that my proposed notion of 'a rule that is unique of its kind' has been defined with sufficient precision could be queried.

I shall not offer a lengthy analysis of the notion in question since anyone who has misgivings about its legitimacy has several other, simpler arguments at his disposal to explain why hypothesis selection rules such as (R$_3$) and (R$_4$) are to be rejected in favour of (R$_1$). Now, we took it as a basic desideratum that any rule to be adopted should result in everyone accepting the same hypothesis. But (R$_3$) bids us assume that the law that will hold in the future is the one designated by a person A$_1$. In order that everyone in the world should be able to apply (R$_3$) it is necessary for every individual to obtain the information about the choice A_1 has made. I may be living thousands of miles away from A_1, and so to find out A_1's decision I would have to rely on the telephone, telegraph, smoke signal or some other means of communication. But I am not in a position to do so unless I have some established hypothesis about whether and how these vehicles for conveying information work. Thus we are forced into the Rylean type of regress or circle discussed earlier in this chapter, with its paralysing effect. I have a list of experimental results and would like to obtain from A_1 a hypothesis covering these results as well as any other of their kind that may be forthcoming. In order to do so I require a preliminary hypothesis concerning what may be regarded as a reliable means for transmitting information. But this hypothesis too cannot be obtained before I consult A_1, and so on ad infinitum. The same argument applies, of course, to all those hypothesis selection rules that require our having information other than the experimental results our hypothesis is to account for.

The set of rules (P), (Q) and (R_1), that is, the inductive method, can of course be applied without the need to obtain any piece of empirical information in addition to the set of observational results to be accounted for. It is part of the inductive method to assume that these results can be reproduced by every person wherever he is. The crucial point to bear in mind is that all the results produced everywhere are to be assumed to be similar where 'similar' is defined by the rules (P) and (Q) and the truth of the assumption itself is vouched for by the inductive principle.

It is, I believe, important that I mention one other fundamental argument why it stands to reason that we adopt (R_1) rather than (R_3), (R_4) and their like. We have made mention before of the central role that the notion of simplicity plays in our methodology. We have seen that if we want a principle which will lead us not to a large set of hypotheses of a comparable degree of simplicity but to a unique hypothesis, we must adopt the principle of always selecting the hypothesis of maximum parsimony. What I have said concerning hypotheses applies to hypothesis selection rules as well. I can, of course, offer nothing like a comprehensive criterion for the comparison of the simplicity of any two rules. But I can confidently proclaim one elementary principle no one will want to dispute. Suppose we are faced with an indefinitely large number of selection rules, each requiring the performance of various operations: the first one requires $O \& O_1$, the second $O \& O_2$, the third $O \& O_3$ . . . the nth $O \& O_n$. There is however one rule which consists of what is a part of every other rule and nothing else, namely, of O alone. Unquestionably this rule, which amounts to the performance of an operation that is a proper sub-set of all the other sets of operations required by the other rules, is the simplest rule.

Now, whichever of the other rules we end up adopting for the selection of the hypothesis that postulates the law that governs the correlation of certain parameters in the past, present and future, the first physical operation required is to find out what their correlation was in the past. The next step will be to submit these results to some select individual with the request that he should designate the hypothesis to be adopted, or slaughter the sacrificial animal with a view to examining its entrails, or visit the countryside to observe the flight of certain birds in order to determine what hypothesis to choose. Thus (R_1), and (R_1) alone, is a hypothesis selection rule which has no next step at all. (R_1) is therefore the simplest rule in a very obvious sense.

Now, it so happens that virtually everyone familiar with my suggestion of how to defend induction is prepared to concede that the assumptions on which it rests are sufficiently innocuous to be unobjectionable and that the argument does go as far as it claims to go, which however falls short of what is required. For even if everything I have said is acceptable it follows that, given our desire to use a universally applicable method, we are inevitably led to the genuinely unique method of inductive reasoning. This may be said to be quite an adequate defence of the rationality of the common practices of scientists. But nothing has been said about the chances of these practices being successful. My argument does not provide the much stronger kind of justification that would be required to support the universally firmly-held conviction that the inductive method is likely to yield true hypotheses. In other words, my argument falls short of a full justification in the same way as Reichenbach's argument, as I explained in the Introduction, does. Naturally, I could offer the answer I gave on behalf of Reichenbach there, that our belief in the efficacy of induction has not been formed as a result of any argument but is a deeply entrenched, innate attitude, and all that philosophers are called upon to do is to provide a rational basis compatible with it. To use Herbert Feigl's famous phrase, what may be needed is not a justification but merely a vindication of induction. [25]

It should, however, be pointed out that while my argument does not approach Reichenbach's in ingenuity, it does have a number of considerable advantages over it. None of the technical objections that have been raised against Reichenbach are applicable to my argument. Furthermore, Reichenbach himself admitted that his central claim – that if any method of prediction will work then induction is bound to work too – is true only in the long run, and he offers no defence of the preference for induction over other methods in the short run. But the really crucial weakness of Reichenbach's central claim is that in a vast number of contexts it is plainly false. There are innumerably many methods that are such that if events are predictable by their use then someone adhering to the inductive method will *never* succeed in adopting the right hypothesis. Such methods have for some reason completely escaped the attention of Reichenbach and all his commentators. To avoid unnecessary technicalities consider:

R_3^* = Assume that the law that will hold in the future is the one designated by the Vice President of the United States.

Suppose that the Vice President employs no method in the selection of hypotheses and that what he does in fact amounts to a series of entirely random acts. This suggests that there is no principle one could articulate whose application would produce all the hypotheses that have been produced by the Vice President. Clearly the consistent application of the inductive method to the past results of our observation of the correlation between various physical parameters will not succeed in yielding such a principle either.

Remarkably enough, even in a case such as this Reichenbach's idea is not entirely irrelevant. For should it turn out that the strange method of letting the Vice President select our hypotheses meets consistently with success then we may apply induction to this very fact and argue that seeing that R_3^* has always been successful in the past it is likely to be so in the future and thus we should adopt it. But of course there is a decisive difference between the way we normally apply the inductive method and the extraordinary way we would apply it under these peculiar circumstances. Normally we observe the correlation between the relevant parameters, describe it and employ the description as the premiss of our argument. But here of course our premiss has to be the ruling of the Vice President. The obvious trouble is that it may never occur to us to request the Vice President to serve as our hypothesis-selector and thus we shall never become aware of the premiss we need for our inductive argument. We shall continue forever applying induction to the premiss we are bound to believe is the right premiss, namely, the actual description of the past behaviour of whatever physical particulars we may be interested in, and we shall get nowhere. Thus we have a simple illustration of a possible universe in which there is a plain method that would always yield the right predictions, but in which – contrary to Reichenbach's claim – we shall never succeed by using induction in arriving at a correct hypothesis because of our ignorance of crucially important information.

Let me conclude by saying that not only is it possible that I have succeeded in providing a vindication of induction free from the defects of Reichenbach's proposal, but we can also envisage a way in which my argument may lead to a stronger kind of defence. Here I have to allude to a metaphysical principle intimately related to our concerns but whose proper treatment would require a chapter of its own. I am referring to the Principle of the Intelligibility of Nature. This principle may be taken to imply that human beings are endowed with the capacity to discover how nature works and that our minds are so constituted that we are attracted to finding, and impelled to believe in, hypotheses that represent true laws of nature. It is clear, however, that the principle cannot be equated with the universal generalization that the human mind has the fortunate property of always lighting on the right hypothesis. There is, for instance, a fairly widespread propensity to believe in superstitions. A great number of people have been fascinated by astrology, and even some famous leaders, for example Hitler, have made important decisions based on horoscopes, often with entirely disastrous results.

Is it possible to formulate a universal generalization that would reasonably well correspond to what has been meant by this fundamental belief in the intelligibility of nature? One might be tempted to say that the belief is a belief in the following principle:

(PIN) = Nature is so constituted that it will yield its secrets when they are sought by the appropriate method.

However (PIN) remains a vacuous statement so long as we do not have a definition of 'appropriate method' not described by (PIN), that is, so long as we can say no more about it than that it is a method that is bound to lead us to success in discovering nature's secrets. Our next attempt might be to substitute 'inductive method' for 'appropriate method'. But this too does not seem to yield a happy result. One way of accounting for our dissatisfaction would be to point out that thus interpreted, (PIN) would seem to lose its significance. But (PIN) has always been regarded as a remarkable feature of the universe; and we are supposed to be filled with wonder at our special good fortune in finding ourselves in such a universe, one which is so vast and complex and yet yields its secrets to our limited minds. But if there are infinitely many practicable methods then, if the laws of nature were discovered by any one of these, nature would have to be regarded as intelligible just the same, and as a result it would be much harder to remain fascinated by the fact that nature is intelligible.

By now, however, we are in a position to realize that the method referred to in (PIN) is the one very special method we are led to adopt as our method of investigating nature on the basis of reasoning alone. That the universe should so be constituted that its nature becomes intelligible through the application of a methodology that may be reproduced with the sole aid of rational argument is understandably a source of wonder.

9

Formal methods, verificationism and the existence of an external world

Mathematical logic in philosophy

In this chapter we shall touch upon some aspects of the fundamental metaphysical belief that our sense impressions are generated by factors external to our minds and independent of them, factors that constitute what is called a real, external world. The philosopher who most notably raised doubts concerning this belief was Descartes, and one of his best-known arguments in this connection is the Dream Argument. Reviewing this argument will provide us with an opportunity to deal with one of the many aspects of what is probably the greatest methodological innovation of this century, the adoption of formal, mathematical logic as a tool for philosophical analysis.

The introduction of formal methods of reasoning into philosophy has on the whole had a very beneficial effect on the discipline, greatly improving the clarity of expression and the rigour of argumentation. Inevitably, as with all good things, these methods can and have been misused; their indiscriminate application has had a variety of ill effects. While there is hardly any need for expatiating on the many obvious virtues of using mathematical methods in the construction of arguments, it would be useful to discuss what is much less often considered, that is, the unhappy results which the excessive use, and in some cases even the abuse, of these methods has produced.

The wholesale mathematicization of the discipline has had various types of unfortunate effect, and a whole book would be required to deal adequately with them. Let me briefly mention a few. One well-known undesirable product has been the blurring of the boundaries between metaphysics and other disciplines. Since the methodology of metaphysics, or of philosophy in general, has come to resemble to such a great extent the methodology of the strictly mathematical and natural sciences, it has become considerably easier to overlook the fact that some works purporting to deal with philosophy are essentially dealing with linguistics, mathematical logic, probability theory, decision theory, theoretical physics and so on.

Another undesirable effect of the undue mathematicization of philosophy is that much that is written, while it may belong to metaphysics proper, deals with trivial issues blown up to an extent that is quite out of proportion to their importance. There are a number of reasons why there is a correlation between the increase in the use of formal methods and the increase in the number of inconsequential discussions. The most obvious one can be seen in a philosophical discussion in which we are led to a statement which is such that if it were presented entirely unadorned its lack of significant content would be transparent. When the same statement is advanced in the context of an elaborate system of formal arguments and expressed in symbolic language with the aid of a couple of longish expressions, we are ready to assign far more weight to it.

It may also be claimed that those who look upon philosophy as a discipline closely related to mathematics tend to discourage the use of arguments that are not rigorously deductive, and this is not always an advantage. I am referring to what some may claim is an undue suppression of fruitful ideas and arguments, brought about by an insistence upon judging everything in the light of formal methodology. A philosopher may move from p to q even though p may not strictly, logically, imply q. However, he may be able to show by skilfully presented and persuasive arguments that the move was reasonable. There are well-known principles of reasoning, as we have said before, that are used only in philosophy and are not quite deductively valid. The most interesting contributions to philosophy are often made when an entirely new form of reasoning is introduced and argued for in so forceful a manner that the reader becomes persuaded of its reasonableness. Often an important proposition is advanced not through the application of logical or quasi-logical rules, but by pointing out that its adoption leads to the illumination of some other proposition or set of propositions which is otherwise difficult to understand, or that it enables us to subscribe to some proposition we find intuitively appealing but otherwise cannot justifiably hold, and so on. Such considerations are not recognized by formalists as valid. Those who are wedded to formal techniques feel inhibited in employing arguments that are merely persuasive and not conclusive, and also discourage others from employing them.

But of all the undesirable results of the excessive insistence on formalization, the one that is of more significance than any of these is that philosophers tend to concentrate on those and only those aspects of a problem which lend themselves to handling by formal methods, regardless of whether they are important aspects of the problem, or aspects whose study can yield philosophical insight. Let me be a little more specific. When a philosopher claims to have arrived at the conclusion that q from the premiss that p, then what is most obviously susceptible to formal analysis is the claim that p logically implies q. The logician will thus translate p into a formal language, supply the extra premisses he thinks may be needed for the actual derivation and describe precisely the sequence of steps that are required in order to arrive at q from p, as well as examine the possibility that there may be alternative sequences, employing different rules, which lead to q from p. The outcome in most cases fails to be very illuminating and has hardly anything to recommend it but complexity or elegance. For in the typical case, the really interesting questions are to be found not around the issue of the logical relationship between p and q but rather in the issues relating to such questions as: what concepts do the terms of p represent? What is the exact meaning of p? Does p adequately represent our beliefs? What precisely are the assumptions on which those beliefs are based? Are those assumptions justified? and so on. These questions, however, are not as a rule amenable to formal treatment and are consequently neglected.

In what follows I shall examine in detail a suggested reconstruction of Descartes' Dream Argument which may indicate the possible perils of formalization.

A reconstruction of Descartes' Dream Argument

A typical summary of Descartes' Dream Argument was given by G. E. Moore:

'You do not know for certain that you are not dreaming; it is not absolutely certain that you are not; there is *some* chance, though perhaps only a very small one, that you are.' And from this that I do not know for certain that I am not dreaming it is supposed to follow that I do not know for certain that I am standing up.[1]

According to this the conclusion of the argument is:

(c) = $\sim KS$ (I do not know that I am standing up)

and one of the premisses is

(p_1) = $\sim K \sim D$ (I do not know that I am not dreaming)

In addition, Descartes seems also to rely on the premiss:

(p_2) = $D \supset \sim KS$ (If I am dreaming I do not know that I am standing up)

for he tells us how often he has been deceived in his dreams concerning matters of fact.

What strikes us at once is that (p_1) and (p_2) do not entail (c)! Admittedly $\sim K \sim D$ may be true for different reasons. One reason may be that D is true and certainly it is impossible to know that $\sim D$ when in fact D is the case. But if D is true, then that together with (p_2) implies by Modus Ponens (c). However, the trouble is that $\sim K \sim D$ may also be true even in the case in which $\sim D$ happens to be true so long as I am not *justified* in believing that $\sim D$. Hence clearly $\sim K \sim D$ on its own does not entail D and thus (p_1) and (p_2) do not entail (c).

Mark Steiner discusses this matter in an ingenious paper[2] and claims that (c) follows if we add a third premiss nowhere mentioned by Descartes, namely:

(*) = If one is committed to $\sim KP$ (P for any sentence) then it is irrational of him to assert P.*

His demonstration is as follows:

(1)	$KS \supset \sim D$	from (p_2) by Counterposition
(2)	$K(KS \supset \sim D)$	(1), Necessitation Rule of Epistemic Logic
(3)	$KKS \supset K \sim D$	(2), Another rule of epistemic logic
(4)	$\sim K \sim D \supset \sim KKS$	(3), Counterposition
(5)	$\sim KKS$	(p_1) & (4), Modus Ponens
(6)	Asserting KS is irrational	(5) & (*)

I shall attempt to subject Steiner's argument as just laid out to closer scrutiny, but the following point already seems obvious.

No one is likely to claim seriously that Steiner's 'reconstruction' represents what Descartes actually had in mind. He employs a number of logical principles that were unknown in the seventeenth century. Admittedly each of them is fairly simple and not necessarily beyond the grasp of a mind like Descartes'. Still, since they had never been explicitly formulated before, he should at least have mentioned them, for he certainly could not assume that they would be known to his readers. Even if all the intermediate steps were common knowledge he should

---

* I do not follow Steiner's numbering.

have mentioned them explicitly. It happens sometimes that a writer neglects to mention an obvious intermediate step in an argument, but surely not six consecutive intermediate steps.

Conceivably an attempt could be made to defend Steiner. One could suggest that his is not a reconstruction of Descartes but rather an effort to show that as a matter of objective fact Descartes' conclusion follows from his premises via six valid steps. Apart from the fact that this is not the impression we get from reading Steiner's paper, for his aim seems to be to explicate Descartes' argument, we could ask whether such an exercise has any point. One is not likely to give an affirmative answer should it turn out that there are other ways in which the conclusion may be shown to follow from the premises, ways that could more plausibly be claimed to represent Descartes' own or ways that were merely simpler than Steiner's.

The flaws in the reconstruction

Let us begin by examining the way Steiner moved from (1) $KS \supset \sim D$ to (2) $K(KS \supset \sim D)$, that is, from (1) to K(1). He says that he has done so on the assumption that if I myself have demonstrated the truth of (1), then surely not only must (1) be true, and I believe it to be true, but I am also justified in believing it to be true and hence K(1). Now in general, given that p is true and that p entails K_q, then in spite of the fact that K_q asserts something about me it is an objective fact that K_q is true irrespective of whether I am or am not aware of the logical connection between p and K_q. However, the move from (1) to K(1) is not facilitated by pure logic alone, it also requires that I myself should have derived (1) from true premises, that is from (p_2). Hence, for any person who is not aware of the fact that (p_2) entails (1) because he does not know the rule of logic called Counterposition, or it did not occur to him that it applies here, and there are such people, K(1) is not true and hence (6) remains underivable. Also (6) does not follow for anyone who does not realize the truth of (p_1) and (p_2).

Let us look at the precise implication of this. Let Kdp stand for 'Descartes knows that p' and Kxp stand for 'x knows that p'. Suppose also that x is the name of a person who is intellectually vastly inferior to Descartes, capable of little reasoning or understanding and knowing hardly any of the basic rules of logic.

We shall let

Dx = x is dreaming.
Sx = x is standing up.

Then it is reasonable for us to assume the truth of the following two premisses:

$(p'_1) = \sim Kx \sim Dx.$
$(p'_2) = Dx \supset \sim KxSx.$

Now, as before, we obtain:

$(1') = KxSx \supset \sim Dx$ from (p'_2) by Counterposition.

The point however is that from $(1')$ it is not possible, for the reason we have mentioned, to derive

$(2') = Kx (KxSx \supset \sim Dx)$

and consequently it is impossible to arrive at the conclusion that

$\sim KxKxSx.$

It may be noted however that we can derive

$(2'') = Kd (KxSx \supset \sim Dx)$

since Descartes is in possession of the relevant information. From this we get

$(3') = KdKxSx \supset Kd \sim Dx$

which is a counterpart of (3) and

$(4') = \sim Kd \sim Dx \supset \sim KdKxSx$

which is a counterpart of (4). We recall that in the original reasoning Steiner applied Modus Ponens to derive from (p_1) and (4) the conclusion that

$(5) = \sim KKS.$

It is, however, clearly impossible in the parallel reasoning process to derive from (p'_1) and $(4')$:

$(5') = \sim KdKxSx$

since (p'_1) is $\sim Kx \sim Dx$, whereas the antecedent of $(4')$ is a quite different proposition, namely $\sim Kd \sim Dx$.

Thus we see that, while it is possible to prove that $\sim KdKdSd$, we are able to prove neither that $\sim KdKxSx$ nor that $\sim KxKxSx$. It also follows therefore that it can be established that it is irrational for Descartes to assert that $KdSd$, but not that it is irrational for Descartes or for anyone else to assert that $KxSx$. This result is paradoxical. The implication is that Descartes, regarded by all as a man of immense intelligence and learning, is forced, contemplating his own state of knowledge, to the conclusion that he cannot claim to be knowing anything at all. However, when it comes to the intellectually vastly inferior x, thought of by everyone as a complete ignoramus, we can find no reason why it is inappropriate for him or for anyone else to assert that he knows a large number of true propositions.

We have already developed some idea of how the ascription of an unduly great usefulness to the formal method of analysis can lead one astray. It is not surprising to find the aforementioned flaws in Steiner's analysis. Given the approach he was determined to take, he was likely to miss the points he seems to have missed. None of our objections have been, after all, formal objections. The assertion that his reasoning is not an authentic reproduction of Descartes' reasoning, or that it may not serve any useful purpose, does not imply that any step in his argument is invalid. Nor does the last objection imply any fault with the logic of Steiner's derivation. The premisses with which Steiner begins are reasonable. Each one of the rules of inference he employs is valid. His conclusion follows strictly from his premisses via the steps he has described. All this is as one would expect from a first-rate logician like Steiner. However, while Descartes happens to be dealing specifically with his own state of knowledge, there are compelling reasons, based on our understanding of such notions as 'knowledge', 'intelligence' and the like, for saying that, whatever cracks we may discover in the foundations of Descartes' knowledge claims, these must surely be present in those of his intellectual inferiors. Our objections, which Steiner was quite liable to overlook, do not affect the formal validity of his arguments but do affect their usefulness and relevance.

A better attempt

Our objections are strengthened by recognizing that there are other, better ways of reconstructing Descartes' Dream Argument so that the conclusion is clearly seen to follow logically from the premisses.

The first way of doing this is to postulate that the sceptic employs no premisses at all that refer to what happens if we are dreaming. The sceptic may well adopt the attitude that the burden of proof is on anyone who claims that we *can* know the truth of any sense-based assertion, rather than on the one who wishes to deny this. It is possible to begin by wondering what prima facie reason there is for the truth of any such assertion. After all, we have direct access only to our own mental world; how do we arrive at assertions about the external world?

Our so-called perception of external objects amounts to no more than our experiencing certain sensations which incline us to attribute their causes to features of the external world. But what is the logical basis for such attributions?

The position I have just described is widely known as the phenomenalistic position. There are a number of well-known moves available to the realist or physicalist who claims that our inner experiences justify us in our belief in an external world. I shall not refer to any specific arguments of the latter and will only state in general that the realist holds that our perceptions bear some distinct mark, which we may denote as ϕ, which somehow guarantees that they are occasioned by suitably corresponding external events. Thus if

$$\phi x = \quad x \text{ is a mental event which has a unique feature of a specific sort}$$
$$\psi x = \quad x \text{ is caused by an external event}$$

then it is not inconceivable that the realist might wish to claim that there is a principle

$$(x)(\phi x \rightarrow \psi x) \ldots \text{(i)}$$

In addition, he may assert

$$\phi \, \Sigma \ldots \text{(ii)},$$

that is, roughly, 'The mental event of having the impression of standing up has the feature ϕ.' From this it follows that

$$\psi \, \Sigma \ldots \text{(iii)},$$

which of course implies that there is an external world. It might be added on behalf of the realist that since S (= I am (*actually*) standing up) has been proven to be a justified belief it follows that KS. To this however Descartes can reply

$$\phi \, R \, \& \sim \psi \, R \ldots \text{(iv)}$$

pointing out that in the past some mental event R which occurred in a dream and which had ϕ turned out unquestionably to be $\sim \psi R$!

While I shall not insist that this must definitely be the argument Descartes had in mind, I do wish to point out that for several reasons my reconstruction has a number of advantages over Steiner's reconstruction and to that extent it is more likely to be a genuine explication of Descartes' argument. First of all, its argument consists of considerably fewer steps. Secondly, it does not require the use of premiss (*) – an advantage since not everyone would grant that (*) was true. For example, some philosophers, as we have seen, insist that for any p, a person does not know that p unless his belief is justified and, furthermore, he himself is in cognitive possession of that justification. Suppose now that X believes that

p = I have a toothache

and X is a layman who does not know what precise feature of p ensures that he is justified in believing it. In other words, though in common parlance it may sound strange that X is capable of being ignorant of having a toothache, X, who may be aware of the principle that a knower must be in cognitive possession of the justification of his belief, may realize that by a strict philosophical criterion $\sim Kp$. Nevertheless, I am convinced that X would have the permission of all philosophers to see his dentist and complain loudly about his toothache. Thus it is not irrational for X to assert p and indeed to insist that he means p in spite of the fact that X is committed to $\sim Kp$. But then we have just denied the truth of (*). Our explication of Descartes' argument makes use of premises upon which everyone will agree without exception. Thirdly, while Steiner's argument is restricted to showing that a sophisticated person like Descartes lacks all knowledge, the argument we have just described leads to universal uncertainty, for it does not require the move from (1) to (2) which depends on the fact that one has oneself derived (1) from (p_2) and is therefore a move which is not valid for all people. Fourthly, the conclusion arrived at represents a firmer kind of scepticism, one which besides being somewhat more interesting also seems more likely to have been Descartes' own conclusion, namely, that not merely is it irrational to assert that KS but that one can definitely proclaim that $\sim KS$.

It is worth noting that according to my reconstruction Descartes' argument does not at any stage involve a claim that he *is* dreaming or that he *may be* dreaming or that he *does not know* that he is not dreaming at this moment or always. According to my reconstruction he may well suppose that he is wide awake. Yet there is no sufficient reason to maintain that sensations are reliable indicators of occurrences which take place in an external world. It could be argued, however, that there is no substantial difference, or indeed any meaningful difference, between the so-called state of wakefulness I wish to assign to ourselves and the possible state of dreaming Steiner wishes us to entertain about ourselves. It would seem that what is being raised is not the possibility that I am dreaming in the sense that I am lying stretched out in a bed, my eyes closed and my body in a state of relaxation typically associated with a state of sleep. Surely Descartes meant to raise the possibility of there not being a bed at all and of our bodies not being in any state whatever, for anything material may only seem to exist and the sole reality is our mental world. His kind of dreaming may well be equated with my state of wakefulness since in both nothing really exists beyond what goes on in our minds.

However, some may wish to argue that Descartes' writings permit an interpretation according to which we do not know that we are not literally dreaming. That is, we may be having a dream from which we may eventually awake and find an external world, but one vastly different from what we envisage at the moment.

Further reconstructions

Now I would like to show that if we wish we could grant that Descartes indeed starts with premisses $(p_1) \sim K \sim D$ and $(p_2)\ D \supset \sim KS$ and still arrives at a sceptical conclusion, but in an entirely different and much faster way than Steiner supposes, and one that seems much nearer to what Descartes might have had in mind. Clearly (p_1) may be taken to imply PR $(\sim D) \leqslant 1 - n,^*$ where n is sufficiently large to create enough uncertainty for D not to be established beyond reasonable philosophical doubt and thus not to be known as true. This, of course, means that PR(D) $\geqslant n$ and by the intuitively given principle that when it is given that $p \rightarrow q$ then PR $(q) \geqslant$ PR (p) it follows via (p_2) that PR $(\sim KS) \geqslant n$, that is, that PR (KS) $\leqslant 1 - n$. This means that KS is uncertain enough to ensure that $\sim$ KKS. But if $\sim$ KKS then by (*) it is irrational for us to assert KS.

The present derivation of Steiner's result has a number of advantages over his. Firstly, it reaches the conclusion in fewer steps. Secondly, it does not make use of the questionable move which led him from (1) to (2) and in consequence of which people who could not derive (1) themselves are not committed to (2). Thirdly, while it does make use of (*), it does so under circumstances no one can object to. Let me explain. Sometimes the reason may be that $\sim Kp$ because I may not be able to justify my belief that p even though I am absolutely certain that p. We already discussed an example of this, that is, when p stands for 'I have a toothache.' In this case (*) may well be said to be invalid, since it is reasonable to assume that it is not irrational for me to assert p. But when $\sim Kp$ results from my being uncertain to a sufficiently high degree whether p is true then we should feel no scruples about agreeing to (*).

---

* PR = probability of.

In the case before us p stands for KS and $\sim Kp$ was established directly from the fact that $PR(\sim p) \geqslant n$ and hence the validity of (*) in our case is not to be queried.

But there is a way of explicating Descartes that seems superior to all these ways. In the passage cited by Steiner, Descartes says 'I see so manifestly that there are no certain indications by which we may clearly distinguish wakefulness from sleep that I am lost in astonishment.' According to this, it seems that the uncertainty attaches to the very question whether he is in a state of wakefulness, since it is quite possible that he is asleep. In other words, his first premiss plainly seems to be 'I may be dreaming.' From this and (p_2) follows 'It may be the case that I do not know S.' If we insist on formalization then the first premiss may be put $PR (D) \geqslant m$ where m is the minimum probability a proposition must have if its truth is to be seriously entertained. Then because of (p_2) it follows that $PR(\sim KS) \geqslant m$ and therefore the likelihood of $\sim KS$ is not negligible and the possibility that $\sim KS$ is the case is not to be dismissed. In this way we make no use of (*) and we arrive at a stronger form of scepticism so that not merely is it irrational to assert KS but we are committed to $\sim KS$.

This last reconstruction makes use of the concept of probability, and Descartes lived before the birth of probability theory. Still, it is commonly agreed that long before the systematic study of probability philosophers had a grasp of certain elementary truths concerning it.

The defence of belief in an external world

When it comes to the constructive task of providing a rational basis for a belief in a physical reality outside our mental world, this proves to be more arduous than providing a basis for the metaphysical beliefs discussed in the previous two chapters. I shall probably not be required to offer a lengthy justification of this claim. It is obvious that different types of scepticism presuppose different extents of unquestioned beliefs, and clearly the less that is being queried the more that is available from among our accepted beliefs for constructing the foundations of the hypothesis to be established. Solipsistic doubts are easier to deal with than the wholesale doubt in the efficacy of our methods of empirical reasoning. For as long as we have confidence in the latter we can make use of some aspects of it, as we have seen in chapter 7 in our attempts to justify the belief in the existence of other minds. But now, rather than other minds or other bodies, nothing except our own experiences are questioned. Thus little room is left for manoeuvre and little stable ground remains for us to stand on while developing a convincing reply to the radical kind of scepticism we are confronted with.

I propose to do no more than provide an outline of what may amount to a plausible answer. First, however, let me point out that while the problem of an external world, one associated with Descartes, is still regarded with considerable interest, Descartes' own solution is rarely thought of as meriting serious study, except of course in the context of the history of philosophy. I shall not examine the reason for this, but make one small point. After discovering the possibility that he might be dreaming, Descartes maintains that the only consideration that can make him doubt his most evident perceptions is the idea of God's great powers. However, he subsequently argues that on a fuller understanding of the idea of God and its implications he has come to realize that it is unthinkable that an all-perfect being should engage in deception. One of the things I find hard to understand is why the notion of deception should be thought applicable in this context. A paradigm instance of being greatly deceived would be if I have a vivid dream in which I am deluded into a variety of expectations. The relevant feature of such an instance is that it eventually comes to an end; I wake up and realize to my chagrin that I am not, for example, stretched out on a deckchair on a luxury yacht but am lying in bed in my humble apartment. Thus I have been cheated out of my expectations. It is not clear that a wholly sustained 'deception' – where all my expectations are fulfilled to exactly the same degree as they would be if there was no deception, where there is no waking up and where there is not now or ever the slightest difference in any of my experiences to what they would be like if there actually was an external world – must still be regarded as a deception in any significant sense.

As I have said, philosophers have usually disregarded Descartes' constructive proposals and have gone on to develop their own. There is a well-known reply to someone who entertains what is called the phenomenalistic position, that of denying the existence of an external world. The reply is based on the claim that the phenomenalist is forced to subscribe to a vastly more complex set of hypotheses than his adversary, the realist. The realist is in the advantageous position of being able to account for his experiences by the use of the established laws of physics. He accepts, for instance, the truth of the relatively simple laws of Newtonian mechanics and explains in terms of these the immense variety of sense experiences he believes to have been induced by the actual motions of material bodies. His adversary, however, denying the existence of the external world, clearly admits the reality neither of material bodies nor of their motion, which he cannot therefore speak of as obeying the greatly unifying and simplifying laws of Newton, or, for that matter, any other laws. The implication appears to be that the principle of simplicity commits us to the realist position.

The phenomenalist may, however, resist this argument without denying the unifying power of Newton's laws or the importance of the principle of simplicity. He could claim that he too, no less than the realist, accepts Newton's laws as well as every other law to be found in standard textbooks. The only point at which he differs from the realist is in reading each one of these laws slightly differently. For example, he will maintain that in reality there are no moving physical bodies; however, our perceptions are such that we are capable of fully describing them by speaking as if moving bodies which obeyed Newton's laws of motion existed.

On the surface, however, the phenomenalistic reply should appear objectionable. We do not in general admit the kind of argument that posits that h is false, but everything behaves exactly as if h were true. Scientists never regard such an argument as legitimate. For example, there have been many opponents to the kinetic theory who maintained the caloric theory of heat and attempted for a long time to defend their position with a variety of arguments. No one, however, ever thought it plausible to maintain that the kinetic theory was false except that gases behave in a manner such that they seem to consist of discrete particles obeying the laws that comprise the kinetic theory. There is a variety of possible explanations for this. One is that it has been assumed to be too improbable that given that h was false, nevertheless everything should by an immensely happy coincidence behave as if h was true. It is at this stage that the phenomenalist may introduce the Dream Argument or the Demon Argument, which refer to situations in which complex experiences, describable with the aid of a fictitious external reality, do take place. It should serve as an illustration of circumstances under which the particular h under review may be false and yet everything appear as if it was true.

The debate need not, however, come to an end at this stage. The realist may go on to advance another suggestion as to how his metaphysical belief in the existence of an external world might be justified. The following is an outline of his suggestion. To begin with, the realist points out that many philosophers have agreed that I may incorrigibly assert 'I perceive that p' where, for example, p stands for 'There is a table in front of me.' This is so when, in uttering 'I perceive that p', I am understood not to be making a direct claim that p actually obtains − that is, when my utterance is not taken to be a direct assertion that there is something to be perceived, but only as a report of what is going on in my mind. In other words, I may incorrigibly assert 'I perceive that p', when all I wish is to convey the information that I am having certain visual or tactile experiences. In this sense, 'I perceive' is not used to imply 'I know' – for if it were I could not be said truly to perceive that which is not the case – but rather it is used merely to report a sense impression. The statement is just an avowal of my immediately felt experience, on which I am, according to many philosophers, an absolute authority. It would be absurd for anyone to attempt to talk me out of it, to try and convince me that I am mistaken, or that it is not a fact that I perceive that p (saying perhaps that it only appears to me that I perceive that p, when of course there is no distinction between 'It appears to me that I perceive that p' and 'I perceive that p').

It is essential to emphasize that the realist would not regard 'I perceive that p' as incorrigibly true irrespective of what p stood for. When p stands for 'There is a table in front of me' then the statement is incorrigibly true because there are two necessary factors present:

1 The kind of sensation I claim to be undergoing is certainly such that you can at will reproduce it in your mind. You know precisely how it feels to have the perceptual impression of there being a table in front of you. I am thus asserting that I am having an experience of a kind with which you are perfectly familiar, and therefore there is not a shadow of doubt that you know what I am talking about.

2 It is out of the question that I am mistaken since I am talking about my immediately sensed experience and it is ruled out that I am untruthful as it is given that I am sincere.

However, when p stands for something like 'The absolute is lazy' then 'I perceive that p' is not true because condition (1) is not fulfilled. When I claim to perceive that the absolute is lazy, you, the hearer, have really no idea what kind of a sensation I report having when allegedly perceiving what I claim to be perceiving. In fact, you have no idea at all what I am talking about.

Thus we may well suppose that the realist would be claiming that in all those cases in which (1) and (2) are fulfilled, and consequently 'I perceive that p' must be accepted as true, p is meaningful. He is, of course, not claiming that if 'I perceive that p' is true then p is also true; only that p must be meaningful. The realist who is supposed to subscribe to verificationism would argue that 'I perceive that the absolute is lazy' is not true, in spite of my being an unquestioned authority on my immediate sense experience, simply because 'The absolute is lazy' is nonsensical and nobody can imagine what sort of sensation I must be having when perceiving the absolute as lazy. Thus if

p is not meaningful, then neither is 'I perceive that p.' But if 'I perceive that p' is not meaningful, then it could not be true, and so ipso facto could not be incorrigibly true.

At this stage the verificationist – realist may propose that we take a crucial step and claim that the verification principle may be put to a use which is the inverse of the use to which verificationists are in general supposed to put it. Usually, it is assumed that what is to be done is to note that a given sentence is verifiable, and hence to classify it as meaningful, or else demonstrate that it is not verifiable, and so exclude it from meaningful discourse. But here the realist suggests that a verificationist may do the opposite: note that a given sentence is undeniably meaningful and hence declare that it must be verifiable. Thus, since we are compelled to judge that 'There is a table in front of me' is meaningful, we must also regard it as verifiable. But, since it is necessarily the case that no other evidence could be available, we are forced to give our approval to the generally accepted evidence, such as testimonies based on sense impressions, as sound indicators that there is a table in front of me. For consider what kind of evidence is commonly regarded as sufficient to establish the truth of p. I may mention a number of typical examples:

1   I perceive with my eyes that there is a table in front of me.

2   I can touch it with my hands and feel that there is a table in front of me.

3   It is dark and I have not touched anything, but just before the lights went out I saw a table in front of me, and not having heard the slightest sound since, I take it that the table could not have been removed.

4   Somebody completely reliable tells me that there is a table in front of me on the basis of the kind of evidence mentioned in (1), (2) or (3). Clearly (1), (2), (3) and (4) are ultimately based on the testimony of my senses, as would be anything else imaginable that would normally be regarded as evidence for p. Thus, if we were permitted to query whether our sense impressions are reliable indicators of conditions in the external world, we could not possibly confirm that p was true.

Suppose the following objection is raised. Admittedly p, which is part of a meaningful sentence, must be regarded as meaningful. Let it also be conceded that since p is meaningful it must also be confirmable. But perhaps it is confirmable because circumstances are describable in which p would be confirmed as false. When, for example, after searching as thoroughly as possible I cannot detect any traces of a table anywhere near me, it could be claimed that there is evidence that p is false. One could possibly even go further and claim that if every p-like sentence were confirmed as false we could well deny then the existence of an external world.

But the realist should not find it difficult to meet this objection. After all, the issue raised by the form of scepticism under review is whether sense impressions are reliable clues to conditions prevailing in an external world. To the extent that our searching hard and not finding a table in the vicinity may legitimately be taken as confirming the falsity of p, to that extent we admit that our sense impressions are not deceiving us. In that case, there is no good reason to cast doubt on the trustworthiness of our senses when we see a table in front of us.

It is clear that the realist's claim implies that there are indefinitely many experiences which confirm the existence of an external world. All those instances in which our senses testify that something is the case outside our mental world may be construed as confirming the existence of an external world.

We must resist any temptation to dismiss this argument too hastily by ill founded arguments. One reason for wanting to reject it might be the lack of seriousness with which most philosophers nowadays view the verification principle. Let us remind ourselves, however, that in chapter 5 we have seen that there is absolutely no basis for the widely shared belief that the principle is incoherent. As we have seen, the principle is no more problematic than the one associating credibility with confirmation. It is by no means unreasonable to demand minimal verification and to insist that a sentence which is not verifiable in any sense is devoid of empirical significance.

Another way of opposing this last move of the realist may be to say that just as we were willing to deny the truth of 'There is a table in front of me', we should be willing to deny the meaningfulness of that sentence. The crucial point is that this route is not available to the phenomenalist. As we have seen, his reply to the challenge that he cannot take advantage of the immense unifying power of science was that he does adopt all the best books written by realists but gives each statement a certain twist. He obviously could not do so if every sentence contained in those books was meaningless!

Notes

1 What is metaphysics?

1 *Metaphysics: An Introduction* (Encino, 1976), p. 1.
2 ibid, p. 17.
3 *Metaphysics: An Introduction to Philosophy* (New York, 1969), p.18.
4 *An Introduction to Philosophical Analysis* (Englewood Cliffs, NJ, 1967), p. 349.
5 *The Nature of Things* (London, 1973), p. 235.
6 *Metaphysics: An Introduction,* p. 5.
7 'The Elimination of Metaphysics' in *Logical Positivism,* ed. A. J. Ayer (Glencoe, Ill., 1959), p. 80.
8 *Language, Truth and Logic* (New York, 1952), pp. 35–75.
9 'The Role of Metaphysics in Contemporary Philosophy', *Ratio,* 1977, p. 162.
10 'In Defense of Metaphysics' in *Metaphysics,* ed. W. E. Kennick and M. Lazerowitz (Englewood Cliffs, NJ, 1966), pp. 331–5.
11 *Encyclopedia of Philosophy,* ed. Paul Edwards (New York, 1967), p. 302.
12 *Metaphysics,* p. 14.
13 *Metaphysics* (London, 1965), p. 183.
14 *English Philosophy since 1900* (Oxford, 1958), pp. 136–7.
15 *Individuals* (Garden City, NJ, 1963) p. xiii.
16 'Metaphysics and Rationality', *Idealistic Studies,* 1972, p. 135.
17 Regis Jolivet, *Man and Metaphysics* (New York, 1961), p. 13.
18 John Kekes, 'Metaphysics and Rationality', p. 135.
19 *The Logic of Scientific Discovery* (London, 1959), p. 433.
20 cf. G. C. Nerlich and W. A. Suchting, 'Popper on Law and Natural Necessity', *British Journal for the Philosophy of Science,* 1967, pp. 233–5.
21 *Metaphysics,* p. 5.
22 'In Defense of Metaphysics', p. 135.
23 'The Elimination of Metaphysics', p. 80.
24 ibid., p. 67.
25 ibid., p. 69.

2 Justification in metaphysics

1 'Other Minds' in *Logic and Art*, ed. R. Rudner and I. Scheffler (Indianapolis, 1972).
2 ibid., p. 83.
3 ibid., pp. 83–4.
4 *On Certainty* (Oxford, 1969), § 559.
5 ibid., § 323, 458, 519.
6 *American Philosophical Quarterly*, 1978.
7 (Ithaca, NY, 1967).

3 Theism and scientific method

1 (Dordrecht, 1977).
2 'Hume on Evil' in *Philosophical Review*, 1963.
3 *After Auschwitz* (Indianapolis, 1966), p. 227.
4 *The Marks Jews Wear* (New York, 1973), p. 199.
5 'God and Evil', in *Readings in the Philosophy of Religion*, ed. B. A. Brody (Englewood Cliffs, NJ, 1974), pp. 174–5.
6 R. W. K. Paterson, 'Evil, Omniscience and Omnipotence', *Religious Studies*, 1979.
7 A. Plantinga, 'The Free Will Defense' in *Readings in the Philosophy of Religion*, ed. B. A. Brody.
8 A. Flew, *New Essays in Philosophical Theology* (London, 1955), p. 96.
9 'Evil, Omniscience and Omnipotence'.
10 ibid., p. 8.
11 R. Swinburne, 'The Problem of Evil' in *Reason and Religion*, ed. S. C. Brown (Ithaca, NY, 1977), p. 90.
12 ibid.
13 'Evil and Omnipotence' in *Readings in the Philosophy of Religion*, ed. B. A. Brody.
14 *Religion and Scientific Method*, pp. 48–51.
15 'God, "Soul Making" and Apparently Useless Suffering', *American Philosophical Quarterly*, 1970.
16 H. J. McCloskey, 'God and Evil', p. 168.
17 'God, "Soul Making" and Apparently Useless Suffering'.
18 E. H. Madden and P. H. Hare, *Evil and the Concept of Good* (Springfield, Ill., 1968), p. 70.
19 'God and Evil', p. 179.
20 See above, p. 51–2.
21 *New Essays in Philosophical Theology*, ed. A. Flew and A. MacIntyre (London, 1955), p. 96. Hare's ultra-progressive position is shared by R. B. Braithwaite, who develops it in his *An Empiricist's View of the Nature of Religious Belief* (Cambridge, 1955).

22   Frank B. Dilley, 'The Status of Religious Beliefs', *American Philosophical Quarterly*, 1976, p. 41.
23   'Religion and Science: A New Look at Hume's *Dialogues*', *Philosophical Studies*, 1978; 'Experimental Atheism', *Philosophical Studies*, 1979.
24   David Hume, *An Inquiry concerning Human Understanding*, ed. Charles W. Hendel (Indianapolis, 1955), p. 133.
25   R. F. Holland, 'The Miraculous', *American Philosophical Quarterly*, 1965, p. 43.
26   R. G. Swinburne, *The Concept of Miracle* (London, 1970), p. 8.
27   Robert Hambourger, 'Belief in Miracles and Hume's Essay', *Noûs*, 1980, pp. 590–1.
28   *An Inquiry concerning Human Understanding*, p. 123.

4   Thought experiments and the flow of time

1   'A Function of Thought Experiments' in *The Essential Tension: Selected Studies in Scientific Tradition and Change* (Chicago, 1977).
2   ibid., p. 261.
3   ibid.
4   'The River of Time', in *Essays in Conceptual Analysis*, ed. A. Flew (London, 1963).
5   'Time and Becoming' in *Time and Cause*, ed. P. Inwagen (Dordrecht, 1980), p. 6.
6   'Ostensible Temporality' in *Problems of Space and Time*, ed. J. J. C. Smart (New York, 1964), p. 332.
7   'The Flow of Time', *Synthese*, 1972, p. 137.
8   ibid., p. 140.
9   'Time and Becoming', p. 3.
10   'A Formal Approach to the Problem of Free Will and Determinism', *Theoria*, 1974, p. 9.

5   The method of counter-examples, possible worlds and the mystery of existence

1   *Aspects of Scientific Explanation* (New York, 1965), p. 273.
2   Cited by Charles G. Montague, 'On Two Proposed Models of Explanations', *Philosophy of Science*, 1972, p. 78.
3   *Aspects of Scientific Explanation*, p. 275.
4   ibid., p. 273, note.
5   'On the Logical Conditions of Deductive Explanation', *Philosophy of Science*, 1963.
6   'Kim on Deductive Explanation', *Philosophy of Science*, 1970.

7 'Selections from *Thought*' in *Essays on Knowledge and Justification*, ed.
G. S. Pappas and M. Swain (Ithaca, NY, 1978), p. 212.
8 ibid., p. 215.
9 ibid.
10 *Counterfactuals* (Cambridge, Mass., 1973).
11 *Philosophical Review*, 1979.
12 'Theory of Conditionals' in *Studies in Logical Theory*, ed. N. Rescher
(*American Philosophical Quarterly* monograph, 1968).
13 'The Trouble with Possible Worlds' in *The Possible and the Actual*, ed.
Michael J. Loux (Ithaca, NY, 1979), pp. 287–8. (I have omitted Lycan's point
(iv), renumbering his (v) as (iv) for convenience.)
14 'Anselm and Actuality', *Noûs*, 1970, p. 186.
15 ibid., p. 185.
16 'Theories of Actuality' in *The Possible and the Actual*, pp. 194–5.
17 ibid., p. 195.
18 (New York, 1954).
19 ibid., p. 30.

6 The problem of universals and linguistic analysis

1 'Statements about Universals', *Mind*, 1977, pp. 427–9.
2 'Particulars and Ontological Purity', *Metaphilosophy*, 1974.

7 Other minds and explanations

1 'Operationalism and Ordinary Language', *American Philosophical
Quarterly*, 1965.
2 ibid., p. 293.
3 'The Simplicity of Other Minds', *Journal of Philosophy*, 1965, p. 578.
(The article is republished in *Essays on Other Minds*, ed. T. D. Buford
(Urbana, 1970).)
4 'The Simplicity of Other Minds', p. 576.
5 *God and Other Minds* (Ithaca, NY, 1967), p. 247.
6 'The Analogical Inference to Other Minds', *American Philosophical
Quarterly*, 1972, p. 172.
7 R. I. Sikora, 'The Argument from Analogy is *not* an Argument for Other
Minds', *American Philosophical Quarterly*, 1977, p. 137.
8 'Inverted Spectrum', *Ratio*, 1973, pp. 315–19.
9 'Systematic Transposition of Colours', *Australasian Journal of Philosophy*,
1979, pp. 211–19.
10 *Between Science and Philosophy* (New York, 1968), pp. 75–6.
11 'About', *Mind*, 1961.
12 ibid., p. 13.

8 Induction, infinite regresses, the uniformity of nature and the intelligibility of nature

1 P. F. Strawson, *Introduction to Logical Theory* (London, 1952), p. 249.
2 ibid., p. 262.
3 ibid., p. 259.
4 ibid., p. 257.
5 'Can Science do without Induction?' in *Applications of Inductive Logic*, ed. L. J. Cohen and M. B. Hesse (Oxford, 1980), p. 129.
6 ibid.
7 *The Structure of Scientific Inference* (Berkeley, Calif., 1974), p. 95.
8 *The Logic of Scientific Discovery* (London, 1959), p. 140.
9 *Probability and Induction* (Oxford, 1949), p. 230.
10 *Induction and Hypotheses* (Ithaca, NY, 1957), pp. 180–2.
11 (New York, 1962).
12 'Plato's Parmenides', *Mind*, 1939.
13 'Universals and Metaphysical Realism' in *Universals and Particulars*, ed. M. J. Loux (Notre Dame, 1976), p. 140.
14 'Abstract Particulars', *Philosophy and Phenomenological Research*, 1973, pp. 328–9.
15 *The Concept of Mind* (London, 1963), p. 31.
16 'Why not Scepticism' in *Essays in Knowledge and Justification*, ed. G. S. Pappas and M. Swain (Ithaca, NY, 1978).
17 *Skepticism and Cognitivism* (Berkeley, Calif., 1978).
18 ibid., pp. 80–1.
19 *Past, Present and Future* (Oxford, 1967), pp. 5–6.
20 (Indianapolis, 1980), pp. 57–8.
21 *Scientific Inferences* (Cambridge, 1931).
22 *Fact, Fiction and Forecast* (London, 1955), p. 74.
23 'Inductive Inference' in *Philosophy of Science*, ed. B. Baumrin (New York, 1963).
24 'On the New Riddle of Induction' in *The Philosophy of Science*, ed. P. H. Nidditch (Oxford, 1968), p. 158.
25 'De Principiis non disputandum . . . On the Meaning and the Limits of Justification' in *Philosophical Analysis*, ed. M. Black (Ithaca, NY, 1950).

9 Formal methods, verificationism and the existence of an external world

1 'Proof of an External World' in *Philosophical Papers* (London, 1959), p. 149.
2 'Cartesian Scepticism and Epistemic Logic', *Analysis*, 1979.

Index